The Bonds of Freedom

Recent titles in

AMERICAN ACADEMY OF RELIGION
ACADEMY SERIES
SERIES EDITOR
Carole Myscofski, Illinois Wesleyan University
A Publication Series of
The American Academy of Religion
and
Oxford University Press

Profile of the Last Puritan
   Jonthan Edwards, Self-Love, and the Dawn of the Beatific
   David C. Brand
Victor Turner Revisited
   Ritual as Social Change
   Bobby C. Alexander
Chinese Women and Christianity, 1860–1927
   Kwok Pui-Lan
The Man in the Yellow Hat
   Theology and Psychoanalysis in Child Therapy
   Dorothy W. Martyn
The Grace of Difference
   A Canadian Feminist Theological Ethic
   Marilyn J. Legge
The Intersubjectivity of the Mystic
   A Study of Theresa of Avila's *Interior Castle*
   Mary Frolich
Narrating History, Developing Doctrine
   Friedrich Schleiermacher and Johann Sebastian Drey
   Bradford E. Hinze
Analogical Possibilities
   How Words Refer to God
   Philip A. Rolnick
Womanist Justice, Womanist Hope
   Emilie M. Townes
Women Don't Count
   The Challenge of Women's Poverty to Christian Ethics
   Pamela K. Brubaker
The Exploration of the Inner Wounds—Han
   Jae Hoon Lee
Comprehending Power in Christian Social Ethics
   Christine Firer Hinze

The Greening of Theology
   The Ecological Models of Rosemary Radford Ruether, Joseph Stiller, and Jürgen Moltmann
   Steven Bouma-Prediger
The Spirit and the Vision
   The Influence of Christian Romanticism on Development of 19th-Century American Art
   Diane Apostolos-Cappadona
The Freedom of the Spirit
   African Indigenous Churches in Kenya
   Francis Kimani Githieya
Bridge-Makers amd Cross-Bearers
   Korean-American Women and the Church
   Jung Ha Kim
God Bless the Child That's Got Its Own
   The Economic Rights Debate
   Darryl M. Trimiew
Energies of the Spirit
   Trinitarian Models in Eastern Orthodox and Western Theology
   Duncan Reid
The Goddess Laksmi
   The Divine Consort in South Indian Vaisnava Tradition
   P. Pratap Kumar
Creative Dwelling
   Empathy and Clarity in God and Self
   Lucinda A. Stark Huffaker
Hospitality to Strangers
   Empathy and the Physician-Patient Relationship
   Dorothy M. Owens
The Bonds of Freedom
   Feminist Theology and Christian Realism
   Rebekah L. Miles

The Bonds of Freedom

Feminist Theology and Christian Realism

REBEKAH L. MILES

OXFORD
UNIVERSITY PRESS

2001

OXFORD
UNIVERSITY PRESS

Oxford   New York
Athens   Auckland   Bangkok   Bogotá   Buenos Aires   Cape Town
Chennai   Dar es Salaam   Delhi   Florence   Hong Kong   Istanbul   Karachi
Kolkata   Kuala Lumpur   Madrid   Melbourne   Mexico City   Mumbai   Nairobi
Paris   São Paulo   Shanghai   Singapore   Taipei   Tokyo   Toronto   Warsaw

and associated companies in
Berlin   Ibadan

Copyright © 2001 by The American Academy of Religion

Published by Oxford University Press, Inc.
198 Madison Avenue, New York, New York 10016

Oxford is a registered trademark of Oxford University Press.

All rights reserved. No part of this publication may be reproduced,
stored in a retrieval system, or transmitted, in any form or by any means,
electronic, mechanical, photocopying, recording, or otherwise,
without the prior permission of Oxford University Press.

Library of Congress Cataloging-in-Publication Data
Miles, Rebekah, 1960–
The bonds of freedon : feminist theology and Christian realism /
Rebekah L. Miles.
p.   cm.—(American Academy of
Religion academy series)
Includes bibliographical references and index.
ISBN 0-19-514416-3
1. Feminist theology.   I. Title.   II. Series.
BT83.55 .M49 2001
230'.082—dc21   00-045279

1 3 5 7 9 8 6 4 2

Printed in the United States of America
on acid-free paper

For my parents,
Jo Ann Ridgway Miles
and
John Pershing Miles I

"*The lines have fallen for me
in pleasant places;
yea, I have a goodly heritage.*"
Psalm 16:6

Acknowledgments

I ONCE believed that academic manuscripts were born in the isolation of the study and nurtured under one set of watchful eyes; now I know better. They come from large, extended families. They are shaped in the noise of the household, encouraged by the praise of friends, whipped into shape by colleagues in the field, rushed along by the calendars of editors, and finally spit-polished by secretaries, graduate assistants, and copyeditors. This manuscript grew under the watch of an unruly and generous family. Though they graciously shared in nurturing this work, they are in no way responsible for any errors in it.

I am indebted to the faculty of the Divinity School at the University of Chicago, particularly to Robin Lovin, William Schweiker, Anne E. Carr, Martin Marty, David Tracy, Don Browning, and Franklin Gamwell. I also give thanks for other professors, Sheila Davaney, Jean Miller Schmidt, and Delwin Brown of the Iliff School of Theology; Jay McDaniel and John Farthing of Hendrix College; and Rose Margaret Summers, Mary Ewing, Francis Sturdy, and many other excellent teachers in the Arkansas public schools. Under their care, I came to appreciate Aquinas's claim that teaching is an "act of mercy."[1]

I am grateful for the encouragement of colleagues at Brite Divinity School, Texas Christian University, where I worked while writing this manuscript and revising it for publication. Deans Leo Perdue and Mark Toulouse offered patient assistance and an occasional swift kick. Terry Inman, Sharlie Tomlinson, Margaret Wintersole, Pam Rose-Beeler, Melanie Moore, Carolyn Herring, Jason Vickers, and Sherry Willis helped with editing. I am thankful for new colleagues at Perkins School of Theology, Southern Methodist University. Dean Robin Lovin, Provost Ross Murfin, and Associate Deans Jouette Bassler and Marjorie Procter-Smith have given generous support. Thanks also go to Carole Myscofski of the American Academy of Religion's Academy Series and Cynthia Read of Oxford University Press.

My friends delivered me through this process. I owe thanks to Susan Simonaitis, Lois Malcolm, Chung Wook "Maggie" Kim, Brad Stull, Susan St.Ville, Todd Whitmore, Charlene Garlarneau, Sarita Tamayo, Joy McDougall, Mary Doak, Heather Miles, and Lisa and Paul Motz-Storey. Aquinas claimed that "likeness" or similarity was the cause of the love between friends; he had evidently never met mine.[2] On the contrary, I say that the love of friends springs from gracious disagreement and amiable conflict. Such conflict is the source not only of these friendships but also of the arguments presented in this book. When I insist that I take full responsibility for all the ideas presented in this text, some of these friends will sigh with relief and say "amen."

My family, the Mileses, Delonys, Rudows, and Vibhakars, offered lively encouragement. I am grateful to my sister Deborah, brother John, and Uncle Warren who tried their best to make sure that this work is feminist (Deborah), orthodox (John), and done (Warren). I dedicate this work to my parents, Jo Ann and John Miles, who have given their lives in ministry to their family and the church. I thank God for the love they have shared with me and so many others. The powerful bonds they nourished in our family allowed us to learn to be free and then to enact that freedom in the world. I am also grateful to the Little Rock Conference of the United Methodist Church which has supported them and now supports me in ministry. My husband, Len Delony, helped in a thousand ways. He listened, edited, cooked, cleaned, danced, prayed, juggled, comforted, cajoled, and reminded me to "rest in the shade of mercy."[3] In the final steps of manuscript preparation, he gave himself in care not only for me but also for our delightful little daughters, Anna and Katherine. For all that and much more, I give thanks.

Finally, I am grateful to you for reading this book. One of the hard truths of writing academic manuscripts is that, in most cases, so few people read them. I have often remembered the sweet, "mad" Dickens character, Mr. Dick, who built kites out of his never completed manuscripts. He explained himself to young David Copperfield. " 'There's plenty of string,' said Mr. Dick, 'and when it flies high it takes the facts a long way. That's my manner of diffusin' 'em. I don't know where they may come down. It's according to circumstances, and the wind, and so forth; but I take my chance of that.' "[4] Both kite flyers and academic writers take their chances. While academic books may be slightly more effective at diffusing ideas, they are surely not as much fun. Given that sobering fact, I thank you for taking a chance and reading this book.

Contents

1 *Freedom and Boundedness*
  A Feminist Christian Realist Account   3

2 *What's So Bad about Reinhold Niebuhr?*
  Feminist Criticisms of Niebuhr   28

3 *Freedom for the World*
  Reinhold Niebuhr's Christian Realism   57

4 *The Evolution of Cooperation and Consciousness*
  Rosemary Ruether's Naturalist Moral Realism   90

5 *Battling for Truth in the Beloved Community*
  Sharon Welch's Relativist Political Realism   120

6 *Dueling Realisms*
  Ruether, Welch, Niebuhr, and a Feminist Christian Realism   147

Afterword   157
Notes   159
Bibliography   191
Index   201

The Bonds of Freedom

ONE

Freedom and Boundedness

A Feminist Christian Realist Account

THE primary issue prompting this feminist realist project is the loss of moral grounding and critical judgment within some North American feminist theologies. I contend that feminist criticisms of appeals to divine transcendence and human self-transcendence, as well as the increasingly radical emphasis on divine immanence and human boundedness, have undercut the anthropological, moral, and religious assumptions on which feminism rests. I further argue that feminist theologians would be better served by critically reappropriating a more positive understanding of divine transcendence and human self-transcendence while maintaining their emphasis on human boundedness and divine presence. These four aspects are crucial to what I call a feminist Christian realism.

My central claim, that a feminist Christian realism is well suited to account for feminist moral experience,[1] is highly controversial. This argument goes against a common feminist assumption that Christian realism is hardly a resource to combat a patriarchal theological ethic; it is, instead, a prime example of one. Indeed, Christian realism and feminism are mentioned in the same breath only as antagonists.[2] In a sharp departure from this common wisdom, I use feminist criticisms not to reject Christian realism but to revise and appropriate it. In addition, I examine the realist arguments implicit in several feminist theologies and suggest that a more fully developed feminist realist position could better account for feminist moral experience and address crucial ethical concerns evident within recent feminist theologies.

This realist position is developed in conversation with three thinkers—Reinhold Niebuhr, Rosemary Radford Ruether, and Sharon Welch. Each figure contributes to the project by highlighting some aspect of human experience that is central to an adequate feminist Christian realism. At the same time, each thinker denies or neglects some aspect of that experience that one of the other thinkers marks as crucial. Therefore, only when they are seen together does a full account of feminist Christian realism emerge.

The theological ethics of Ruether and Welch illustrate a common feminist move toward human boundedness and divine immanence and exemplify two types of feminist realism.[3] Both women, along with most other feminist theologians, charge that many aspects of Christian ethics and theology, including common Christian claims about divine transcendence and radical human self-transcendence, promote domination.

Both Welch and Ruether propose new models for theological ethics designed to lessen domination and promote mutual empowerment. For Ruether, a naturalist moral realist, the locus of moral reflection and the divine is a natural and historical evolutionary process within which human consciousness and altruism emerge as the "growing edge." Human moral action takes place in relation to this process and is an expression of it. Responsible moral persons recognize their interdependence in this system and go on to further the evolutionary development through acts of social and ideological transformation.

For Welch, a relativist political realist, the locus of moral reflection and the divine is radically particular, finite human communities. Human moral action and the radically relative norms that guide it develop out of these particular communities. No shared human nature or revealed norm bridges these particular communities. The interactions between communities reveal the limits of all perspectives. These proposals represent two options within feminist theology—Ruether's naturalist moral realism and Welch's relativist political realism.

Reinhold Niebuhr is the primary resource both for feminist realism's third component, a theological realism, and for its further understanding of the components of political and moral realism. For Niebuhr, the locus of moral reflection is the tension between human boundedness and freedom.[4] Human moral action and the norms that guide it develop out of the free self's reflection on and judgment of its boundedness and its freedom. While this tension is not the locus of the divine, it is a point of "revelation." The free and bound self longs for that which is not bound. As a theological realist, Niebuhr understands God to transcend, to relativize, to give meaning to, and ultimately to unify all human projects and desires. Thus, genuine moral responsibility is possible when the tension between human boundedness and freedom is set in relation to God. Niebuhr combines this theological realism with both the grounding of moral claims in human experience (moral realism) and a deep suspicion about the embeddedness of self-interest in moral claims (political realism).

Though my realist position draws on all three figures, its success depends on a crucial feature taken from Niebuhr. Niebuhr's focus on the transforming capacity of human freedom and the unifying and relativizing character of divine transcendence provides an internal critical mechanism within his system. Through this mechanism, a realist model not only helps to resolve tensions within other feminist models but also can modify itself in the face of feminist criticism. My critical feminist modification of Niebuhr, using his broader framework, exemplifies the success of his realist argument. The self-critical, transformative capacity of this system illustrates not its weakness, but its power and flexibility. Likewise, my ultimate reliance on Christian realist assumptions does not weaken my feminist argument but rather strengthens it.[5]

Even so, Niebuhr's Christian realism is not fully adequate for a feminist theological ethic. As we will see, Niebuhr fails to account for some central facets of feminist moral experience and, indeed, human moral experience. The features neglected by Niebuhr are central to the theological ethics of Ruether and Welch. I develop a feminist Christian realism, then, out of a critical and synthetic engagement with Niebuhr, Ruether, and Welch.

Because Niebuhr has been so widely criticized by feminist theologians, a critical retrieval must first examine the extensive charges against him. To this end, chapter 2 outlines feminist criticisms of Niebuhr and develops a framework for a feminist reappropriation of Niebuhr that takes into account feminist criticisms. At the conclusion of chapter 2, I suggest that feminist criticisms of Niebuhr's understanding of gender roles do *not* fundamentally challenge Niebuhr's model of the free and bound self. Indeed, these criticisms actually *exemplify* the need to recognize the moral significance of both our given bodily reality and our human freedom to partially transcend and transform that givenness. Niebuhr's understanding of human moral experience provides a framework for that recognition.[6]

Chapter 3 begins with Reinhold Niebuhr's claim that human experience is both bound and free and goes on to examine the broader ethical implications of this claim for feminist theologians and others. Though I draw on Niebuhr as the primary resource for this position, my alternative is not simply Niebuhr dressed up in feminist vocabulary or feminism disguised by Niebuhrian concepts. Niebuhr's "hermeneutic of suspicion" creates a greater ambivalence about the moral status of the natural world and human communities than is necessary in a realist position. Instead, the alternative, a feminist Christian realism, accounts both for feminist criticisms of Niebuhr and for feminism's positive contributions to a realist ethic.

In chapter 4, I examine Ruether's naturalist moral realism. Her naturalist, ecofeminist ethic locates both God and human norms in natural processes, particularly evolution. Transcendence of immediate context and experience is possible through conscious participation in natural evolutionary development into the future. Her moral realism is evident in her confidence that humans can know the good by looking to nature, including human nature.[7] This same confidence makes her an idealist about the potential to eliminate domination by creating new selves, theologies, and social structures. Moreover, Ruether's description of normative human nature focuses on boundedness to nature and the self's unique faculty of consciousness as an expression of nature; it does not include the human capacity for radical transcendence of or freedom over nature and consciousness. Thus, I argue, Ruether offers grounding for moral norms in her naturalist moral realism, but she lacks a mechanism to judge those norms and to account for the resilience of human sin and the potential of human creativity to transmute nature.

Chapter 5 examines Welch's political realist position. We will see that Welch, in contrast to Ruether, locates moral norms and the divine in particular human communities. All moral claims are radically relative to those particular contexts. Appeals to an experience or reality that transcends our interactions in communities are illusory justifications of our own relative positions.[8] Only within community interaction can we transcend ourselves as we see the limitations of our understandings through the criticism of others. Welch is a political realist in the sense that she is suspicious of the power interests hidden behind truth claims. She is cynical in her skepticism of any substantive grounding for moral claims. I will attempt to show that each of these proposals undercuts a crucial aspect of feminist moral judgment and, thus, does not lessen, but rather unintentionally supports, further domination.

The final chapter points toward an alternative position that critically retrieves the realisms of Ruether, Welch, and Niebuhr and finds a middle way between the idealistic realism about moral grounding found in Ruether and some early feminists, and the radically relative political realism of Welch and some other postmodern feminists. This alternative joins an appeal to human self-transcendence and divine transcendence with an affirmation of human boundedness and divine presence. At the same time, it takes seriously Ruether's turn to creation and Welch's turn to community. In this alternate model—a feminist Christian realism—I hope to maintain both substantive grounding for moral claims and critical judgment of them.

Christian Realism: Background and Definitions

Historical Background

Feminist Christian realism is a critical heir to a larger realist movement in twentieth-century American theology.[9] In its earliest stages, this movement defined itself in contrast to the "faith of modernism."[10] Christian realists turned away from modernist confidence in the human potential to radically transform social institutions for lasting peace and Christlike love, and they retrieved an Augustinian emphasis on the limits of the moral life in the earthly kingdom.[11] While social gospel modernists confessed their "faith in the possibility of a new social order,"[12] Christian realists, grimly observing social disorder, claimed that "nothing is too terrible to be possible."[13] The Christian realists of the midcentury, as well as their secular realist counterparts, took pride in their "temper of mind which . . . prefers objective realities however disagreeable, to subjective fancies, however glorious."[14] And Reinhold Niebuhr, the best known proponent of Christian realism, defined *realism* as the willingness to "take all factors . . . into account, particularly the factors of self-interest and power."[15] Because of the focus on the "disagreeable" realities of self-interest and power, realists came to be regarded as pessimists who lent support to the status quo through their suspicion and criticism of idealistic social projects.[16]

Liberation theologians have criticized Christian realists for this same pessimism. Rubem Alves blasts the Christian realism of North American theology as the "ideology of the establishment."[17] In a lively defense of "utopianism" and reproach of realism, Alves (in good realist style) unmasks the power dynamics and self-interest that lie hidden behind the realists' moralizing.[18]

Likewise, feminist theologians have charged that Christian realism is "the product of patriarchal mentality."[19] According to Ruether, Christian realism's insistence on human limitation leads ultimately to "conservative complacency."[20] Beverly Harrison maintains that Christian realism's pessimistic view of human nature finally denies the possibility of the historical development and change that is central to feminism and other liberation movements.²¹ Christian realist positions are seen by many, then, as a deterrent to significant social change.

Admittedly, Christian realism *has* emphasized human limits and *has* included some politically conservative branches.²² I will argue, however, that the sort of revised Christian realism that I am proposing can support movements for political liberation.²³

Unfortunately, the stereotypical focus on its pessimism has obscured other aspects of realist positions that offer greater hope for significant moral judgment and social change. Realists claimed to "take *all* factors into account," not just the grim ones.²⁴ While the midcentury realists *did* counter the modernist enthusiasm for human virtue and progress with an oddly exuberant declaration of human sin and failure, they *did not* ignore the human moral capacity for the good. For example, John Bennett's realism went beyond his declaration that "nothing is too terrible to be possible."²⁵ Bennett also insisted that the Christian suspicion about sin and power should always be balanced by a "faith in human possibilities" through responsiveness to God.²⁶ Moreover, Walter Horton maintained that though the realist's analysis of life starts with the difficulties and limitations, it does not stop there. He wrote, that the realist had

> a resolute determination to face all the facts of life candidly, beginning preferably with the most stubborn, perplexing and disheartening ones . . . and then through these stubborn facts and not in spite of them, to pierce as deep as one may into the solid structure of objective reality until one finds whatever ground of courage, hope, and faith is actually there, independent of human preferences and desires, and so cast anchor in that ground.²⁷

Horton joined his suspicious political realism about human sin with an empirical moral realism about an "objective reality" as a ground of human hope. Likewise, Niebuhr's insistence that all factors should be taken into account included both human limitations *and* human possibilities as free and bound creatures.²⁸ Thus, midcentury realists, though stressing human limitations to counter the optimism of the modernists, also affirmed some grounding for human hope and human good.

Recent interpreters of Reinhold Niebuhr have emphasized this multifaceted nature of his Christian realism.²⁹ Robin Lovin insists that Niebuhr is a helpful resource for contemporary theological ethics precisely *because* Niebuhr's realism goes beyond the pessimism with which he and other realists are so closely associated. Lovin describes three facets of Niebuhr's Christian realism: political realism, moral realism, and theological realism. I draw on his division in the definitions that follow.

Definitions

As we have seen, Christian realism refers to a disposition to attend to the full range of factors in a given situation.³⁰ Three aspects of this attention are central to realist analysis: political realism, moral realism, and theological realism. As we will see, these three components are related to an understanding of human nature as bound and free and of God as transcendent and immanent. Moreover, our three thinkers are distinguished from each other by their varied configurations of these themes.

Political realism is an attentiveness to the factors of human self-interest and power in any moral or political process.[31] Political realism's suspicion about human possibility for pure virtue and its focus on human limitation stem not from any ambivalence about human boundedness but rather from a recognition of the human tendency to deny that boundedness. Political realism notes the disposition of the human self to hide its own sin, often masking it with language of morality, religion, or political right. Humans cover their self-interested actions with appeals to virtue or to divine will, in the attempt to delude others and even themselves.

Each of our thinkers is, at least partially, a political realist. Niebuhr's focus on the realities of power and self-interest in human communities and ideologies is a type of political realism. Welch's insistence on the radical embeddedness and formation of all truth in particular systems of power is a relativist political realism. Likewise, Ruether's insistence on the self-interested nature of patriarchal theologies is partially politically realist. She is more confident and even idealistic than either Welch or Niebuhr, however, about the formation of *new* theologies and social structures that are built around altruism and not self-interest.[32]

Though political realism, with its suspicion and pessimism, is most closely associated with Christian realism, it is only one component. Niebuhr and other Christian realists also emphasized *moral realism* that considered not only the grim facts of human distortion but also the full range of shared human experience, including moral experience.[33] Moral realism assumes that human ethical claims can be true or false. Though all moral claims are limited by human context and finitude, they are not simply radically relative to that context.

Niebuhr, Ruether, and Welch offer contrasting perspectives on moral realism. Niebuhr's theological ethic is based on an analysis of human experience as such. His understanding of human nature as bound and free grounds normative claims; he is a naturalist moral realist. Yet because freedom (with its creative and destructive aspects) is a part of essential human nature, any attempts to overdefine natural law are questioned. Likewise, Ruether's feminist ethics is a type of naturalist moral realism. As we will see, Ruether is more confident that moral laws can be read directly from nature. Moreover, her emphasis on the uniqueness of human consciousness as an expression of nature rather than on the uniqueness of self-transcendence makes her understanding of human and social development quite different from Niebuhr's. For Ruether, consciousness does not so much transcend but emerges *from* and expresses the natural evolutionary process. Unlike both Niebuhr and Ruether, Welch rejects moral realism. Moral truths are radically embedded in and relative to particular contexts; they are created by the powers of each age.

Christian realism includes a third component, *theological realism*.[34] The purposes and desires of different humans stand in conflict within community. Indeed, within the individual self these conflicts are also evident. Yet moral claims assume some higher call than the balancing of finite desires. According to

Niebuhr, our values and desires are unified, relativized, and given meaning by their relation to God, who is always beyond them. This model of God is quite different from Welch's model. For Welch, God does not relativize and unify finite claims but is, instead, a "quality" of the finite. Likewise, Niebuhr's theological realism stands in sharp contrast to that of Ruether. Ruether speaks of the divine as the ground or matrix of the natural evolutionary process. So, she places much greater focus on immanence and relation to nature than on transcendence and discontinuity. Unlike Welch, however, she is a theological realist. God is somehow beyond or more than human communities and lives, relativizing and unifying them.

Given these three definitions of realism, what roles do divine transcendence, divine immanence, human freedom, and human boundedness play within a Christian realism? For Niebuhr, these four ideas are profoundly interrelated. Because of their boundedness and self-transcendence, humans long for an end that is not finite, but as finite creatures this end is beyond their reach. *Divine transcendence*, then, has a moral purpose in Niebuhr's realism. Human lives and finite choices can find their end, meaning, and unity only in a God who is ultimately beyond those lives and choices. At the same time, God's transcendence also relativizes any attempts to claim too much for any finite positions or structures.

Yet God is not only transcendent. God's transcendence is expressed most fully in *God's immanence* in the world. Through God's presence in Christ, especially in the cross, humans are given a "transhistorical norm." The transcendent norm of agape love stands over human relationships, judging and inspiring them.

Human creation in God's image is also a factor in moral life. For Niebuhr, humans are created *bound and free*. Human self-transcendence or freedom reflects the image of God. It plays both a critical role and a grounding role. The tension between the givenness of human finitude and the capacity of human freedom to transcend, judge, and transmute the finite is the source of both human distortion and human creativity. This freedom provides a critical mechanism for social transformation and for the criticism of all systems, including Niebuhr's own.[35] As we have seen, freedom also grounds normative claims and carries ethical and theological requirements. But even though Niebuhr draws on and grounds some moral claims in human experience, his emphasis on self-transcendence leaves him ambivalent about grounding moral claims in human boundedness to nature and society.

A feminist Christian realism, by contrast, has a more positive moral role for human boundedness to body, nature, and community. At the same time, the natural human capacity for freedom or self-transcendence checks any overdefinition of or undue optimism concerning claims about nature or community. Because of human self-transcendence and because of the human tendency to act from hidden self-interest, any natural claims are relativized by the creative and distorting aspects of freedom.

Moreover, this emphasis on freedom or self-transcendence provides an internal critical mechanism for Niebuhr's ethic itself. I will argue that Niebuhr's ethical model "works" precisely because of this emphasis. As we will see, because Niebuhr's ethic offers this internal critical mechanism, it not only is able to account for the internal problems in other positions but also can be revised in response to external criticisms of its own weaknesses. Thus, this model's openness to modification in the face of criticism and its capacity to account for inconsistencies in other arguments demonstrate the efficacy of this understanding of freedom. Ironically, then, my feminist *revisions* of Niebuhr exemplify the success of his realist model.

In summary, Christian realism contains three components, political, moral, and theological realism. And these three components are related to a multifaceted understanding of four other categories: human freedom and boundedness and divine transcendence and immanence. The varied configuration and weighing of these features mark the differences among our thinkers and focus the development of a feminist Christian realism.

Assumptions and Methodology

The entire project is influenced by assumptions suggested in the name "feminist Christian realism." First, this project grows out of Christian realist understandings of the distortions of human power, shared human experiences as a ground for normative claims, and the reality of a God who relativizes, unifies, and gives meaning to contingent human choices and desires.[36] Because the assumptions are Christian, the understandings of God, human nature, and the moral life draw on Christian language and are formed by the perspective of that faith tradition. At the same time, central to Christian realism is an analysis of human experience as such. Though realists recognize the embeddedness of all human experience (including claims *about* experience) in cultural context, they *do* begin from broad claims about shared human moral experience. Consequently, their arguments, though couched in and formed by Christian understandings, claim wider relevance. Thus, Christian realism is a type of revisionist theology that seeks to correlate theology with human experience and to engage in public discussion about human good.[37] I will claim, then, that the feminist Christian realism that emerges from this study has relevance for any feminism, not just Christian feminism.

Though feminist Christian realism draws on Christian language and concerns—particularly Niebuhrian language and Niebuhrian concerns—it is not a simple makeover of Christian theology or Niebuhr into feminist garb. Because my position is unabashedly feminist, it carries a loyalty to women's flourishing (as well as to the flourishing of men, children, and other parts of creation) that overrides any loyalty to particular traditions or figures, including Niebuhr (or Ruether or Welch, for that matter). I critically examine the work of Ruether, Welch, and Niebuhr in the interest of prior feminist commitments. I draw on those aspects of their work that I judge to promote the flourishing of women and others.[38] Consequently, while at one level Christian realism provides the critical lens by which feminist theology is examined, that Christian realist lens is itself scrutinized by prior feminist commitments and modified by feminist criticisms. Thus, feminism and Christian realism are not simply "synthesized" in a feminist Christian realism but stand in mutually critical relationship to each other.

As I noted before, a feminist Christian realism has the capacity to engage in this critical exchange because it draws on Niebuhr's model of freedom as an internal critical mechanism. Therefore, even though the three figures stand in mutually critical relation to each other, Niebuhr's model is the crucial factor that creates the context for that interaction.

The mutually critical interaction between Christian realism and feminism is a central aspect of the methodology of this project. Thus, the critical examination and synthesis of the theological ethics of Ruether, Welch, and Niebuhr both emerge from and shape a feminist Christian realism. While this process and my alternate model draw significantly from the language and assumptions of Christian realism, they are driven by feminist commitments and concerns.

From Transcendence to Boundedness: A Composite Feminist Account

Commonality and Difference in Feminist Theologies

In this section, I sketch a general argument about transcendence and immanence that is common to many, though not all, feminist theologies.[39] While the composite nature of this account reflects a genuine tendency within feminist theology, such generalized claims also run the danger of overlooking the extraordinary divergence that is obvious within feminist theologies.

The diversity of voices among feminist theologians can hardly be overestimated. Because feminism is built around appeals to particular experiences and contexts, it is not surprising that it has spawned theological positions that are as varied as women's experiences. This appeal to diverse experience is reflected in the early pages of most feminist books, which highlight a description of the author's identity, including class, ethnic background, geography, and sexual orientation.

Many feminist theologies are shaped by the particular experience to which they appeal. Sara Ruddick and Bonnie Miller-McLemore reflect on theology and ethics from the experience of motherhood.[40] Kathryn Rabuzzi explores the sacred dimensions of "housework."[41] The domestic arts of cooking, quilting, and weaving are central experiences around which Grace Cumming Long delineates a feminist theological ethic of freedom.[42] Rita Brock asks what difference female sexual abuse makes for Christian theology.[43] Lesbian experience is a primary resource for theological reflection in Mary Hunt and Carter Heyward.[44] Clearly, the focus on particular experiences is one of the primary factors in the diversity of women's theologies.

Though most feminist theologians appeal to women's experience, other feminists criticize this appeal because it often assumes that there *is* a common women's experience.[45] These claims to commonality are said to universalize white female experience and ignore the differences among women. Out of these appeals to particular experience have emerged a variety of women's theologies that sometimes distance themselves from European American feminism. African American womanists, Hispanic mujeristas, Asian women, and others have developed diverse theologies out of diverse contexts.[46] Yet even these particular groups are not of one voice. African American womanist theologians diverge on many topics, including even their understanding of the word *womanist*.[47] And Hispanic mujerista theologians have cautioned one another not to gloss over the differences between Cuban American, Puerto Rican, and Mexican mujerista perspectives.[48] Clearly, diversity and particularity reign.

In spite of the overwhelming diversity, however, common themes and groupings are evident among many feminist, womanist, and mujerista theologians. This project focuses on two groups of mainstream European American feminists who respond to Christian theology. Disagreements among European American postmodern feminists are evident, for example, in a collection of essays on the use of French feminisms in feminist theologies.[49] Likewise, there are significant disagreements between Ruether's naturalist ethic and the naturalism of some Goddess feminists.[50]

Given these caveats about the extent of diversity and disagreement among womanist, mujerista, and European American feminists, there are commonalities within many of these theologies, particularly those of the European American feminists. What are some common assumptions within feminist theology?

Ironically, one commonality is the appeal to diverse experiences. The diversity of feminist theologies reflects a common turn to particular, concrete social location. Most feminists contend that theologies spring not full grown from the mind of God or from the facts of some abstract, universal experience; they are shaped instead by the singular experiences of particular theologians. Moreover, theologies are not innocent reflections on that experience but instead often further the interests of the theologians and the elites who support them.

Thus, traditional Christian theologies, while claiming to be universal, are fashioned, so a common feminist argument runs, from dominant male experience and often for the benefit of dominant males. The allegations leveled at this dominant male theology are legion. The exclusion of women from social and political equality, the denigration of the body and sexuality (especially women's bodies and women's sexuality), the threat of nuclear war, the ecological crisis, world hunger, homophobia, racism, slavery, and the holocaust have all been included in the charges made against dominant male ideologies.[51] Feminist criticisms and reconstructions extend to beliefs about God, human nature, sin, scriptural authority, Christ, Mary, redemption, eternal life, the ordained ministry, and many other aspects of Christian theology and practice.[52]

While the criticisms and reconstructions of traditional Christian theologies are strikingly varied, the ethical assumptions are quite similar. Clearly, ethical concerns drive feminist theology. A particular doctrine of God is accepted or rejected largely according to its supposed ethical effects. Feminists often use the well-being of women as the primary norm for evaluation.[53] Yet many of the arguments of feminist theology center on a broader concern. The criterion of well-being is often extended to all humans and even to all of creation.[54]

As many feminists articulate the content of this well-being or flourishing, their models often center on the full and responsible use of power. The rejection of domination and powerlessness and the affirmation of mutual empowerment is central to many feminist theologies. Within recent feminist discussions, this conversation has centered on the rejection of "power over" and the affirmation of "power with."[55] "Power over," which is thought to be central to patriarchy, is domination and competitiveness. It is always accompanied by the "powerlessness" or passivity of the subjugated group. "Power with," on the other hand, is mutual empowerment and support.[56] The assumption, then, is that bad social systems or theologies are those that promote domination (the overextension of human power or agency) or powerlessness (the failure to fully exercise human power or agency).[57] Good social systems and theologies, by contrast, are those that promote empowerment on behalf of self and creation. Many feminists, including Ruether and Welch, use this kind of analysis of power to evaluate understandings of divine transcendence and human self-transcendence.

From Domination and Transcendence to Mutuality and Immanence

Most feminist theologies emphasize both divine immanence and human particularity and boundedness.[58] Divine immanence reflects feminist values of relationality and mutual empowerment. Daphne Hampson notes that a "transcendent monotheism" suggests the male values of "freedom, power and independence." This conception, she writes, "would seem to fit singularly ill with the feminist vision."[59] The emphasis on divine immanence is a "given" in most feminist theologies. Indeed, one feminist declared, "If there is any one theme that emerges most clearly [in contemporary women's theologies], it is the assumption of the immanence of the divine. The indwelling of the divine is the foundational assumption on which numerous other concepts rest."[60]

Human finitude and boundedness to the world, to body, to natural processes, and to human community are also celebrated within many feminist theologies. Human ethics and theology are radically tied to the particularity of human lives in daily experience, body, social structure, history, and/or nature.[61] The extent and "location" of human boundedness varies in different feminist works. Some thinkers emphasize bodiliness or nature. Others focus on human ties to cultural or ethnic identity. But for most feminist theologians, traditional claims that humans can somehow transcend bodily and cultural environment are suspect. Such claims, the argument runs, devalue the finite world, discourage moral responsibility for the finite, and encourage hierarchical dualism.[62] This radical boundedness to particular experience casts suspicion on any assertions claimed to be made from and about abstract, universal human experience. For some feminists, male universal claims both express and mask male interests. Theological and moral claims are always formed out of particular contexts. Diverse human experiences and communities shape human life, theology, and morality in radically different ways. As we have seen, this focus on diversity of experience is central to feminist theology. Claims of individuals to stand out from nature or community are even rejected as deluded and immoral.[63]

This common emphasis on divine immanence and human boundedness is balanced by a rejection or radical remodification of divine transcendence and human self-transcendence. For many feminists, appeals to transcendence are projections of the male ego. According to Carol Gilligan, Nancy Chodorow, and other feminists, many males experience relationships as threatening.[64] They find their identity not in community but as free, autonomous individuals. Generally speaking, then, male sin is the failure to identify with others and the tendency to separate from others and use them for one's own benefit. Conversely, many women are thought to understand themselves and find their identity in relation to others. Their sin tends to be that of overconnectedness with others and the failure to find a free, acting self. (See chapter 4 for further explanation of this theory.)

Divine transcendence and human self-transcendence, then, can be expressions of male desire for radical separation and freedom.[65] Catherine Keller writes that "the absolute separateness of deity has symbolized the separative aspirations of Mankind, created in his image."[66] Thus, divine transcendence is a projection of male desires and anxieties. Daphne Hampson writes, "His power, freedom and self-sufficiency know no bounds. Is He, one wonders, the reflection of what have been many a man's wildest dreams?"[67]

According to some feminists, the concepts of divine transcendence and human self-transcendence were made by male elites in the ancient world to sacralize their own power and to stave off their anxiety about finitude.[68] They grounded their power in a transcendent realm that was associated with the good and virtuous. The less powerful (women, slaves, the poor, animals, etc.) were associated with the bad and impure. This hierarchical division served to justify other forms of domination and is thought to be a primary cause of many environmental and social problems today.

By either theory, divine transcendence is a projection of male sin and separation. The male ego denies its boundedness to the world by imagining that it can transcend its finite condition. This self-transcending ego further projects itself onto the divine. Ruether writes that this picture of God is "the guilty conscience of a self-infinitizing spirit."[69] A sick God is created in the image of a sick man. A sick world characterized by domination and exploitation is the result.[70]

Many feminists have charged that classical Christian understandings of divine transcendence further this sickness.[71] The Christian understanding of God becomes "the legitimating construct of the patriarchal desire to dominate and control the world."[72] God's otherness is said to devalue the finite world. A hierarchical dualism between God and the world sanctions hierarchical dualisms that subordinate women to men, nature to humans, and body to mind. Moreover, an emphasis on divine transcendence and power is said to discourage humans from taking responsibility for problems in this world. Likewise, appeals to human self-transcendence are thought to devalue the finite and to deny the reality of our human boundedness in nature, history, and relationships. Thus, divine transcendence is the pinnacle of a whole web of hierarchical dominations. Judith Plaskow writes,

> If the image of God as male provides religious support for male dominance in society, the image of God as supreme Other would seem to legitimate dominance of any kind. God as ruler and king of the universe is the pinnacle of a vast hierarchy that extends from God "himself" to angels/men/women/children/animals and

finally the earth. As hierarchical ruler, God is a model for the many schemes of dominance that human beings create for themselves. . . . The image of God as dominating Other functions as a fundamental authorizing symbol in a whole system of hierarchical dualisms.[73]

Many feminists argue that these concepts lie at the heart of the patriarchal system of domination. If the world is to be made better and if human lives are to be led in mutuality and abundance, a new understanding of God and human nature is required. The centerpiece of this new understanding is the concept of divine immanence. Feminist models for God often illustrate this focus on immanence. The divine is understood as friend, lover, matrix, erotic desire, and the power of human relationship.[74] God is radically present in and sacralizes the world. Sallie McFague writes of "the world as 'God's body.' "[75] For many feminists, human relationships, nature, and historical development are the sites of God's holy presence. Indeed, in some cases, God is human relationships, nature, or historical development.[76]

Examples of this move to more immanent, relational models of God are numerous. Sallie McFague uses the image of the divine as lover to express a dynamic relationship of mutual need, desire, and responsibility.[77] Likewise, her turn to the metaphor of "friend" suggests reciprocity, companionship, and mutual care.[78] Similarly, Mary Hunt draws on the language of "friends" or "many women" to reflect the relationality, multiplicity, and mutuality of a "friendly divinity."[79] She turns to plural images for the divine because she suspects that monotheism promotes domination and because she wants to affirm the power of women's communities.

Other feminist models of God also reflect this focus on community. For Carter Heyward, God is "our power in mutual relation." This relational power includes human sexual desire and is the locus of the highest expression of human creativity.[80] Sharon Welch understands divinity to be "relational power" of community and not a power or source or ground outside the community.[81] She also refers to *divinity* not as a noun or verb but as an "adjective or adverb." Divinity, she writes, "connotes a quality of relationships, lives, events, and natural processes that are worthy of worship."[82] For Ruether, on the other hand, "God/ess" refers to "the primal matrix of being" or the source and lure of natural evolutionary process.

For some feminists, God or Goddess refers to an aspect of the self. In an article on the importance of "the Goddess" for feminism, Carol Christ says that some feminists see the Goddess as "the symbol of the affirmation of the legitimacy and beauty of female power."[83] Likewise, Emily Culpepper notes that while some feminists refer to Goddess as a maternal divine being, many others understand Goddess as "a name for woman's spirit or fullest sense of Self."[84] In a similar move, Mary Daly speaks of divinity as "the Self-affirming be-ing of women."[85] Whether the focus is on an aspect of the self, community, or natural processes, all of these examples illustrate a common feminist turn to relational, immanent models of God.

This common move toward boundedness and immanence should not cause us to overlook fundamental disagreements even on this issue. As we saw before, there are great differences among many feminists regarding the "location" and extent of this immanence and boundedness. The theological and ethical assumptions of many moral realists like Ruether or McFague and those of Welch and several other more recent relativist political realists stand in sharp contrast. This division can be seen in several works by postmodern feminists.[86] Certainly these are not the only two groups among feminists.[87] And, as groups, they are not of one voice. Even so, these are two major options within current feminist discussion. The positions of Ruether and Welch illustrate these two clusters.

Although many "earlier" European American feminist theologians (including Ruether) are keenly aware that all theology and ethics come from and are shaped by the theologian's context, they are, for the most part, theological and moral realists. God is somehow beyond human construction; ethics is something more than contingent human choice. There are better and worse ways of living—better and worse moral decisions. And certainly, in the case of a naturalist moral realist like Rosemary Ruether, humans have considerable access to moral knowledge through observation of the natural world, including their own human natures and experiences.[88]

For Ruether, both human moral responsibility and the divine are radically bound to the natural evolutionary process. Her naturalist ethic is morally realist in the sense that the good can be known through the examination of nature (including shared human experience) and enacted through proper social adjustments. Her idealism about nature is not fully politically realist. Her optimism about human knowledge of and potential to enact the good leaves her unable to account for and counter the continuing self-interest and evil evident in the very domination she wishes to fight. Moreover, this idealism makes it difficult for her to maintain a consistent critical perspective by which to judge even her own system. Her ethic emphasizes the growing goodness of creation in a way that makes it difficult to account for distortions of human power. She speaks a Catholic "yes" without a Protestant "no."[89]

By contrast, Welch and several more "recent" feminist theologians are much less confident about the correspondence of our claims about God and moral truth to something beyond human construction.[90] Both God and moral judgment are radically located in human communities and contexts. The postmodern feminist combination of strong political commitments and a tendency toward ethical relativism, or in Welch's case "qualified nihilism," makes it difficult to explain basic feminist ethical assumptions and judgments about patriarchy and to account for the possibility of feminist moral experience (or any moral experience).

For Welch, finite human communities are both the source of human morality and the location of divinity.[91] Moral truth is formed within each age in a battle among various perspectives that are often driven by their own political or economic interests. No moral truths are found in nature, experience, or revelation that will cross history and cultures. Welch's ethic is politically realist in the sense that she is acutely aware of the use of morality and religion to cloak human self-interest and power. Because of the relativism of her political realism, however, she is unable to account for her hope to advance liberation and to curb domination. To put Welch's postmodern position in more traditional language, she speaks a Protestant "no" without a revelatory or natural "yes."

Ruether and Welch, then, represent two very different options in a common feminist move away from appeals to transcendence. For both thinkers, humans are radically bound to, and God is radically immanent in (or even, perhaps, collapsed into), community relationships or the natural evolutionary process. Classical Christian formulations of divine transcendence and otherness are rejected or radically modified.

In my reflections on these two figures and on Reinhold Niebuhr, I contend that the turn away from divine transcendence and human self-transcendence poses difficult problems for feminist theologies. In the interests of *curbing* human domination, some feminist theologians have undercut a primary *check* on human pretense and domination. As we will see, a few feminists insist that divine transcendence relativizes patriarchal claims about God and about human power.

I maintain that the common feminist emphasis on human boundedness and rejection of human self-transcendence have undercut the very assumptions about human freedom on which feminism depends. How is it possible to judge patriarchy, to account for the radical transformations of societies, or to make sense of feminist moral experience without presupposing human freedom or self-transcendence? Indeed, I argue later that freedom is a condition of feminist moral experience. A feminism without radical freedom is not logically or practically possible.

Feminist Reality and Feminist Assumptions

A Summary

At the heart of my feminist realist project is the argument that common feminist rejections of radical human self-transcendence are bad for feminism because they undercut that which makes feminist experience possible. Out of the reality of freedom, feminists reject domination and the structures and theories that support it. Divine transcendence and radical human self-transcendence are, for reasons examined previously, rejected or radically modified because they are thought to encourage domination. But the rejection of radical human self-transcendence in the interest of curbing domination undercuts the very thing that makes feminist experience possible. An affirmation of the human capacity for radical self-transcendence, for radical freedom over culture and nature, is necessary to make sense of the realities of feminist moral experience. Feminism, by rejecting that radical freedom, thus undermines itself. In addition, the rejection of divine otherness and radical transcendence entails the loss of a critical or relativizing principle over and against any human system of domination, including both patriarchy and feminism.

The Realities of Feminist Moral Experience: Oppression and Transformation

Any adequate feminist theology or theory must account for the facts of history and of feminist moral experience. These facts include (1) the extensive restrictions and limitations placed on women across cultures and throughout most of human history, (2) the extraordinary emergence of greater freedom for women, especially in the twentieth century, and (3) the reality that these gains are only partial and contingent (i.e., that they have not been fully extended to all women and are not guaranteed in the future for any women). After reviewing the realities of feminist experience, I will attempt to show that these facts carry normative implications for feminist theology and ethics.

The historical reality of women's oppression and emerging freedom is difficult to ignore. The extension of political, personal, vocational, educational, and economic freedoms to women in this century has been staggering. For example, women were almost completely excluded from voting a hundred years ago. Yet in the course of this century, women's suffrage has been widely expanded. Now most electoral processes in major countries around the world allow women voices and votes.

Closer to home for feminist theologians, theological education offered only limited opportunities for women until recently. Women's existence as scholars is largely dependent on the radical individual and social transformations of this century. Clearly, the destruction of barriers to women's agency or freedom has been one of the great social changes of the twentieth century.

The historical reality of women's oppression is not only in the past, however. Today in many communities, women's opportunities to enact their own freedom are severely limited.[92] Moreover, many feminists have traced a movement of backlash against women's freedoms within American culture.[93] Whatever freedoms have been gained might easily be lost. This is the historical and present context of feminist discussion.

Given the facts of oppression and freedom, what are the implications for feminist theology? To account for these facts—widespread oppression, increasing freedom, and the possibility of backlash—feminists must make sense of several concepts. Any adequate feminist ethic or theology must account for human distortion (sin), human wholeness, and the possibility of moving from one condition to the other (conversion).

Feminist examinations of sin and evil are common and extensive.[94] Likewise, many feminist theologies develop models of human wholeness and imagine new structures and ideologies that will encourage our transformation toward wholeness and away from sin.[95] The problem is not that these realities and concepts are ignored. The problem is that the presuppositions that help to make sense of these realities are sometimes rejected. To account for human distortion, wholeness, and transformation, feminism needs both minimal grounding for human moral claims and an affirmation of the human capacity to transcend (and thereby to reflect on and judge) the givenness of culture and nature. The postmodern feminist suspicion of moral grounding makes it very difficult to explain feminist judgments. Moreover, the common feminist rejection of appeals to individual self-transcendence or radical human freedom undercuts the possibility of the judgment and transformation that are necessary for feminism to exist.

Conversion or transformation for the good assumes some human capacity to radically transcend the given (whether cultural, ideological, natural, or historical) in order to reflect on, judge, and change circumstances and even consciousness. The possibility of feminist conversion or transformation itself assumes a radical human freedom or self-transcendence within the context of our undeniable boundedness and finitude.

Thus, the reality of oppression and freedom carries normative weight for feminists. Feminist theologians reflecting on moral selfhood and God must begin from the fact that if they had been born a century before or perhaps a century later, they would probably not have the structural opportunities to enact their own agency as theologians. From the experience of freedom, we see that it might have been, and might still be, otherwise. A normative commitment to freedom is entailed by the very experience of oppression, judgment, and liberation.

Do many feminist theologies adequately account for this experience of freedom that is so crucial to feminism itself? I claim that feminist rejections or radical modification of the concepts of divine transcendence and human self-transcendence undercut the presuppositions about freedom on which feminism rests.

In summary, feminist moral judgment (or any moral judgment) and feminist hope for social transformation presuppose some human capacity to transcend the givenness of culture and nature. Thus, freedom is the condition of feminist moral experience. And if freedom is so central, then its disavowal or slighting carries serious implications for feminist theological ethics. Therefore, I will attempt to develop a feminist realist ethic that affirms both radical human freedom and human boundedness.

Feminists on Freedom

An appeal to human freedom or self-transcendence should hardly be surprising within feminism. Until a generation ago, most feminist theory shared a liberal or Enlightenment understanding of the individual self as a free and rational being.[96] Indeed, feminism grew out of the extension to women of Enlightenment understandings about human freedom and rationality. Nineteenth-century feminist thought assumed both the human capacity for freedom and some natural grounding of claims about human rights and dignity. Indeed, freedom itself was considered a natural capacity and right.[97] These early feminists were clearly moral realists.

In this century, Simone de Beauvoir continued the feminist emphasis on freedom. De Beauvoir argued that self-transcendence is crucial for women's full development. Because women are more closely associated with nature and are defined as the "other" by more powerful males, they face greater obstacles than men in becoming active subjects in the world. She writes,

Now, what peculiarly signalizes the situation of woman is that she—a free and autonomous being like all human creatures—nevertheless finds herself living in a world where men compel her to assume the status of Other. They propose to stabilize her as object and to doom her to immanence since her transcendence is to be overshadowed and forever transcended by another ego . . . which is essential and sovereign.[98]

De Beauvoir does not stop with the givenness and oppression of women's situation but asks, "How can a human being in woman's situation attain fulfillment?"[99] The answer lies in self-transcendence. Though women are always caught in the tension between the "swoon of immanence" and the "challenge of transcendence,"[100] de Beauvoir suggests that they can maintain moral agency. She writes, "I believe that she has the power to choose between the assertion of her transcendence and her alienation as object."[101] And only by the transcendent act of choosing to assert her transcendence does woman find fulfillment. De Beauvoir also recognizes, however, that the possibility of choosing transcendence is influenced by the oppression of the context. She notes that political, economic, and social independence foster women's transcendence.[102]

Some contemporary feminists have criticized both Simone de Beauvoir and nineteenth-century feminists for their reliance on Western understandings of the self. Postmodern feminists have questioned their "modern" assumptions about individual self-transcendence and freedom, as well as their ethical appeals to nature or human commonality.[103] These "modern" arguments are not liberating for women, the argument runs, but are a central part of Western patriarchal ideology. De Beauvoir's rejection of immanence and affirmation of transcendence, for example, are seen as a "subtle form of co-optation" to male identity and understanding of the world.[104] Instead, there is a call to celebrate women's boundedness to the world (especially to social communities) and to recognize the particularity of all truth claims and experience.

Other feminists have questioned these postmodern attacks on some "Enlightenment" aspects of feminism.[105] These critics of the critics have charged that the common postmodern focus on particularity and the rejection of these appeals to freedom and to some minimal grounding for moral claims may be dangerous for women. This project shares similar concerns.

We have seen, then, that some feminists have emphasized the importance of radical freedom. The goal of this study is to find a way to affirm freedom and to ground moral claims without denying the boundedness and contextual nature of human experience, including moral experience.

Feminists on Divine Transcendence

As we have seen, not all feminists reject the possibility of radical human freedom or self-transcendence. Likewise, some feminist theologians have affirmed the importance of divine transcendence.[106] A few have even suggested that an appeal to divine transcendence can benefit women. Their reappropriation often involves significant redefinition of the concept of transcendence to fit more closely with feminist concerns and themes. Others have suggested that even more classically Christian understandings of transcendence can be helpful within a feminist framework.

Anne Carr, for example, notes that God's transcendent otherness can be a check against the idolatry of patriarchal attempts to use God to support male privilege. On the one hand, she acknowledges that "the idol of a male divinity in heaven issues in a divinizing of male authority, responsibility, power, and holiness on earth."[107] God as transcendent or other should not underwrite but rather should undermine such idolatry. She sees in "the symbol of God . . . the ultimate source of all that is, the name of the hidden one who remains mystery, who transcends and relativizes all our human images and concepts of God."[108] Transcendence, then, should not support patriarchy but should relativize it.

Neither is God's otherness a block to God's immanence. Carr writes of "God as the fully transcendent mystery who encompasses *all* of creation, *all* of our lives in universal presence."[109] Thus, Carr's feminist theology incorporates both transcendence and immanence.

Likewise, Roman Catholic theologian Elizabeth Johnson affirms the idea of God's "holiness and utter transcendence" as not only central to Judaism and Christianity but also helpful as a limit to "patriarchal dominance in naming God."[110] With Carr, Johnson insists that God's hiddenness relativizes all human theologies and projects. God's transcendence reminds us that all of our understandings of God are partial. Transcendence is relevant not only critically or negatively, however. With Karl Rahner, Johnson suggests that human fulfillment needs divine transcendence. "God's inexhaustibility is the very condition for the possibility of the human spirit's self-transcendence in knowledge and love."[111] Thus, for Johnson, human self-transcendence is grounded in divine transcendence.

Ghanaian liberation theologian Mercy Amba Oduyoye affirms both God's greatness and otherness, as well as God's immanent presence. Her hope for liberation is grounded in her belief in a God who is both greater than and active in the transformation of the world and its powers. Her claims about human worth, particularly the worth of women, are based on our creation in the image of God and our redemption by Christ. Human freedom is grounded in God's liberating presence and activity. Oduyoye delineates a classical Christian model of God that incorporates transcendent and immanent elements as liberating for women.[112] For these three feminists, more traditional understandings of divine otherness and mystery are affirmed as beneficial for women.

Other feminists have offered more radical redefinitions. British theologian Grace Jantzen, for example, redefines divine transcendence through the Stoic metaphor of the world as God's body.[113] God is understood to transcend the world as humans transcend their own bodies. By turning to this human model, Jantzen attempts to avoid either "cosmic dualism" or "materialistic mechanism."[114] The analogy from human transcendence provides a tool to speak of a transcendence that is, ironically, radically present.[115]

Jantzen insists that many of the problems associated with classical models of divine transcendence stem from understanding transcendence as the opposite of immanence or of presence. For Jantzen, transcendence is, instead, the opposite of "reducible." Humans, while fully embodied, are not reducible to their bodies. She points to human "consciousness, human personality, freedom, feelings, and a sense of moral responsibility" as examples of transcendent aspects of the self which, though not reducible to the material, are also radically embodied.[116] She writes that "though they transcend the material world, [they] are rooted in that very physicality which they transcend."[117] Analogously, to say that God is transcendent is simply to say that God may not be reduced purely to that material reality in which God is radically present and "embodied."

Jantzen clearly does not want, however, to turn to a dualistic understanding of either divine transcendence or human self-transcendence as somehow "*other* than matter."[118] Transcendence "does not posit an incorporeal extra something of another substance than the body."[119] Indeed, she rejects models of God as over or even "*other*" than the world.[120] Even "*contrasts*" between God and the world are suspect because they result in human domination and the devaluation of the material[121]

If contrasts are denied, is Jantzen finally pantheistic? On the one hand, she affirms that "there is a sense in which it is true to say that God and the world are a single reality."[122] Yet, she also notes a certain "asymmetry" between God and the world; God is not "reducible to mechanism and physical statistics any more than personhood is reducible to physiological data."[123] If pantheism is "reductionism," she rejects it. But if pantheism can acknowledge asymmetry, she affirms it. Indeed, Jantzen describes her model as a type of Christian pantheism. She writes,

> If pantheism is thus understood as an affirmation that all reality is God's reality, that there can be nothing without God or utterly apart from him or independent of him, then pantheism is not an alternative to Christian theology but an ingredient in it. The idea of the universe as God's body draws out this aspect of pantheist thought, stressing as it does God's immanence and totality while still rejecting reductionist accounts which plunge us into mechanistic determinism.[124]

Thus, God is not "other" than or in "contrast" to the world. Neither is God fully reducible to the world any more than human personality is reducible to biological, mechanical processes. It is not clear exactly what this transcendence is or how it is more than the world. It is clear, however, that Jantzen wants to avoid any contrast or discontinuity between God and the world.

While Jantzen's metaphor of the world as God's body compares God to human personhood, Judith Plaskow's community metaphor gives transcendence a different twist. Plaskow seeks to redefine divine transcendence by turning to the model of community.[125] In company with other feminist theologians, Plaskow objects to the hierarchical model of God as "dominating Other."[126] Because this model defines God's power as "power over" (or domination), it encourages humans to either dominate others or give up their responsible exercise of power in an almost childlike dependency.[127] Plaskow writes, "The image of God as dominating Other functions as a fundamental and authorizing symbol in a whole system of hierarchical dualisms."[128] Instead, Plaskow suggests that theologians and worshipers use many images—anthropomorphic, natural, and communal—to express the all-encompassing but not exclusive reality to which monotheism points. She focuses on community images for God because of their relative neglect within feminism and because of the importance of community in Judaism.

Plaskow recognizes the importance of keeping some sense of divine otherness within feminist theology. How may one maintain some sense of God's "otherness," she asks, in the face of the "warm and intimate" metaphors that are commonly used within feminist theology?[129] She is clearly rejecting hierarchical understandings of otherness or transcendence that see God as "a dominating sovereign manipulating the world from outside it and above."[130] Instead, otherness is recast as "moreness" and mystery. "Moreness" need not support hierarchy, she insists. Indeed, the image she uses to explain divine otherness is one of mutuality in community. She writes, "Just as a community is more than the sum of its members, for example, without controlling or dominating them, so God as the ultimate horizon of community and source of unity is more than all things—also without needing to control or dominate them."[131]

So, God is more than or other than the parts of the world, just as a group is more or other than its members. Yet a community is composed of its parts though it functions as a whole. Is God's otherness or moreness, then, simply the uniting of the world's parts into a whole? If so, has Plaskow fallen into pantheism?

God is one with and includes the whole web of life, according to Plaskow. "God is present in the whole of reality—all the processes of development and transformation, growth and decay that make up cosmic existence."[132] God's oneness with the world has implications for divine otherness. First, Plaskow reexamines monotheism. God is "one" in the sense that God unifies and includes everything within God just as a community includes smaller groups within it.[133] Thus, within Plaskow's monotheism, God's otherness does not make the world or its parts into no God but, instead, embraces all things within the oneness of God.[134] Second, because God includes all that is, God is also adversarial. Evil, pain, and death are a part of God that is both "other" and also very familiar to human life.[135] Clearly, for both Jantzen and Plaskow, divine transcendence is dramatically located in the world. As we will see, these arguments about the nature of divine transcendence carry significant ethical implications.

These feminist discussions are a part of a larger debate about divine transcendence in twentieth-century theology.[136] The general feminist emphasis on divine immanence parallels a similar move in many nineteenth- and twentieth-century liberal theologies. Ruether's "location" of God as the ground and source of natural evolutionary process is dependent on the work of Teilhard de Chardin.[137] The common feminist link with process theology makes sense, given the shared emphasis on divine presence in nature and the lure toward the future.[138] Likewise, the postmodern feminist suggestion that the divine *is* some aspect of finite life (including Welch's claim that God is human relationships) is similar to other postmodern arguments.[139] And my own emphasis on divine transcendence is related to my appropriation of Christian realism and Reinhold Niebuhr as resources. Thus, this feminist discussion does not take place in a vacuum but is a part of broader movements in twentieth-century theology.

Reinhold Niebuhr as a Feminist Resource

Niebuhr and Feminist Theologies: Commonalities

Many feminists claim that Reinhold Niebuhr is not a resource for feminist solutions; rather, he is a part of the problem. As we will see in chapter 2, feminists have criticized Niebuhr for subtle as well as outright sexism and male chauvinism. His understandings of God and the self are said to underwrite "the myth of the masculine hero" and to express a "false consciousness."[140] Before examining these charges in the next chapter, I emphasize here the often overlooked similarities between Niebuhr and many feminists.

For both Niebuhr and most feminist theologians, experience is the primary starting place for theological reflection, serving both as its source and its norm. Though appeals to universal human experience are suspect for many feminist theologians, there are frequent appeals to experiences of women or, more recently, to the experiences of particular groups of women (such as lesbian women, middle-class white women, or African American women). Feminist ethical norms, generally drawn from some aspects of women's experiences, drive theological reflection. For both Niebuhr and many feminists, theology begins with experience and is in the service of ethics.

In addition, both Niebuhr and many feminists emphasize the social nature of human sin. Both define human participation in structures and systems, including Christian systems, that dominate others as sin. And for both, any genuine transformation includes the transformation of institutions and structures.

For Niebuhr and many feminists, power analysis is primary in ethical, political, and theological discussion. As children of the twentieth century and its massive suffering and organized evil, they are attuned to the ways that ideas and structures are used to undergird power. Consequently, they suspect that most institutions, including the church, are self-interested. This suspicion leads them to support extra moves to balance power, checking the power of the dominant and giving greater power to the weak.

This suspicious political realism extends to the language of religion and virtue. Both note the use of religious language (as well as appeals to reason or ethical systems) to hide selfish interests. And both reject religious ideologies that promote a flight from the world and its responsibilities by placing greater value in some spiritual realm or afterlife. Yet both appeal to religious language within their own proposals for political transformation.

In addition to these similar concerns, they also share an insistence on the contextual nature of all human language and thought, a commitment to social change, a suspicion of static definitions of human nature and ethics, and an affirmation of the unity and goodness of human life. Though there are numerous points of disagreement, as we shall see, it is helpful to remember the many points of similarity.

Freedom and Boundedness in Niebuhr's Ethic

Like most feminist theologians, then, Niebuhr begins with human experience. As humans reflect on themselves and their world, they experience themselves as bound and free. Humans recognize that they are bound by the givenness of bodies, culture, and natural environments. They are bound by the moral truths of their age, by the needs of their communities, and by the concrete limitations of space and time. Nevertheless, humans also experience themselves as moral actors who reflect on, judge, and transform themselves, their cultures, and their natural environments. The human experiences of reflecting on the value of life, examining the significance of rational processes, and judging and transforming history and community all point to a unique human capacity to transcend self and culture. The tension between human boundedness and human freedom is central to Niebuhr's theological ethic.

For Niebuhr, freedom and boundedness are essential parts of human nature given in creation. Human boundedness is a good gift of God. Human freedom or self-transcendence reflects human creation in the image of God. Freedom, a part of creation and our essential nature, pulls us beyond the natural. This tension is the ground of creativity and sin. In freedom, humans imagine that the world might be different; they transform nature and create and change history. The self-transcendent human is never fully satisfied with the finite creation, looks for a truth greater than the relative truths of the culture, and searches for meaning beyond the limits of the finite world. Sin occurs when, in its self-transcendence, the self exalts something finite, particularly itself. The self, though trying to deceive itself, is dissatisfied. Because of its self-transcendence or freedom, it sees the limits of any finite end and longs for a transcendent end. Freedom longs for a "center of value" or a "principle of comprehension" beyond itself.

Thus, for Niebuhr, faith in God, as well as hope for the future and love of others, is finally a requirement of freedom. Only when the self trusts in a center of meaning, a principle of comprehension, a pure love beyond itself and the finite world, is true creativity, true selfhood, true hope in the future, and true relationship possible. By the analogy of human personality—particularly freedom and engagement in structures—Niebuhr attempts to understand God's transcendence over and immanent presence with creation. Because of our limitations as humans, however, God is never comprehended. Indeed, faith is required because human vision is imperfect.

The longing of the free and bound human has further ethical implications. Seeing the limits of all human norms, the self yearns for a norm beyond history. In Christ, the transcendent norm of agape love is revealed in history. While not a full possibility for human life, agape love is relevant to all human relationships, judging human loves and drawing them toward a purer form of concern for other. Only by striving for this transcendent norm are real justice and mutual love possible. As we have seen in this summary, the tension between human boundedness and freedom drives Niebuhr's theology and ethic. In chapter 3, we examine this tension and its implications more closely.

Feminist Christian Realism

Given my affirmation of human self-transcendence as a condition of feminist moral experience, it is not surprising that I turn to Niebuhr as a resource. Still, even though Niebuhr's Christian realism is a helpful tool for feminism, it is finally inadequate to account fully for feminist moral experience. Niebuhr's ambivalence about the positive moral role of our boundedness to body and to community raises problems for feminists. Only when Niebuhr's Christian realism is revised by feminist criticisms and emphases is it adequate for a feminist theological ethic. Likewise, the theological ethics of Ruether and Welch present both invaluable resources and troubling problems for a feminist Christian realism. Only when the three figures are set in mutually critical interaction does one distinguish the outlines of a feminist Christian realism. What problems and possibilities does each figure offer to this critical synthesis?

Niebuhr's understanding of human nature as bound and free offers a sort of antifoundational foundationalism or antiessentialist essentialism by which to make sense of feminist moral experience. For Niebuhr, human freedom is a part of nature and grounds substantial theological and moral claims. At the same time, freedom undercuts any attempt to overdefine that grounding in nature and makes the transformation of nature and social structure possible. The reality of human freedom also explains the extent of our distortion and sin. The focus on freedom provides an internal critical mechanism for a realist ethic. A feminist Christian realism will appropriate Niebuhr's model of the self as bound and free, while reflecting more fully on the positive moral content of human boundedness in nature and in human community.

Similarly, Niebuhr's emphasis on God's otherness, which unifies, gives meaning to, and relativizes all human projects, is a crucial part of a feminist Christian realism. Niebuhr's focus, however, on the indwelling of the transcendent in the sacrificial love of the cross has been highly criticized by feminists. Thus, a feminist Christian realism will broaden the focus to God's love manifest not only in the cross but also in creation, liberation, judgment, incarnation, and community. As I will argue later, a revised version of these affirmations of divine transcendence and immanence, as well as human self-transcendence and boundedness, would be compatible with and beneficial to feminist theology.

Niebuhr's ambivalence about the positive moral role of human boundedness in nature is balanced by Ruether's naturalist ethic. A feminist Christian realism will critically retrieve Ruether's natural moral realism, which understands the human moral life to reflect and make conscious the natural laws of cooperative interdependence and relationality. Because human moral life is an expression of the natural evolutionary process, it is difficult within her system to account for evil and the radical potential of human freedom to transmute the natural. As we will see later, these problems are especially troubling from the perspective of feminist experience. A feminist Christian realism will attempt to retain some notion of radical human freedom and to avoid Ruether's idealistic optimism about nature and social change. It will give Ruether's naturalist moral realism a more consistent political realism.

Finally, Welch's insistence on the positive role of community interactions is a helpful balance to Niebuhr's ambivalence about the moral capacity of communities. While Niebuhr argues that groups lack a capacity for self-transcendence and are therefore unable to reach the moral level of the individual, Welch insists that the only transcendence possible is the interaction in community discourse. For Welch, the group is the only context and source of moral activity. As we will see later, Welch's relativism and her denial of the moral capacity of individuals raise serious questions for feminists. A feminist Christian realism would appropriate Welch's understanding of transcendence in community interaction while avoiding her relativism and her denial of individual moral responsibility.

Hence, a feminist Christian realism emerges from a mutually critical interaction among Niebuhr, Ruether, and Welch. An additional factor in this critical engagement is the feminist criticism of Niebuhr. A feminist realism must carefully weigh the many charges against his work. To these arguments I now turn.

TWO

What's So Bad about Reinhold Niebuhr?

Feminist Criticisms of Niebuhr

ANY feminist appropriation of Reinhold Niebuhr must begin with the indisputable fact that he has been widely criticized by feminist theologians.[1] Niebuhr's model has come under fire and has, indeed, "gained him a special infamy" among feminists.[2] Because he focuses on the individual self, critics claim that his realism is "an expression of false consciousness"[3] and "a product of the patriarchal mentality."[4] His entire theological ethic is said to reflect and support patriarchal understandings that are damaging for women.[5] Indeed, according to some feminist critics, his thought not only *reflects* patriarchal mentality but also may even *create* patterns of distorted power that might not otherwise be a part of human life.[6] The implicit patriarchal bias pervading his ethic is "no accidental sexism," charges Catherine Keller, but is reflected in the outright sexism of his understanding of family life and motherhood.[7] On consideration of some of the charges against him, Beverly Harrison christens Niebuhr as "prototypical *liberal male chauvinist.*"[8]

A feminist turn to Niebuhr must account for these criticisms. Therefore, the immediate task of this chapter is to outline and analyze four primary feminist criticisms of Niebuhr. In each case, I will look to Niebuhr's work to evaluate briefly the accuracy of the criticisms. In most cases, my response is carried further in the next chapter. The broader goal is to develop a feminist Christian realism that takes seriously both Niebuhr and feminist criticisms.

Though some feminists have labeled Niebuhr as a primary antagonist, the distance between Niebuhr and many feminist theologians is not as great as it might seem at first blush. As we have seen, he is an obvious foil for feminists in part because so many presuppositions are shared. Their theological reflection begins from the starting point of experience. They emphasize the contextual nature of human knowledge, affirm the goodness and unity of creation, insist that the demands of justice are essential to faith, and suspect that the language of religion and morality often hides the interests of the powerful. The significant overlap of argument and concern does not, however, negate the differences between Niebuhr and many feminists.

What's So Bad about Reinhold Niebuhr?
A Summary of Feminist Criticisms

What *is* so bad about Reinhold Niebuhr? What earns Niebuhr the infamous title "prototypical liberal male chauvinist"?[9] Though feminist criticisms of Niebuhr are widespread and divergent, I will focus here on a few central questions. First, is Niebuhr's model of the self so fundamentally individualistic and atomistic as to be irrelevant or even harmful from the perspective of women? Second, is Niebuhr's emphasis on sin as pride inapplicable to women's experience and even detrimental to women? Third, does Niebuhr's transcendent norm of agape love set up a standard that is dangerous for women? Moreover, does his model encourage a conservative cynicism about the political realm and an oppressive romanticism about the private realm, especially the family? Fourth, is Niebuhr explicitly sexist? Do his reflections on gender roles, particularly motherhood and fatherhood, support the oppression of women by men? In outlining these criticisms, I present both dubious and compelling feminist arguments.

The most questionable criticisms center on the charge that Niebuhr's understandings of gender roles in the family are thoroughly sexist and dangerously romantic. An exploration of this point is important not simply as an opportunity to examine the charges of overt sexism.[10] Niebuhr's understandings of family life and gender roles also illustrate larger Niebuhrian themes and tendencies that are directly relevant to the concerns of this project. In these reflections, Niebuhr tries to make his way between self-transcendence and boundedness, between the possibilities of freedom and the limits of nature and community, between the ideal of familial love and the reality of familial power and distortion. In his examination of family relationships and gender roles, Niebuhr attempts to hold boundedness and freedom in tension. We see in these arguments between Niebuhr and his feminist critics the uneasy intersection of the realities of natural creation, social construction, and creative freedom. As we will see, the inconsistencies of both Niebuhr's argument and feminist criticisms underline the need to maintain the tension between human freedom and boundedness in order to account for the full range of human experience.

Niebuhr's Autonomous Self

The Feminist Critics

Many feminists criticize Niebuhr's model of the human self.[11] At the core of Niebuhr's theological ethic, the argument runs, is a highly individuated self that is only secondarily in relation to others. These critics acknowledge that Niebuhr valued and wrote about social relationships and structures. Indeed, a commitment to social transformation drives both his theological ethic and his political activities. They argue, however, that his model of the self that enters the social realm is first and primarily an autonomous individual.

In contrast, according to most feminist models, the self is essentially relational.

From this perspective, the Western conception of an autonomous individual is highly suspect. According to some feminists, this individualistic model is an expression of male anxiety about relationships and a subsequent drive toward separation.[12] Feminists have criticized this individuated self on several grounds. First, an overfocus on the individual as separate is thought to encourage oppressive relationships. If the self fails to recognize its fundamental relationality and attempts instead to emphasize its separation from other selves, it is more likely to hurt others or fail to care for them. Ultimately, this model of the self threatens the whole ecosystem. Second, a fundamental, if unspoken, assumption of many of these arguments seems to be that an individualistic model of the self is simply wrong. It does not correspond to the actual nature of human life, which is relational.[13] Thus, an individualistic model of the self is problematic both normatively and essentially.

These problems with the individualist model are compounded when the uniqueness of the self is understood to be its capacity to transcend itself. Thus the self not only is separated from others but also in its highest form is split off from itself. This situation is worsened by two other tendencies. First, God is also understood to be transcendent to and even somehow separate from the world. Second, maleness is associated with the divine and the transcendent realm, while femaleness is associated with a finite and immanent realm. Through this projection, separation and maleness are sanctified, and relationality and femaleness are denigrated. Many feminists argue that the emphasis on the separate individual and the separate transcendent God pervades the whole patriarchal Christian system and supports oppression.

One of the earliest feminist critics of Niebuhr's model of the self was Ruth Smith. In a comparative study of moral agency in Marx and Niebuhr, Smith criticizes Niebuhr's free, autonomous self. She claims that Niebuhr has "two unreconciled forms of individuality: the social-historical individual who is determined and the free-transcendent individual."[14] His understanding of the self is inadequate, she claims, because of his failure to reconcile these two different models of the self.[15] She writes that Niebuhr's focus on the self both as finite and as transcendent (which she incorrectly associates with the capacity for reason) leads to a division of ethics into individual and collective realms. He never fully develops or incorporates his understanding of community, focusing instead on the individual identity of the self. Finally, his model "involves the basic assumptions of the autonomous perspective. The division of nature and spirit replicates the Kantian distinction between the empirical contingency of relations in time and the transcendent ego which exists beyond them."[16]

Likewise, Judith Vaughan's criticisms hinge on her claim that Niebuhr begins with a model of the moral self as a "free autonomous individual."[17] In a comparison of Niebuhr and Rosemary Ruether, Vaughan argues that Ruether's theological ethic is preferable to Niebuhr's because she begins with a model of the self as fundamentally social. For Ruether, moral decisions are made socially because moral agents *are* social. Because humans are "selves-in-relation," there are "no autonomous individuals acting apart from others."[18]

If selves are so tied to social structure, how is radical change of that structure possible? According to Vaughan, Ruether is able to allow for transformation of society by an individual. The agents of transformation are not autonomous individuals, however, but "social individuals: ethical agents acting out of a specific social context at the same time they are seeking to transform it."[19] Thus, the individual is always intimately tied or bound to the social context. There is no noncontextual, nonsocial perspective.

Why is Ruether's self-in-relation preferred to Niebuhr's so-called autonomous moral agent? Vaughan offers several reasons.[20] First, Niebuhr's model promotes a division of the private and public realm that is "oppressive for women and . . . encourages irresponsibility in social relations." Second, Niebuhr's conception of the individual self is an expression of "false consciousness," while Ruether's self-in-relation is an "expression of a more adequate consciousness." Niebuhr's consciousness is false, Vaughn claims, because his system discourages the transformation toward a new self and society. Vaughan writes that Niebuhr's ethic is

> an expression of false consciousness which supports the very system he wants to change. The vertical and horizontal dimensions, the two moralities, the two norms, the notions of sin and salvation all foster an awareness of individuals as separate and apart from others, and deny the power and responsibility that persons-in-relation have for creating a new humanity and a fundamentally different society in history.[21]

Thus, Vaughan rejects Niebuhr's model because it is thought to be conservative. By contrast, Ruether's self-in-relation is preferred because it promotes individual and social transformation.

Drawing on the work of Vaughan and others, Daphne Hampson also criticizes Niebuhr's understanding of the individual self as "atomic," "monadic," and "isolated."[22] Acknowledging his focus on social relationships, she still insists that Niebuhr had "an extraordinarily individuated concept of the human being, who finds himself essentially caught up in competitive relationships."[23] According to Hampson, this individualistic, competitive model of the self reflects male tendencies to separate from relationships. As a model, then, it is not applicable to women's experience. Moreover, because of its fundamental competitive nature, it supports further relationships of domination. In contrast, feminist models, according to Hampson, assume an "essential relationality."[24] Human selves do not choose to be in social relationships; they are of necessity socially constituted.

Catherine Keller also challenges Niebuhr's model of the self. According to Keller, Niebuhr's individualism springs from his focus on self-transcendence. Indeed, self-transcendence *is* an aspect of individuation or separation. Niebuhr's model, she claims, values "the ability to make oneself an object and to divide oneself from the 'others.'"[25] She notes the irony of Niebuhr's individuated model of the self.

> How odd that the author of *The Nature and Destiny of Man*, which features an extended, often brilliant, critique of modernity, never spots the mote in his own eye: he has reduced self-transcendence to Cartesian reflexivity. He decries the "autonomous individual," of the modern epoch . . . yet both the Cartesian and the Kantian edifices of autonomy are built on the foundation of the self-objectifying and separate ego. . . . Nowhere . . . does Niebuhr recognize the ego's discreteness is the foundation of its egocentricity.[26]

For Keller, Niebuhr's understanding of sin as pride makes sense only within the context of a separate, individuated view of the self. And yet this individuated self refuses to see that its sin is partially in its own understanding of itself as autonomous. Keller writes that the focus on sin as pride "derives precisely from the self-enclosure of a separate self, paradoxically seen as the self's virtue."[27] This move is especially troubling for Keller when it is confirmed in Niebuhr's model of God as primarily transcendent and separate from the world. Human "self-objectification," she writes, is made "in the image of a separate God." Keller insists that Niebuhr continually emphasizes God's separation from the world.

> Niebuhr's consistent substitution of the "intimate relation to" for "immanence in" the world is in this context obviously intended to guarantee God's separateness from the world. And upon this discrete independence of Creator from Creature the entire scheme of self-transcendence hangs: there is to be no interrelation of beings, no blurring of the boundaries between God and the world, self and God, self and Other. God's curving in on himself comes full circle, in the continuing creation of discrete, self-reflecting selves in the image of the God they keep creating.[28]

Keller questions the linkage of human separateness and divine separateness because it is a conservative force in social and political life. Keller is not surprised that many conservatives have appropriated Niebuhr's work. She claims that his profound individualism ultimately underwrites the status quo. That is precisely why patriarchy supports it. She writes, "The politics of individualism is not accidentally sprung from a theology of sheer transcendence. Both express the power plays of patriarchal masculinity, a masculinity that we begin to suspect of a chronic separatism."[29] Keller insists that "traditional" understandings of gender identity are affirmed by this patriarchal theology. Male identity as separate is linked to divine transcendence. Female identity of relation is associated with the finitude of the created order and serves to buttress male separation and power. Keller writes, "Man mirrors the immutable transcendence of his God. And so as human transcendence opens into an unlimited sphere of possibilities, it is sealed back into self-objectification, mirroring the self-objectification of God the Father. What we may now call woman's sin of solubility and man's sin of separation are within patriarchal religion touted as virtues."[30]

To deny his interdependence with creation, the male not only subjugates women and posits his own self-transcendence but also associates this transcendence with the divine. As the autonomous male projects "the sphere of immanence onto the fleshly woman below him, he simultaneously projects his transcendence onto an other worldly spirit above him."[31] If this patriarchal system is supported by an entire theological and philosophical system, what hope is there for changing human understandings of selfhood? For many feminist theologians, the hope lies in the emergence of a new self-in-relation supported by a theology of immanence and relationality.

In summary, many feminist theologians have criticized Niebuhr's model of the self as overly isolated and autonomous. It promotes a division between the public and private realms and is ultimately conservative. Niebuhr's focus on the self-transcendence of the individual is thought by some to reflect elite male needs for separation and control, as well as male denials of finitude. Divine transcendence, then, is a corollary and support to this distortion in the male psyche. In contrast, a more relational feminist model of the self necessitates new models for the divine and, particularly, a focus on divine immanence.

A Feminist Realist Response

As we will see in the next chapter, these readings of Niebuhr overemphasize the individualism of his model of the self. Throughout his work, the social nature of the self is recognized. Certainly in his later writings, he describes the self as fully formed in relationship and bound to the context of its communities.[32] In fact, Niebuhr's understanding of the self in these later writings is closer to the contextually shaped self-in-relation that Vaughan applauds in Ruether than to the caricature of the overindividuated self found in many feminist criticisms of Niebuhr. Yes, Niebuhr does retain some notion of the capacity of the individual self to transcend community and self in a way that groups cannot. This insight, however, is no affront to feminism but is, as I argue later, a crucial piece of a feminist realist argument.

Ruth Smith claims that Niebuhr has two models of the self—bound and free— that are in tension and never reconciled.[33] But Niebuhr is emphatic, as we will see in the next chapter, that the self is a unified whole. Yes, this unified self has two aspects—freedom and boundedness—but it is not two selves or two models of the self. In addition, the tension that he maintains between freedom and boundedness is not bad for feminism. For Niebuhr, this irreconcilable tension is central to our human condition. Moreover, it provides his ethic with an internal critical mechanism that leaves it open to critical modification. (Contra Smith, the tension is based not on an exaltation of reason but on an affirmation of human freedom.) That said, feminist insights about transcendence in community relationships are a helpful counter to Niebuhr. Sharon Welch and others insist that communities do have a capacity for transcendence through mutual criticism and engagement. This, too, is an important piece of a feminist realism that is missing from Niebuhr.

Finally, then, I believe that the common feminist argument is in part true, if overstated. Niebuhr does *emphasize* human individuality. And in his early work, he is overly suspicious of the constructive and transforming possibilities for community engagement. This problem may emerge, as some feminists argue, from a tendency of males toward overindividuation and separation.

But if this feminist argument is true, then surely the opposite could also be argued. As noted previously, some feminists have argued that "women's sin" is a failure to find a self or a tendency to lose self in relationships. Perhaps, then, much feminist theology does reflect a female "sin" in its emphasis on human community and relationality and its suspicion of the actions of individual selves.[34] If this is so, the best antidote to the problem would be the affirmation of a stronger sense of the self as an individual within the context of relationality. Carol Gilligan makes a similar point when she insists that women need to find a sense of self within their relationality.[35] (And perhaps the theological corollary for this need to

Niebuhr on Sin

The Feminist Critics

Feminist criticisms of Niebuhr's doctrine of sin are widely known.[36] Catherine Keller notes, for example, that Niebuhr's understanding of sin has "gained him a special infamy" among feminists.[37] Because Niebuhr and many feminists begin with such contrasting models of the self, it is not surprising that they define sin (and therefore salvation) so differently. Many feminists have argued that Niebuhr's understanding of sin, especially sin as pride, is not adequate to the experiences of women and other oppressed groups. Indeed, Niebuhr's model of sin as pride is thought to be bad for women.

What does Niebuhr say about sin? Niebuhr's reflections on human sin grow from his prior understanding of human experience as self-transcendent and bound. In its broadest definition, sin is the denial of either of these crucial aspects of human identity.[38] The sin of pride is primarily the overextension of self-transcendence and the consequent denial of finitude. The self exalts itself at the expense of others. The loss of one's sense of self-transcendence or one's self in some aspect of the finite world is also understood as sin—the sin of sensuality.

What are the major points of disagreement between Niebuhr and many feminists on this point? Many feminists argue that Niebuhr's definition of sin as pride is unfitting to women's experience. Sin as pride, the argument runs, is more relevant to the experience of powerful males than to that of many females or members of other less powerful groups. Daphne Hampson, for example, claims that the idea of the sin of pride is better suited to "a male dynamic" because "men have been the ones who have been in a position to be proud."[39] Those within less powerful social groups—women, for example—sin not from an overdeveloped sense of self but from a lack of self. According to this argument, the definition of sin as pride is also dangerous for women. By associating pride with sin, Niebuhr discourages women and others from developing an adequate sense of self. Thus, a lopsided focus on the sin of pride may encourage greater passivity in the powerless, thus protecting the position of the powerful.

Some feminists note that Niebuhr's definition of sin as sensuality is more adequate for the experience of women. If the sin of pride or overextension of self is a greater problem for powerful males, the argument runs, then the sin of failing to be a self or to enact one's freedom may be the greater problem for women and others with little social power. Valerie Saiving, Judith Plaskow, and Daphne Hampson, for example, claim that the primary sin for women is not pride but "the failure to take responsibility for self-actualization."[40] Sue Dunfee calls it the "sin of hiding."[41]

Though feminists note that Niebuhr's sin of sensuality is similar to this second feminist model of sin, they also raise several important questions about the particulars of his model. First, though Niebuhr has two understandings of sin, he emphasizes pride more heavily and develops it more fully.[42] Second, when Niebuhr does define sensuality, he focuses almost entirely on the loss of self in physical excess (particularly sexuality.)[43] Thus, he fails to consider fully the loss of self in care for others or in the routine tasks of daily existence so typical in the lives of many women, especially the mothers of young children.

Third, Niebuhr's definition of sin as sensuality is considered inadequate because sensuality is defined as secondary to or derivative of pride. Niebuhr responds to a long tradition in Christian theology in which pride is seen as *the* primary sin.[44] The self turns away from freedom and to outside things or pleasures because of a basic self-centeredness. According to Judith Plaskow, Niebuhr's insistence on the derivative nature of sensuality is not necessary in his larger argument.[45] If Niebuhr focused on his broader definition of sensuality as loss of freedom or self-transcendence rather than the more particular associations with bodily excess, then he could consistently see them as complementary but opposite sins in relation to one's true self, a denial of finitude (pride) or a denial of freedom (sensuality).

Judith Plaskow suggests that Niebuhr's understanding of sensuality as derivative may stem from his ambivalence about creatureliness or finitude. Though he has insisted on the goodness of the created world, Plaskow and others suggest that his ambivalence about creatureliness is evident in the language he uses to refer to it. Human finitude or creatureliness is "an unpleasant fact for Niebuhr."[46] Plaskow links this ambivalence with his claims about the derivative status of the sin of sensuality. "The fact that Niebuhr ignores the positive features of human naturalness may prevent him from fully appreciating sensuality's temptations. Not seeing human beings as continually, positively involved in the world's vitalities, he is less likely to view loss of self in some aspect of these vitalities as a clear and ever present danger."[47] On the contrary, we will see later that his reflections on traditional Christian claims about sensuality center around his trust in the goodness of creation.

Likewise, Niebuhr's understanding of salvation has come under fire. For Niebuhr, the self-transcendent human, tempted to make itself the center, finds its true self by losing self in relation to God and to others. The loss or breaking of the self, then, is necessary to salvation.[48] Feminists criticize this understanding of salvation because it does not reflect women's experience and because it is dangerous for women and for all of creation. The world would be better served by a model of salvation as a healing of the self in relationships.

A Feminist Realist Response

Though a constructive response to these criticisms will be developed more fully later, several general points must first be summarized. The feminist charge that Niebuhr gives greater attention to the sin of pride and does not fully or adequately develop the idea of the sin of sensuality is undeniable. This deficiency in Niebuhr is a problem not only for women but also for the consistency of

Niebuhr's larger system. This lopsided discussion of sin does make Niebuhr less adequate for and appropriate to the experiences of some people.

Moreover, because Niebuhr does tend to overfocus at least part of his discussion on the bodily aspects of sensuality to the neglect of sensuality as the failure to enact freedom, he limits its applicability. It has been suggested that recent Western culture has particular problems with the sin of sensuality as the loss of freedom, as well as with the sin of pride.[49] Thus, a broader definition of sensuality might be more relevant both for many women and for the wider culture.

I also agree with Plaskow that the insistence on sensuality's derivative nature is unnecessary. However, Plaskow and others claim that Niebuhr is unambiguously arguing for the derivative nature of sensuality. As we will see later, Niebuhr does not give unqualified support to the tendency of the Christian tradition to make sensuality derivative; indeed, he openly criticizes it.

Finally, in my analysis of Niebuhr's understanding of human boundedness, I will argue that Plaskow is wrong to suggest that Niebuhr devalues creatureliness.[50] As we will see in the next chapter, Niebuhr affirms the goodness of creation. As Plaskow notes, his language about our created nature is negative at times, but it is also true that his language about transcendence and freedom can be quite negative. Both aspects carry the possibility for great good and great destruction. Moreover, the goodness and unity of creation is a central part of Niebuhr's argument and is evident throughout his work.[51] Even so, Niebuhr does express some ambivalence about creation and about its place as a ground for moral claims. Furthermore, Niebuhr does not fully develop the "requirements" of our boundedness as he does the requirements of freedom. This is a crucial point for a feminist reappropriation of Niebuhr.

Niebuhr's Transcendent Norm: Public Cynicism, Private Idealism, and the Status Quo

The Feminist Critics

Many feminists criticize Niebuhr's appeal to a transcendent norm. Niebuhr claims that agape love, seen in Christ, is the highest ethical norm. This fully self-giving and disinterested love transcends human history and can never be fully enacted by humans because of human sin. Consequently, mutual love and justice are affirmed as more realistic norms for human communal life (though they, too, can be only partially realized). Mutual love (not to be confused with selfishness) normally entails some level of reciprocity. Justice, by contrast, is the balancing of power and interests. They both lack the purity of the transcendent norm of agape love that stands over these less perfect norms, judging them and drawing them toward a greater fulfillment. Though agape love is not fully and perfectly achieved in human lives, it may sometimes be approached, partially and imperfectly, especially in more intimate relationships. In political relationships, the appropriate norm, also only partially approached, is justice or a balancing of interests and power.

Niebuhr's turn to a transcendent norm has prompted several criticisms. First, some feminists claim that this transcendent norm is finally irrelevant to human ethical life.[52] By placing the standard beyond history and claiming that humans will never fully achieve it, Niebuhr is said to deny the possibility of substantial change within history. Thus, the argument runs, his realism is finally conservative. Because Niebuhr believes that power interests will always play a part in human political systems and therefore finds the higher norm to be inappropriate for governing them, he is accused of being essentially conservative and patriarchal.[53] Sheila Collins writes:

> Niebuhr's realism failed to penetrate to the edges of the reality system in which it was immersed. Christian realism is still very much a product of the patriarchal mentality . . . it is essentially pessimistic about the ability of human beings to shape creatively a more humane destiny; and its solution to the human dilemma is to accept and work within the limits of the status quo. . . . Thus, realism positing a kind of ontological determinism offers no new vision by which to understand reality and therefore no new hope for the oppressed. The result is that Christian realism tends to become the ideology of the establishment masquerading as a universally valid world view.[54]

So Niebuhr's transcendent ethic not only fails to help in the struggle for social change but also actually hinders the work for such change. Likewise, Beverly Harrison notes that the focus on a continual assertion of power in all social relationships leaves Niebuhr and the realists with "little or no moral ground for choosing between sides" in political struggles.[55] Realists are finally "ahistorical," she claims.[56] Their pessimism about the inevitability of human power struggles finally denies "the particularity of historical process and the shifting history of institutions largely drops out of the picture."[57]

In a related argument, feminists have also charged that Niebuhr's emphasis on transcendence is dangerously dualistic.[58] By claiming that individuals, because of self-transcendence, have a greater capacity for moral reflection than groups and by suggesting that love may be partially enacted in intimate relationships while justice is the highest possibility for broader political communities, Niebuhr established a divide between the personal and the political. This division of moral expectations for the public and private realm has two negative ramifications, say many feminists. First, this dualistic split dilutes moral obligation in the public realm and leaves it devoid of value.[59] Second, the claim that love as an ethical norm is more relevant to intimate, private relationships romanticizes personal relationships, particularly in families, and thereby fails to recognize the distortion and injustice within them.

Harrison claims, for example, that Niebuhr's "entire" ethic is based on this "presumed discontinuity" between the "dynamics of power" in large social and political communities on the one hand and in more personal communities such as families on the other.[60] This division leaves Niebuhr oddly idealistic about family life. Harrison writes, "Like many a male ethicist, Niebuhr romanticized the family. He characterized familial relationships as the sphere of human life in which mutuality and sacrifice can express themselves directly in human action."[61]

This division is not morally neutral or harmless but blinds Niebuhr to the difficult realities of family life for many women. Harrison notes that Niebuhr recognized some of the social and political problems of sexism, but the possibility that those social injustices against women were also "operating in the supposedly blissful arena of the family never occurred to him."[62] She writes, "It never occurred to him that the 'beatific' arena of interpersonal relations in families was maintained largely by a dualism of gender role expectations, values, and norms that was itself deeply unfair to women. . . . He did not notice that this private/public split legitimized both a capitalist mode of political-economic organization and female subjugation in personal or domestic life."[63] So, these critics argue, the leading realist, who saw the power dynamics in all other communities, failed to recognize them in the family. His affirmation of sacrifice as the highest norm for women within the family simply adds insult to injury.

Ruether also criticizes Niebuhr for dividing public and private morality.[64] She claims that this split in Niebuhr's ethic reflected a larger social pattern in capitalist society. Bourgeois culture artificially divides the workplace and the home. Niebuhr not only furthers the split but also becomes its primary spokesperson. This division was "sanctified in Protestant theology, the theology of bourgeois society, in the form of the split between 'moral man and immoral society.' Reinhold Niebuhr became the chief formulator of this essential dichotomy in bourgeois culture between the home and public life."[65] This bourgeois dichotomy has profound ethical implications for women and for anyone concerned about social change. Morality is banished, claims Ruether, to the private sphere, where it "becomes appropriate only to the individual person-to-person relation exemplified by marriage."[66] On the other hand, this private "love morality" is unfitting for the public realm, where the "the only possible morality is that of a 'justice' defined as a balancing of competitive egoism."[67] The public realm of men is associated with masculinity and brutality, while the private sphere of the home is associated with women, who through self-sacrifice come to symbolize and embody "altruistic morality."[68] Ruether writes, "The male sphere of public life becomes rational in a way that is emptied of human values. Morality is privatized, sentimentalized, and identified with the 'feminine' in a way that both conceals the essential immorality of sexism and rationalizes a value-free public world. A morality defined as 'feminine' has no place in the 'real world' of competitive male egoism."[69]

This division of public and private spheres serves to legitimate—or at least to excuse—male brutality and injustice in the public spheres of business and politics.[70] Expectations of greater change are considered naive and unrealistic. And though the idealization of women as pure and virtuous is ostensibly affirming, it actually serves to restrict them to the home, where they are expected to sacrifice themselves for their husbands and children and to forgo concerns about justice or the balance of power.[71]

Sheila Collins also criticizes Niebuhr for separating the private and public realms.[72] With Ruether, she claims that Niebuhr "gave voice" to a prior move in bourgeois culture "to split the consumer home off from the alienated world of work and to make the home the locus of morality, while decisions based on 'rationality' and a balance between conflicting power forces operated in the world of work."73 By placing morality in the home and associating it with women, Collins says, Niebuhr and bourgeois culture ask women to bear an unfair moral burden that leaves them feeling guilty, dissatisfied, and angry.74 Men, by contrast, are given free rein to operate in the political and economic realm without moral restraint. The division of the public and private realm "has led to an attitude today which derides any attempt to apply moral standards to public life."75 Many church people accept this division without criticism or question. Indeed, she insists that "Christian realism" has given it a "'sacred' legitimation."76 By sanctifying this dualistic model of social reality, Niebuhr and "other realists reveal their immersion in the patriarchal reality system."77 Feminists recognize that the division is false and

> that there is no difference in kind between the personal and the political attitudes and behavior of men in patriarchal societies, but that, in fact, they are beholden to the same reality paradigm with its psychic model of a hierarchically ordered world, its view of the relation between things as governed by a superordinate-subordinate pattern, its distrust of the nonrational and its heavy emphasis on reason and will, its mind/body dualism, its linear view of history, and its tendency to exclusivity and definition through differentiation.78

Thus, for Collins the dualistic split between the moral expectations of home and public life is a part of a much larger patriarchal system that supports hierarchical domination and hinders struggles for liberation and for the enactment of new ways of being. The division is, itself, basically conservative, supporting the dominating patterns present in the status quo.

Daphne Hampson also argues that Niebuhr has romanticized the family in his division of the morality of public and private spheres. Niebuhr's division of love and justice has implications for women because they are limited to home and are the bearers of love. The "private sphere," she writes, "is of course understood to be the sphere of women, who should aspire to freedom and equality only in so far as this does not interfere with their function of motherhood."79 As mothers, women are thought to have a greater capacity than others for agape love. She highlights Niebuhr's claim that sacrificial love is "a moral norm relevant to interpersonal (particularly family) relations, and significant for parents (particularly mothers, heroes and saints), but scarcely applicable to the power relations of modern industry."80

Hampson holds that this equation of mothers and sacrificial love is dangerous for several reasons. First, the focus on sacrifice as the supreme value for women and home discourages any move toward equality for women in the family. She encourages a greater emphasis on justice, in addition to love, as a family value. "Not simply love but justice too, feminists would maintain, must reign in the private sphere."81 Second, Hampson rejects the idea that love is irrelevant to political life. With Ruether and other feminists, she denies the dualistic split between love and justice, insisting that justice is a demand of love in all human communities.82

Thus, many feminists criticize Niebuhr for emphasizing a transcendent norm that is "irrelevant" to human life. They claim that his focus on an unrealizable transcendent norm is fundamentally pessimistic and denies human hope for significant change in this world. As we will see, Niebuhr insists that the transcendent norm is relevant for human history. He claims that justice and mutual love are made possible by the influence of agape love.

Feminists have also criticized the focus on sacrifice in Niebuhr's transcendent norm. They have suggested that this norm encourages women to greater sacrifice of self. Thus, the transcendent norm of agape love is said to lead women further into the sin of the loss of self. I will argue later that Niebuhr's focus on self-sacrifice as the highest norm is not only bad for women and others but also unnecessarily narrows the focus to the suffering love of the cross. It thereby neglects other aspects of love that are expressed in the biblical witness of creation, liberation, incarnation, and community.

The second set of charges relates to Niebuhr's claim that love is somewhat more possible in intimate relations—such as marriage and parenthood—than in political structures, where justice is the best hope. Niebuhr thereby undercuts, so Collins and Ruether suggest, the force of morality in public life. And, on the other side, out of sentimentalism and perhaps male blindness and self-interest, he ignores the injustices done to women in the family, encouraging still greater sacrifice on the part of women and thereby conserving hierarchically ordered gender roles that serve male arrogance and need.

A Feminist Realist Response

How fair are these criticisms to Niebuhr's larger argument and to his specific statements about the family and women's role within it? Is Niebuhr the "prototypical liberal male chauvinist" who sanctifies patriarchy and "formulates" the ideology of bourgeois culture through an appeal to a transcendent norm?

First, as we will see later, these criticisms overdraw Niebuhr's distinction between public and private life, especially in his later work. Niebuhr's point was certainly not to suggest the perfection of love in family life or the absence of value in political life. All human relationships contain possibilities both for distortion and for moral responsibility. Even mutual love and justice (much less agape love) are not perfectly enacted in human life. He does claim, however, that love is more possible in intimate relationships. Surely this is not an unthinkable claim. For example, good parents normally love and take greater responsibility for their own children than for children they do not know. And Niebuhr does note, as we will see later, that families, like all other human communities, must have an element of justice within them, balancing power and competing interests. The distortion and domination evident in human families is both described and derided by Niebuhr. Perhaps what Niebuhr fails to say is that compared with political relationships, intimate relationships may have a greater capacity not only for love and responsibility but also for distortion and evil. Moreover, at times it may be easier to love strangers and humanity in the abstract than the particular humans with whom we are intimate.[83]

On the political side, feminists claim that Niebuhr's division has left the public realm devoid of morality. But Niebuhr's point is not to divide morality artificially so that power interests may have greater freedom to play themselves out without moral restraint.[84] He argues instead that political life cannot be built around the dubious assumption that people will act out of love toward each other. Though humans do sometimes act out of love, even in the political arena, one cannot run political life on the assumption that they always will. Such an assumption would be dangerous for those with little power when the powerful did not act out of love. Consequently, for Niebuhr, political structures should secure justice or the balancing of powers and interests for the sake of the weak. Contrary to Ruether and Collins's argument, this move certainly does not leave the public realm devoid of morality. Justice is a moral value, even if it is not the highest value.

Feminists are correct that for Niebuhr humans tend to operate differently in personal, intimate relations. He hardly "romanticizes" or "idealizes" family life, however. He is not naive about the presence of injustice in the family.[85] He recognizes the injustice of male "tyranny" in the family and also suggests that parental relationships with children are not devoid of manipulation and distortion. Even parental love, he notes, can be used as a tool to extend parents' power in the family. Contrary to the claims of Ruether, Harrison, and others, Niebuhr often recognized the injustices done to women within the family. Indeed, he thought that many arguments about gender differentiation and roles were myths promulgated by males to ensure the continuation of their own domination within the family. According to Niebuhr, males have used religious language to sacralize and sanctify their unjust authority.

Niebuhr referred to the family many times to illustrate the distortion of power in all human relationships. Even the family, he wrote, "does not perfectly coordinate power and love."[86] Indeed, he claimed that fathers often relate to their families as a "projection" of their own egos or as a means for "self-aggrandizement."[87] This imbalance is seen not just in the relationships between men and women. Relationships between parents and children are not free from the "will-to-power" that one finds in other social groups.[88] Consequently, justice is crucial in family life. The balance of power and calculations of rights and justice are as applicable to the life of the family as to larger social groups.[89] Niebuhr writes, "Without the balance of power even the most loving relations may degenerate into unjust relations, and *love may become the screen which hides injustice.* . . . There are Christian 'idealists' today who speak sentimentally of love as the only way to justice, whose family life might benefit from a more delicate 'balance of power.' "[90]

We see here that Niebuhr is not simply criticizing families in which open brutality reigns. Strong, loving parents are also guilty of distortions of power. Love itself is not untainted by parental control and can, in fact, be a tool for the extension of power. It can be an especially dangerous vehicle for power because it tends to disguise the reality of the power and its distortion, becoming a "screen which hides injustice." He notes that children resent the control that comes with parental love. Adolescents naturally rebel against "the power impulses even in the love of the best parents."[91] Children are right, he notes, "in suspecting that power impulses have been subtly compounded with love in the motives of their parents, and that the justice which their parents mete out is least sufferable if the parents are wholly unconscious of this mixture of motives."[92]

We see again that for Niebuhr the *distortion* of love is not the primary difficulty. Blindness to this distortion, so common in families, intensifies the problem. Here, too, Niebuhr is hardly naive about family love. He writes, "There are also many possibilities of using the loving relationship of the family as an instrument of the parental power impulse on a higher or more subtle level. The 'saints' may not be conscious of the fault; but the children who have to extricate themselves from the too close and enduring embrace of loving parents know about it."[93]

Niebuhr is equally critical of male domination of women in the family. When describing the unfair place of many men in traditional family structures, he speaks of male autocracy or "the tyranny of the husband and father in the family."[94] Again and again, he affirms the growing economic and political independence of women that has given them the power to "challenge the unjust dominance of the male in traditional society."[95] He writes, "Women did not gain justice from men, despite the intimacy of the family relations, until they secured sufficient economic freedom to challenge male autocracy."[96] Men not only have been hesitant to give over any power but also have rationalized their possession of it. He notes, for example, that in the suffrage debate men opposed the extension of rights to women by appealing to

> the same arguments . . . which privileged groups have always used in opposition to the extension of privilege. They insisted that women were not capable of exercising the rights to which they aspire, just as dominant classes have always tried to withhold the opportunity for the exercise of rational functions from underprivileged classes and then accused them of lacking capacities, which can be developed only by exercise.[97]

Niebuhr is also suspicious of male attempts to justify domination by appealing to the order of creation.[98] He rejects natural law theories about male headship in the family.[99] Male authority, he claims, is an "*historical contrivance.*"[100] He even suggests that theories about the hierarchical order of gender roles are tainted by "the sin of male arrogance."[101]

In summary, Niebuhr argues that both power and love are defining elements in familial relationships. The love of parents, even good parents, is not free from dominating power and control. Likewise, male authority in traditional families is used as evidence of the way that the will-to-power distorts love and mutuality. These distortions in both spousal and parental relationships are made all the worse by human blindness and rationalization. Niebuhr does not argue that love alone is appropriate for the family and that justice is irrelevant. Justice, involving a balancing of power and the calculation of rights, is necessary in the family, just as it is in all other human communities. But good, healthy intimate relationships cannot be built only around the balance of power and calculation of rights. All human relationships need justice. In our most personal human relationships, it is better if justice can grow out of love and if love can aim toward something more than the calculation of rights. Indeed, for Niebuhr, "Love must strive for something purer than justice if it would attain justice."[102] Therefore, agape love does not deny justice; it makes justice more possible.

Clearly, Niebuhr hardly romanticizes or idealizes the family as the embodiment of perfect love. Contrary to the feminist criticisms previously summarized, Niebuhr has seriously considered and supported the demands of justice within the family. As we will see in the next chapter, his concern for justice in the family is in keeping with his broader ethical argument.

I also disagree with the charge that Niebuhr's transcendent norm leads to a pessimistic support of the status quo. He notes again and again the transformative possibilities of an appeal to transcendent norms. I agree that Niebuhr's focus on the transcendent norm as expressed in the suffering love of the cross raises problems for feminists. But I question the contention that this norm leads to the romaniticizing of family life and the loss of values in the public realm. These claims simply do not fit the textual evidence within Niebuhr.

Niebuhr on Gender Roles: Paternal Dominion and Maternal Constraints

A Summary

In the previous sections, I have examined feminist criticisms that relate to Niebuhr's stress on human self-transcendence. These arguments challenge the idea of an autonomous, self-transcendent individual who experiences sin as a prideful overextension of self and finds that its highest values transcend the finite and hence are only remotely applicable to the world. Perhaps only in the most intimate relationships can this "impossible possibility" of agape love be partially realized. As we have seen, many feminist theologians have criticized this worldview as a reflection of patriarchal mentality. Such a model of human life devalues the finite, ignores the fundamental human relatedness in community, romanticizes the family, is cynical about political community, supports the status quo, and underemphasizes the possibility of sin as a basic loss of self and freedom. All of these criticisms strike at half of Niebuhr's anthropology, the human experience of self-transcendence. Feminist criticisms on gender differentiation relate to the *other* half of Niebuhr's anthropology, the experience of the self as finite or bound. To these feminist criticisms we now turn.[103]

Niebuhr occasionally reflects on gender differences in his discussions of the roles of parents within a family. In many discussions of natural law theory, he points to "the dominion of the father" and the biological limitations on the freedom of mothers. Several feminists have claimed that Niebuhr's grounding of family roles in creation or biology serves as a patriarchal justification for both the constraint of women's freedom and the extension of male authority and privilege. We have already seen that many feminists have criticized Niebuhr's understanding of the family. The charges examined previously (that Niebuhr has romanticized family relations and failed to recognize the need for justice within it) are carried even further here. His definitions of gender roles are seen as a reflection of patriarchal attempts to limit women's freedom and undergird paternal authority. Judith Vaughan, for example, argues that Niebuhr, like other Protestants, has failed to challenge "the patriarchal view of the role of women" in families. This traditional role, claims Vaughan, includes bearing children and being dominated by husbands. Niebuhr furthers this patriarchal view, she insists, when he affirms the natural dominion of the father and when he "contends that the primary function of a woman is motherhood."[104]

In this section, I focus on feminist criticisms of Niebuhr's arguments about paternal dominion and maternal constraint.[105] An examination of feminist criticisms and the relevant Niebuhr texts reveals mistakes, inconsistencies, and odd twists in the arguments of both Niebuhr and his critics. The problems and reversals evident in their arguments illuminate the larger purpose of this project and offer further insight into the relationship between freedom and boundedness.

What were the problems and reversals revealed in this examination? First, some critics base their arguments on oversimplifications and even misreadings of Niebuhr. In fact, as we will see, his claims about motherhood, fatherhood, and the family are often in keeping with feminist models. Niebuhr consistently criticizes male domination and supports the extension of greater freedom and power to women inside and outside the family. Critics who charge that Niebuhr ignores the sexism of the family, advocates the dominion of the father, and ties all women to the vocation of motherhood have simply misread Niebuhr.[106]

We will also examine other texts in which Niebuhr *is* sexist, overdefining the traditional roles of mothers and fathers in the care of children. The surprise is that in most cases his sexism reflects not so much a weakness of his broader realist argument as a failure to carry it through consistently. When Niebuhr pushes the responsibilities of motherhood too far, he contradicts his own claims that human freedom radically transforms nature and culture. He is most consistently Niebuhrian when he is most explicitly feminist.

The examination also reveals reversals in the arguments of Niebuhr and his feminist critics when they come to the subject of motherhood. Feminists who were emphasizing human boundedness in the previous sections suddenly emphasize freedom. And Niebuhr, who moments before was stressing the radical nature of human freedom, abruptly insists on the limits to freedom encountered in human boundedness. Niebuhr and his feminist critics offer, then, conflicting lines of argument. Both anthropology and theology are shaped by their divergent points of departure; one side stresses boundedness, and the other radical freedom. But in the discussion of motherhood, we find an unexpected reversal. Feminist critics are suddenly advocates of women's radical freedom over the limitations of motherhood. Niebuhr suddenly ties the mother closely to biological capacity and the raising of children. The examinations of motherhood, particularly the reversals in their arguments, illuminate the tension between freedom and boundedness in their models of the person.

This reversal returns us to a larger theme of this project—an exploration of the tension between human freedom and boundedness. The most fruitful point for the larger argument is that the discussion of motherhood and fatherhood, particularly the reversal of positions, reveals kinks or problems in their lines of argument. Both sides are unable to account for crucial aspects of human experience because of weaknesses in their models of the self as bound and free. Feminist critics neglect radical freedom; Niebuhr neglects boundedness, particularly as a positive expression or ground of freedom. Reflecting on their kinks and insights, I propose a revised model of the self. Before moving to the larger question of human selfhood, we now turn to an analysis of the textual arguments concerning paternal authority and maternal constraint.

Paternal Dominion

As we have seen, Vaughan charges Niebuhr with promoting the dominant patriarchal view of the family (including women's subjugation) that was a part of his legacy from the Christian church. She carries these charges of sexism further, contending that Niebuhr directly affirms classical Christian arguments for paternal authority. Niebuhr fails to challenge "the patriarchal view of the role of women" that includes bearing children and being dominated by husbands. According to Vaughan, he affirms the dominion of the father as one of "two inexorable bounds set by nature for relations in the family."[107] To support her claim, Vaughan submits two damning references. In the first passage, Niebuhr writes that "nothing in history, except perhaps the authority of the father, belongs to the 'order of creation.'" In the second, he claims, "Every form of dominion, except possibly the first dominion of fatherhood, contains an embarrassment to the moral consciousness of man."[108]

Though these quotations are disturbing, they are not the full story. If we examine these references in the light of his further comments in the same section, Vaughan's claim is considerably less persuasive. Indeed, in the same section, Niebuhr flatly *rejects* natural law arguments for the dominion of the father. Moreover, both the context of the chapters in which these and similar passages fall and the stridency of his broader claims about male injustice in the family reinforce a more generous reading of Niebuhr.

What does Niebuhr say about paternal authority?[109] He often illustrates his reflections on nature and freedom with two examples from the family: the dominion of the father and the biological limitations placed on the freedom of the mother. In several cases, he locates his comments about paternal authority in discussions of human political authority and natural law.[110] Niebuhr claims that self-interested rulers try to justify their power and veil their base impulses by appealing to nature, particularly to the so-called primordial dominion of the father. Niebuhr writes, "The authority of the father as the primary source of all dominion has been a perennial theme in the political theories of the West."[111] Niebuhr insists in these passages that appeals to a pure order of creation deny the role of human freedom and "contrivance" in reworking nature. Because humans throughout history have changed nature—for good and for ill—it is difficult to know what forms are the earliest or most natural, much less to claim that something is legitimate *because* it is natural. Such claims are further suspect when we realize that they are often driven by self-interest.

At first, Niebuhr appears to hedge when he comes to paternal authority. He writes, "Nothing in history, except *perhaps* the authority of the father, belongs to the 'order of creation.'"[112] One might think, as Vaughan does, that we have found convincing evidence that Niebuhr advocates paternal authority. But Niebuhr pushes the contrivance of freedom further, extending its corrupting influence to fatherhood itself. Niebuhr writes "that *male authority is probably itself an historical contrivance* and that a purer nature or history closer to nature, had evolved [from] matriarchy rather than patriarchy. For the mother is the more obvious parent of the two; and in kinship groups it is the *mother's—rather than the father's— authority in which dominion first expresses itself in community.*"[113]

Paternal dominion is neither the natural form nor even an early social form. "Paternal authority, even more than the family itself, is not only an historical development but a comparatively late one." Whatever forms of authority came first, human freedom so changes nature that it is difficult to determine natural patterns for families and "any other human community."[114] Rigid definitions of "natural law" for human societies deny this unavoidable reality.

Niebuhr draws on arguments about paternal authority to illustrate the *destructive* aspects of freedom. He claims that paternal authority, a product of historical contrivance, is subject to the same temptations to pretense and abuse as other forms of power. Male arguments about "supposed absolute standards" for gender differentiation and paternal authority always reflect "something of the sin of male arrogance."[115] Vaughan's claims notwithstanding, Niebuhr's point is not to affirm male dominion but to question natural claims to power, even the claims of fathers.

Niebuhr's criticisms of traditional arguments for paternal dominion conform with his broader rejections of male injustice within the family. As we noted before, even though he is charged with romanticizing the family, Niebuhr refers to the family and fatherhood many times to illustrate typical distortions of power.[116] He criticizes the male "autocracy" and "tyranny" common in family life and charges that fathers often relate to their families as a "projection" of their own egos or as a means for "self-aggrandizement."[117] As we saw previously, he repeatedly supports the increasing economic and political independence of women and criticizes men not only for hesitating to share power but also for rationalizing their sole possession of it.[118]

Because of these problems, the family, like other communities, is subject to imbalances of power and consequently needs the calculations of justice and rights.[119] As noted before, justice is demanded not only in openly abusive families but also in the most loving ones. Indeed, the love of parents for their children can descend into tyranny and injustice. Niebuhr insists, as we saw previously, that love can "*become the screen which hides injustice.*"[120] This is one source of children's resentments toward their parents.[121] For Niebuhr, then, the injustices and distortions of love are not the only problem. Families, even good ones, are not only unjust but also blind to their injustice.

Niebuhr's challenge of traditional gender roles extends beyond the family and the economic and political communities to religious institutions. Niebuhr called for churches to grant women full rights within the church.[122] Niebuhr criticized Episcopalians for refusing to seat elected women delegates to their general convention. Because churches have been slow to grant such equality to women, Niebuhr suggests that they look beyond themselves for guidance and "let secular idealism speak the 'word of God' on occasion."[123] But Christians who are sexist not only go against the "bourgeois standards" of equality for women but also are guilty of "disobedience" to the Bible.[124] Thus, women's equality is given scriptural as well as secular grounding. Niebuhr often refers to Galatians 3:28 to affirm the rights of women and others. In a discussion of the relevance of Christian faith for social justice, Niebuhr writes:

> The vision of universal love expressed by St. Paul in the words: "There is neither Greek nor Jew, there is neither slave nor free, there is neither male nor female, for ye are all one in Christ Jesus," is meant primarily for the church. But it cannot be denied that it is relevant to all social relationships. For the freedom of man makes it impossible to set any limits of race, sex, or social condition upon the brotherhood which may be achieved in history.[125]

Niebuhr insists that the Galatians text is more timeless than the Pauline passages on male headship. Those who still give authority to biblical arguments for male headship are suspect for Niebuhr.[126] The "Bible may thus become the instrument of, rather than the source of judgment upon, the sinful pretensions of men—in this case of the sinful pretensions of the male toward the female."[127] Thus, Niebuhr recognizes the patriarchal nature of some biblical texts but explicitly denies their authority for modern life. He not only rejects male headship but also insists that such arguments express male pretense. Niebuhr was suspicious, then, of the self-interest hidden behind the "dominion of the father," both in the church and in the family.

Niebuhr does not, as Harrison and Ruether charge, fail to see injustice and sexism within the family. He notes that injustice and pretense taint even the most loving families. Neither does he advocate the "dominion of the father." On the contrary, claims for male dominion are expressions of male sin. Niebuhr expressly turns to arguments about "paternal authority" to illustrate the destructive and deceitful aspects of radical human freedom.

Freedom transforms human life not only destructively but also positively. The most natural patterns or the earliest social forms are not necessarily better. Freedom's positive transformations of nature or early social patterns include monogamy, shared marital authority, and sexual fidelity.[128] Monogamy, for example, is not natural for males who are less closely tied to childbearing. But as freedom changes social patterns toward monogamy, the impulses of the "vagrant" male are transformed into something better.[129] Niebuhr also applauds the move away from the single rule of the husband and toward the shared authority of husband and wife. When "there are two centers of authority rather than one . . . the resulting family relation will be on a higher plane than the traditional family."[130] Thus, Niebuhr not only *rejects* paternal dominion but also explicitly affirms mutual authority between wife and husband. We see, then, that for Niebuhr, radical freedom has both positive and negative aspects.

His objections to male dominion are typical of one side of his realist model—the destructive aspects of radical freedom. The free self—in this case, the father—may seek to extend his own power at the expense of others and then conceal the sin by contriving justifications from nature. Niebuhr's focus on the negative aspects of freedom helps to account for destructive elements of human history. His model offers a critical mechanism making it possible to understand, interpret, and watch for the distortions of patriarchy or any other system, including realism and feminism. At the same time, the positive aspects of freedom, exemplified in monogamy and shared marital authority, allow us both to account for the extraordinary transformations in culture that have benefited women and to hope for their further extension. The positive and negative expressions of radical freedom help to make sense, then, both of feminist arguments and of feminist experience.

Maternal Constraint

When Niebuhr writes about paternal authority, he focuses on the limits of natural law and the radical extent of freedom's transformations. When he writes about motherhood, he reverses the emphasis, stressing the limits of freedom and the extent of the mother's boundedness to natural processes. Niebuhr appeals to motherhood to illustrate the inescapable reality of "organic fact" in human life.[131] Critics level three related charges at Niebuhr's model of motherhood. They contend that his model severely limits women's freedoms and binds them closer to nature and parenting, that it makes motherhood the main function of all women, and that it depicts fatherhood as an avocation without any comparable constraints on freedom.[132]

According to Vaughan, Niebuhr draws on an older patriarchal model from the Christian tradition in which childbearing is the primary role for married women. For Niebuhr, she contends, the role of a woman as mother is one of "two inexorable bounds set by nature for relations in the family." Vaughan writes, "Regarding sex differentiation, Niebuhr contends that the *primary function of a woman is motherhood*."[133] Daphne Hampson claims that Niebuhr supports women's "freedom and equality only insofar as this does not interfere with *their function of motherhood*."[134] Keller echoes these concerns, charging that Niebuhr unnecessarily restricts women's freedom. "For women he subsumes with one blow the freedom of the spirit's potential under the biological necessities of a 'primary function.' The unique human individuality Niebuhr so cherishes as the legacy of Christian faith remains barely applicable to women, who *all share the same vocation*."[135]

Keller also objects to Niebuhr's failure to mention similar natural limitations in men. This failure places Niebuhr, in spite of his professed intention, in the long tradition of associating women more closely with nature and men with spirit or freedom. "Men merely share with women the general fact of finitude, but retain their freedom of individual vocation. If it is true of the normative human that *he* 'is at the juncture of spirit and nature,' he has forced woman off the path and into nature."[136] Because Niebuhr emphasizes the so-called fixed obligations of motherhood, critics charge that he commits the very sin he seeks to avoid by extending male freedom at the expense of female freedom and then trying to excuse the injustice by appealing to nature.

What *does* Niebuhr say about motherhood? Niebuhr draws on the example of motherhood to show that radical freedom is sometimes limited by the "facts" of human boundedness. In the passages referred to by Hampson, Keller, and

Vaughan, for example, Niebuhr is attacking natural law arguments and stressing freedom's power to transform natural and social patterns. He turns to the example of motherhood to illustrate the other side of life; human freedom *does* run up against fixed organic limits. He writes, "The natural fact that the woman bears the child binds her to the child and partially limits the freedom of her choice in the development of various potentialities of character not related to the vocation of motherhood."[137] Niebuhr goes on in the next sentences to affirm the growth of freedom for women within the family as long as it is "not incompatible with the primary function of motherhood." Sex differentiation is an unalterable part of biology; the attendant differences in procreation mean that the role of mother always includes greater constraints on freedom. Those who ignore these limitations deny organic fact.[138]

Referring to motherhood, Niebuhr writes of the "necessities of life's organic relationships," the "given facts of nature," and "the organic facts of sex."[139] His descriptions of the "facts" of motherhood can be strikingly negative. In addition to the language of limitation and necessity, he writes of "restraint" and "disability." Because a *"biological restraint"* is placed on women that *"inhibits"* their freedom, they do not share full equality with men. Human efforts, he continues, can go part of the way "to circumvent nature in diminishing the *disabilities* from which women *suffer* in the development of talents which transcend their maternal vocation."[140] Thus, the demands of motherhood are described as deprivation and disability. For Niebuhr, then, freedom transforms nature but does not eliminate the stark givenness of nature, particularly the different roles of men and women in procreation. In these passages, he tries to maintain his characteristic tension between the realities of both our creative freedom and our boundedness to natural and social forms. But in this case (as much as in any other), the weight comes down on the side of boundedness to nature.

Clearly, some aspects of Niebuhr's arguments about motherhood are troubling. Are his detractors correct when they charge that he makes motherhood the primary function of women and unnecessarily restricts women's freedom without offering a comparable limit for men? My analysis focuses on two questions. How extensive are the limits and responsibilities of motherhood? What does Niebuhr mean by the primary function or vocation of motherhood?

If Niebuhr means by primary function that motherhood is the first and most appropriate role for all women, then anyone concerned about human equality and freedom would be right to object. But Niebuhr does not say that in the texts to which his critics refer or, to my knowledge, in any other texts. Niebuhr does *not* say that "the primary function of a woman is motherhood."[141] He nowhere argues that motherhood is the vocation of *all* women. On this issue, Vaughan's and Keller's charges do not stick. In fact, Niebuhr acknowledges that women may rightly take other paths. "Women may choose another vocation besides that of motherhood or they may exchange the vocation of motherhood for another vocation."[142] He goes on to note, however, that because of "biological facts" these vocational choices are more difficult for a woman than for "a mere male."[143]

How extensive are the limits set by the "biological facts" of motherhood? If Niebuhr is simply suggesting that the freedom of a pregnant or lactating woman is constrained by biological necessity in a way that it is not for nonpregnant women and men, then he is descriptively correct.[144] This is a demand not of patriarchy but of biology. Pregnancy can be considered to be *immediately* primary for a pregnant woman without being understood as the primary permanent vocation for the mother herself, much less for all women. The texts reviewed here, particularly when seen in the light of Niebuhr's model of radical freedom, can be consistently read as referring to the straightforward physical demands of pregnancy and lactation. This reading also finds additional support in Niebuhr's own life. During the years when he began writing about the organic limits placed on mothers, his wife not only bore two children but also miscarried several times and subsequently underwent surgery.[145]

But we cannot let Niebuhr off the hook so easily. In a few passages, he pushes the limits and the fixed responsibilities of motherhood beyond the basic biological facts of pregnancy. Though his critics do not refer to these passages, the additional texts provide evidence to support their claim that Niebuhr unnecessarily limits the freedom of mothers. Niebuhr contends that mothers have a special bond and responsibility for children that extends beyond infancy.[146] This longer connection is not, however, a strictly *natural* part of motherhood but is a *social* form that has grown out of "biological facts." "The difference between *fatherhood* as a kind of *avocation* and *motherhood* as a *vocation* has a biological basis which can never be completely overcome. The mother bears the child in her body; and even when she no longer suckles it, the bond between the two is of a special order. *Biological facts* subtly but also *irrevocably determine* certain *social and moral issues.*"[147] Thus, Niebuhr contends that the mother's freedom is limited not only by biology but also by the subsequent social patterns of child care. Mothers are "closer to the heart of the family" and "more necessary to the children."[148] This social form, though not a biological necessity, is not easily changed; indeed, it is determined "irrevocably."

Because of the early physical bond, are mothers subsequently more connected to and responsible for children? Many feminists, including myself, would disagree that the biological facts of pregnancy "irrevocably" determine later patterns of child rearing in all cases. The striking point, though, is not simply that Niebuhr's argument is sexist or unjust but that it is internally inconsistent. His argument for fixed maternal responsibility contradicts his broader assumptions about the radical nature of freedom. A more consistent Niebuhrian argument would allow for the possibility of a change in *this* social form, just as it has in others.

On the other side, feminists can consistently argue for the possibility of *profound* social transformation of parenting roles while acknowledging that biological facts *do* influence social construction in deep and long-lasting ways. The "fact" that women—and not men—bear and nurse children does profoundly shape (though probably not "irrevocably" determine) social structure. In human communities across cultures and centuries, women generally bear greater responsibility for the care of children.[149] This social fact may not be *irrevocable*, but it is certainly *tenacious*. While working for change, feminists can acknowledge this social reality and attempt to improve the lives of women and children within it.

Reflecting on the Discussion: A Feminist Realist Response

In these discussions of motherhood and fatherhood, we find wild inconsistencies *within* Niebuhr's argument, faulty readings *of* Niebuhr in feminist arguments, and odd turns and reversals *in everyone's* argument. These reversals point to illuminating problems or kinks in the arguments of Niebuhr and his critics, particularly in their models of the self. After a brief summary of the misreadings and inconsistencies, I will examine the reversals and kinks more closely.

FEMINIST MISREADINGS AND NIEBUHRIAN INCONSISTENCIES

Through close textual analysis, I have shown that critics have misread Niebuhr. He does *not* say that motherhood is the primary role for all women but maintains instead that women may rightly choose other vocations. Niebuhr does not advocate male dominion in the family. He not only doubts that paternal authority was natural and suggests that maternal dominion was earlier but also charges that male justifications of their authority reflect male arrogance. Moreover, the shared authority of women and men in marriages is a higher form than sole male authority. Throughout his work, then, he sees and challenges sexism both in the family and in broader society.

Of course, this is not the whole story. Though Niebuhr criticizes injustice in traditional models of the family, he does not *fully* see it (much less eliminate it) in his own model. Niebuhr refers to motherhood to note the minimal givenness of organic fact, but he pushes too far when he suggests that mothers bear the primary responsibility for the long-term care of children. The most interesting point is not simply that Niebuhr is sexist but that his sexism springs from inconsistency and incoherence in his argument. He does not suggest that patterns of maternal responsibility are simply tenacious and quite *difficult* to change but that they *cannot* be changed. If freedom radically transforms other social patterns, why is this pattern determined "irrevocably"? If the impulses of the "vagrant male" can be channeled into monogamous sexual relationships, there is no reason to claim that patterns of child raising could not also be changed. Niebuhr not only has no *reason* to limit the transformative capacities of freedom in this way but also has no *grounds*. His radical notion of freedom simply does not square with an "irrevocably" determined social pattern. The sexist Niebuhr is an inconsistent Niebuhr.

Why is Niebuhr inconsistent on this point? One possible answer may come from his own life. The primary references we examined concerning the differences between maternal vocation and paternal avocation were written when Niebuhr's children were approximately ten and fifteen years old. As a realist, it is hard to read those passages and to think about the context of his family life without remembering Niebuhr's own words: "No definition of the natural law between the sexes can be made without embodying something of the sin of male arrogance into the standard."[150] Perhaps Harrison and Ruether are partly right to charge Niebuhr with blindness to sexism in the family, even in his own family.[151]

But I believe that the inconsistencies run deeper. The problem is not simply that Niebuhr ties mothers more closely to the care of children. The *way* he describes the maternal tie or bond is also troubling. As we saw, Niebuhr not only depicts motherhood as a limit to freedom but also turns to negative language, noting the "disabilities" and "restraints" that women "suffer." Moreover, he suggests that the vocation of motherhood constrains freedom, while males or nonmothering females may exercise their freedom to choose other vocations.[152] But why is maternal vocation any *less* an expression of freedom or *more* of a limit than other vocations? And why is the vocation of care for children so linked with pregnancy that it can be only an avocation for fathers? Most important, why is motherhood considered a limit at all? Why isn't the care of children, by any or all members of a community, the highest expression of freedom? I will argue later that these problems point not simply to unacknowledged sexism or minor inconsistencies but to a flaw in his model of the human person as well.

FEMINIST AND NIEBUHRIAN REVERSALS

Behind the Niebuhrian inconsistencies and feminist misreadings, lies the larger problem with which this study began. How do humans hold freedom and boundedness in tension? How can feminism retain a model of radical freedom while avoiding the problems of some traditional Christian models? The arguments about gender roles and family life illustrate beautifully the tension between human freedom and boundedness to social relationships and nature. Who could ignore the radical possibilities for transformation of the natural through the exercise of human freedom? Even in the roles of parenthood, which are as surely tied to biology as any other, the line between nature, culture, and freedom is difficult to discern. Yet though the line is dim, the difference that biology makes for parenthood cannot be denied. In these most familiar human relationships, the tension between freedom and boundedness is unavoidable.

The surprise is not that the tension exists but that it plays itself out so strangely in their lines of argument. On one side, we find the man who normally criticizes natural law arguments and insists on the capacity of the individual to transcend nature, context, and self. On the other side, we find feminists who have affirmed the radical connection of humans to nature and/or society while rejecting claims of radical individual transcendence over context. Yet in the argument here, the roles are reversed. Niebuhr insists that in the case of motherhood, at least, biology and social structure limit the freedom of mothers, and feminist critics are suddenly arguing for women's radical freedom in relation to constricting biological and social roles. What is going on here? These reversals in direction point not simply to minor adjustments but to significant kinks or problems in their lines of reasoning. This small, concrete example from the family illustrates deeper problems in their models of the human person and its relation to the world.

MODELS OF THE HUMAN PERSON

The feminist reversal of argument reveals a weakness in the model of the "connective" person in relation. Because many feminist models of personhood reject self-transcendence or radical freedom and stress full human boundedness, they have difficulty accounting for the extraordinary transformations of the given that are crucial to feminist experience. The discussion of motherhood illustrates why feminists need to maintain a sense of radical freedom in relation to biological function and social expectation. Without this capacity for radical freedom, women are too easily tied to profoundly limiting roles. The reversal toward freedom points to a kink in feminist anthropologies that reject or neglect radical freedom; the reversal, then, is a necessary correction to the model of the connective person in relation.

This insistence on radical freedom is not *antithetical* or even simply *incidental* to feminist moral experience; it is a *central reality* of that experience. As we noted in our examination of Niebuhr, a model of human personhood that incorporates radical human freedom helps not only to account for past transformations of so-called fixed social or natural structures but also to work and to hope for future transformation. In addition, a recognition of the destructive and deceitful capacities of radical freedom offers a tool for understanding the distortions not only of *patriarchy* but also of *any other* human system, including feminism and realism.[153] Thus, a model of the self as radically free is able to account for human capacities both to transform the given in positive and negative ways and to practice internal and external criticism.[154] Feminists who reject models of the self as radically free inadvertently undercut central assumptions necessary to feminist experience. The discussion of motherhood and fatherhood underscores the need for feminists to develop a model of the human person as radically free. Can radical freedom be included in their model without losing their insistence on the goodness and interdependence of bound life?

Initially, Niebuhr's problems appear to be the mirror image of his feminist critics. These critics turn toward freedom in the discussion of motherhood, illustrating the need for a model of the self that includes radical freedom and its transforming relation to boundedness. Niebuhr turns in the *opposite* direction, revealing a need to account more fully for boundedness and its relation to freedom. At this level, the reversal is simply a corrective to his usual emphasis on freedom. Though boundedness is a crucial element of Niebuhr's anthropology, he neglects it as a positive resource for moral reflection; in comparison to freedom, boundedness is a thin resource. So, Niebuhr's turn to motherhood as an example of the moral significance of human boundedness is not so surprising; he is simply working out an often neglected part of his argument.[155]

The surprising part of the reversal is not *that* he turns to boundedness but *how* he does it and *why* he does it that way. Why does Niebuhr describe the maternal vocation not as an *expression* of freedom but as a *negative limit* to freedom? I contend that Niebuhr's negative descriptions of motherhood spring from a weakness in his model of the self. Because of the way he has separated boundedness and freedom within the self, he is unable to account for ordinary human experiences in which boundedness relates to freedom in profound and positive ways. Though radical freedom and boundedness are both essential, created parts of a unified human nature, for Niebuhr, they are distinct elements that exist in uneasy relation.[156] This uneasy relation between them makes it difficult for Niebuhr to account for certain aspects of their interaction. The freedom of the self is, at some level, *estranged* from or extraneous to its own boundedness. Though freedom acts on boundedness both positively and negatively, boundedness relates to freedom as a negative limit. His model can account for experiences in which freedom transforms the bound or in which boundedness limits freedom, but it fails to account for common experiences in which freedom finds its positive ground, meaning, and expression in the bound. The estranged person is unable to reconcile the two elements of its nature. Because of their uneasy relationship, boundedness is a limit to freedom, not its source and fulfillment.

There is another side to Niebuhr's arguments. Occasionally, motherhood and other bonds of human life are described as expressions of freedom, even its highest expression. When humans love sacrificially, giving of themselves for another (particularly in family), they are approximating agape love, the highest expression of freedom.[157] But even here, human bonds are expressions of freedom when they involve loss or *negation* of the self. Thus, even when freedom *does* find expression in boundedness, it is as a limit or negation in extraordinary and difficult circumstances, not as fulfillment and joy in ordinary experience.

We see a parallel in Niebuhr's understanding of God. God's transcendence or freedom finds its highest expression in the cross.[158] Here, too, then, freedom *does* express itself or find its end in boundedness, but primarily as negation and loss, not as joyful creation and abundance. The cross is a necessary companion to Niebuhr's estranged self, with its uneasy relation between freedom and boundedness. It is no surprise that he neglects the doctrines of incarnation, creation, and pneumatology. For Niebuhr, human freedom is expressed in boundedness as loss and negation; God's freedom is expressed in creation as limit and sacrifice.[159]

Niebuhr's model of the "estranged" person is a problem not only because it leads to the neglect of classical Christian categories like creation and incarnation but also because it fails to account for ordinary human experiences in which human freedom finds its positive expression and ground in ordinary bound relationships of human life. Niebuhr has so separated the elements of freedom and boundedness in an uneasy tension that he cannot account for their intimate and positive interaction in human experience. Thus, to make sense of ordinary experiences of human life, including parenthood, an adequate realist ethic needs a model of personhood in which freedom can find in boundedness not only its limit but also its positive fulfillment and source.

Many feminists offer a model of the connected person in relation that partially corrects the deficit in Niebuhr. Their model emphasizes the bound experiences in which humans find meaning and identity. But because many feminist models neglect radical freedom, they are unable to account for crucial aspects of feminist experience. What they neglect, then, Niebuhr partially offers. What model of human personhood could draw on the insights and avoid the problems found in Niebuhr and his feminist critics?

An alternate proposal, the transforming person, synthesizes the models of Niebuhr and some feminists. It maintains both the unity and full boundedness of the feminist connective person and the transforming capacity of Niebuhr's radically free person. In contrast to Niebuhr's model, freedom is not a second element, distinct from boundedness, but is *fully* located and finds its source and meaning within it. In contrast to some feminist models, this free person can radically transcend the bound environment. This model of personhood allows us to make sense of crucial human experiences. By incorporating radical freedom, the model can account for experiences in which boundedness is radically transformed, both positively and negatively. Radical freedom also gives this model a critical mechanism for evaluation. Because freedom is not estranged from boundedness but is a quality of the fully bound person, we can account for those experiences in which freedom finds its positive source, expression, and end in boundedness. This alternate model will be explored more fully in the final chapter.

A Feminist Christian Realist Response: A Summary

Because the next chapter builds on the analysis of the feminist criticisms presented in this chapter, here I review my assessment of the major arguments. First, I partially disagree with feminist claims that Niebuhr worked from an isolated, nonsocial understanding of the self. Niebuhr, particularly in his middle and later work, understood the self to be profoundly socially constructed. Moreover, the maintenance of some understanding of the individual nature of human selves and the capacity for that self to transcend community expectations and roles is important for feminism to account for and promote the transformation of societies to feminist ends. Even so, I agree with feminist claims that Niebuhr focuses on the moral role of the transcendent self so much that he neglects and sometimes even denigrates the positive moral role of the community.

Second, I agree with the general feminist criticism that Niebuhr's preoccupation with the sin of pride and his relative neglect of the sin of sensuality makes his position less relevant for the experiences of some people. At the same time, I take exception to Plaskow's insistence that Niebuhr's discussion of sin reveals his ambivalence about human createdness. I also suggest that some aspects of Niebuhr's understanding of sin can be very helpful for a feminist ethic.

Third, feminist criticisms of Niebuhr's transcendent norm also form part of this analysis. I agree that Niebuhr's focus on the transcendent norm of the self-sacrificial love of the cross as primary is troubling for any feminist argument. I disagree, however, that an appeal to a transcendent norm is finally irrelevant for human life and ultimately supports the status quo. Moreover, the textual evidence does not support the common feminist assertion that Niebuhr promotes a division in which the public realm is devoid of value and the private realm is devoid of justice. Niebuhr clearly saw the corruption of the family and the need for justice within it and was remarkably supportive of women's freedoms in family, church, and public realm. Moreover, in contrast to many feminists' criticism, Niebuhr's insistence that love is more possible within intimate relations is not evidence of sexism but of common sense. What Niebuhr fails to acknowledge, however, is that intimate relationships may carry *greater* possibilities not only for love but also for hatred, distortion, and destruction.

Fourth, I have refuted charges that Niebuhr promoted male dominion in the family or the primary role of motherhood for all women. The texts simply do not support this argument. Moreover, Niebuhr's occasional sexism is fully inconsistent with his larger argument. The conversation between Niebuhr and feminist critics on this issue points to the tension between boundedness and freedom that is crucial to Niebuhr, to feminism, and to a feminist Christian realism. The failure of each side to account for crucial experiences of human life points to problems in their models of the person and suggests the need for an alternate model that maintains the tension between human boundedness and freedom. We will return to this alternate model in the final chapter. The primary task of the next chapter is to explore this tension between boundedness and freedom in the theological ethic of Reinhold Niebuhr.

THREE

Freedom for the World

Reinhold Niebuhr's Christian Realism

THIS chapter explores Reinhold Niebuhr's Christian realism as a resource and a problem for feminist theology. As we have seen, feminist theologians and ethicists have charged that Niebuhr is a "prototypical liberal male chauvinist" whose ethic is an expression of "false consciousness" and a "product of patriarchal mentality."[1] His understandings of the self, sin, a transcendent norm, and fixed gender roles have all come under fire. While this examination of Niebuhr will provide further evidence to *refute* some of those criticisms, it will *substantiate* others. Thus, this chapter continues the task of setting Niebuhr and feminist critics together in mutually critical interaction. I will claim that Niebuhr's reflections on human boundedness and self-transcendence, as well as on divine immanence and transcendence, are a crucial resource for feminist theology. Consequently, this analysis of Niebuhr is also a response to feminist criticisms of appeals to divine transcendence, to human self-transcendence, and to common human experience explored in chapter 1. The task of this chapter is to examine Niebuhr's theological ethic as it develops from his central claim about human boundedness and self-transcendence and to ask what aspects of this ethic are helpful or detrimental to feminism. The larger purpose is to move toward a feminist Christian realism.

Niebuhr's Task: A Summary

Reinhold Niebuhr is a helpful resource for feminism precisely because this crucial tension between freedom and boundedness is evident throughout his theological ethic. He affirms both the fact of our boundedness and our freedom to reflect on and reshape the meaning and social ordering of that boundedness.[2] Niebuhr offers some hope for minimal moral grounding through the reflection on common human needs and experience. At the same time, the creative and destructive capacities of freedom to transform nature always relativize our attempts to say too much about that common experience and need. As we saw before, even the relationship of mother and child is so formed and transformed by human freedom over nature and biology that we cannot say for sure what is natural and what is socially constructed. Even so, Niebuhr insists that our creatureliness makes a difference. Freedom, a part of our nature, enables us to transform our natural and social boundedness. Freedom serves a critical role in Niebuhr's ethic. By emphasizing both freedom and boundedness in moral experience, Niebuhr offers a critical moral realism that is particularly relevant to recent debates in both feminist theology and theological ethics.

As we will see, freedom serves more than a critical or negative role in Niebuhr's ethic. Human self-transcendence, though subject to distortion, is a part of the self's essential nature.[3] It carries with it certain political, theological, social, and moral demands. Politically, the fact of human freedom points to the importance of self-government and the protection of inquiry and expression.[4] Morally, the free self, seeing the contingency of all human norms, longs for a norm beyond its finitude.[5] Theologically, the reality of human freedom requires faith in God.[6] Because of our radical self-transcendence of all finite structures and desires, we long for some ultimate end or "principle of comprehension beyond our comprehension."[7] Without God who transcends human finitude, the tension between our freedom and our boundedness would lead to destructiveness. Only by relying on that which is greater than all of our systems, theologies, finite desires, and plans can we find our own true natures and norm and relate to others responsibly.

Niebuhr draws on the analogy of "personhood" to talk about the biblical conception of God's transcendence and immanence as God's freedom over and engagement in the structures of the world.[8] Divine transcendence and immanence are central to Niebuhr's reflections on the human relation to the divine. This tension between transcendence and immanence, as well as between freedom and boundedness, drives the development of Niebuhr's theological ethic and makes that ethic particularly relevant for feminist theology.

Freedom, Finitude and Religious Language

Niebuhr's use of the language "divine personality" must be understood within the context of his discussion of myth and symbol. Because humans are self-transcendent and finite, they long for some ultimate meaning that transcends the finite. Yet humans can understand and express the infinite only in finite language and myth. Myths speak to the truths of and beyond human experience not by denying the paradoxes and incoherencies of that experience but rather by pointing beyond them. When Niebuhr draws on the myths and images of the "biblical witness" to point to the infinite, he recognizes both their truth and their deception. Niebuhr insists that a "temporal" expression of the eternal can be accomplished "only by symbols which deceive for the sake of truth."[9] Because of the limits of finite language and the paradoxical nature of human life, myths are always partial.

Mythic language is possible because Christian faith assumes that the temporal and eternal are somehow related. "The eternal is revealed and expressed in the temporal but not exhausted in it."[10] Mythical language is somehow "verified" by experience but not by rational or empirical investigation. Niebuhr writes that symbols "describe some meaning or reality, which is not subject to exact analysis but can nevertheless be verified in experience . . . usually in the realm of history and freedom beyond the structures and laws of existence."[11] Thus, the experience to which the symbol relates is the paradoxical experience of freedom over structure. To express this paradoxical relation, the language must carry the tension of finitude and transcendence within it. Human myth attempts to point toward an ultimate coherence or a relation between the temporal and the eternal without denying the tension between them. The myth allows the tension to remain without rejecting or conflating the eternal and the temporal.

Niebuhr's insistence on both the truth and the deception of Christian myths is a response to liberalism and orthodoxy. He rejects the tendency among "orthodox" Christians of his day to accept Christian myths as literally and scientifically true and then to identify them with their own finite moral codes.[12] On the other side, he criticizes the liberal attempt to deny the mystery of the myths and to insist on their immediate relevance to human life. "The original tension of Christian morality is thereby destroyed; for the transcendent ideals of Christian morality have become immanent possibilities in the historic process."[13] Instead, Niebuhr wants to retain the tension between the transcendent and the finite. Thus, when Niebuhr writes about divine freedom (or even human freedom, for that matter), he is using finite language that is both deceiving and true. The free self "stands over" and judges its own finite language and understanding while drawing on that same finite language and understanding to speak of the transcendent. We see here that Niebuhr's understanding and use of religious language emerge from his model of the self as bound and free.

Methodology and Structure

As we have seen, Niebuhr's ethic and theology develop out of his interpretation of human experience as bound and self-transcendent. The tension between these two components forms the locus of moral reflection. The self's reflective moral processes emerge from its partial freedom to view, reflect on, judge, and even transform its boundedness. The self acts responsibly only through an attentiveness to both its freedom and boundedness. And this attentiveness draws the self beyond itself and to God. Through this process, the self is able to be in more genuine relationship with itself and with others.

Niebuhr develops his understanding of experience and his subsequent ethic and theology by contrasting his positions with broad historical options. For example, Niebuhr formulates his positions in contrast to idealists and cynics, liberals and orthodox Christians, Aquinas and Luther.[14] On the one hand, he has a higher view of human nature than Aquinas because he affirms human freedom as an essential part of our created natures not lost in the Fall. Thus, the theological virtues of faith, hope, and love are not extra gifts of grace but requirements of natural freedom. On the other hand, he is closer to Luther than Aquinas in his pessimism about the human ability to know the natural law. But, *unlike* Luther, the problem lies not in the taintedness of natural capacities after the Fall but in the exercise of the natural capacity of freedom. Natural law is questioned, then, because of the "natural" capacity of the self-transcendent human to reflect on and transmute that which is given and the tendency of the self-transcendent human to use the language of virtue and nature to hide its self-interestedness.[15]

In this example and elsewhere, Niebuhr structures his arguments around the tensions between several historical options. In *The Nature and Destiny of Man*, for example, Niebuhr compares his "biblical" understanding of human nature as created (bound) in the image of God (self-transcendent) with the classical Greek focus on human reason, the modern naturalist emphasis on human boundedness, and the idealist exaltation of human self-transcendence to the point where it is lost or unified with universal mind or reason. In response to these positions, he affirms human boundedness to a good creation and the human capacity for self-transcendence in relation to that creation.

Likewise, in *Faith and History,* Niebuhr develops his understanding of history's meaning in contrast to the "classical Greek" attempt to find the meaning of history in the infinite realm of ideas and the modern attempt to find that meaning within the rationality of history itself. Niebuhr claims that Christianity finds the meaning of history in a sovereign God who is transcendent and immanent. God's transcendence or "radical otherness" stands beyond history and all human norms and systems.[16] Out of God's freedom, God discloses God's self in history, giving a glimpse of meaning, unity, and coherence that the world cannot know on its own. Because God's freedom gives meaning to history, it "makes room for the freedom of man."[17] In these examples, we see the importance of Niebuhr's emphasis on divine transcendence and human self-transcendence and boundedness, as well as his use of contrast with broad historical options to clarify his own mediating position.

Both Niebuhr's structure and methodology are profoundly influenced by his focus on the human capacity for self-transcendence. Because Niebuhr begins with human experience as deeply bound yet profoundly free, he *attempts* to sidestep some traditional questions of theological ethics. Whether this move is successful or not, it is important to note that the attempt stems directly from his emphasis on freedom.

Niebuhr does not set out to respond to the question of *how* we know ourselves to be bound and free or, for that matter, how we know anything at all. Epistemology is not his starting point. As Paul Tillich complained, "Niebuhr does not ask, 'How can I know?'; he starts knowing."[18] Likewise, Niebuhr does not begin with questions of methodology. James Gustafson remarks that Niebuhr's theological ethic is not "methodologically self-conscious." He writes, "One looks in vain for a specific articulation of his 'method' of practical reasoning."[19] Likewise, Niebuhr rejects ontologies because he claims that they deny the dynamic freedom of human life.[20] His notorious aversion to epistemology, methodology, and ontology stems not so much from some antiphilosophical bias (as Tillich claims) but directly *from* his understanding of human experience as self-transcendent. Our essential freedom to transcend all theories about being denies their finality. Niebuhr objects to ontologies because he sees them as static. He writes in response to Tillich:

> I do not believe that ontological categories can do justice to the freedom either of the divine or of the human person, or to the unity of the person in his involvement in and transcendence over the temporal flux. If it is "super-naturalistic" to affirm that faith discerns the key to specific meaning above the categories of philosophy, ontological or epistemological, then I must plead guilty of being a supernaturalist.[21]

Of course, Tillich and others have rejected Niebuhr's "rejection of all kinds of ontologies."22 Tillich charged that Niebuhr's insistence on the essentially free nature of human existence does not undercut ontology at all but is, in fact, a prime example of one.23 Speaking of Niebuhr's objection to ontology, Tillich remarks, "What is so interesting is that which I find so often in all anti-philosophical theologians: in the moment in which they start speaking and using abstract terms, they immediately become ontologists against their own will. I prefer to be an ontologist with my will."24 Ironically, whether or not Niebuhr becomes an ontologist "against his will," it is *because* of the will that Niebuhr so objects to ontology. The crucial point here is *not* whether Niebuhr has an implicit ontology. (I believe that he does.) The primary point is that his hesitation about the language of ontology stems directly from his emphasis on radical human freedom. Further, Niebuhr's focus on self-transcendence or freedom entails the questioning of any theory about the nature of being or knowledge—including his own.

Yet the experience of self-transcendence or freedom to reflect on and judge theories does not only relativize or limit any theory, including one about self-transcendence. For Niebuhr, our ability to reflect on and judge our theories of being and knowledge suggests a prior capacity to transcend ourselves, our communities, and our ideas. Thus, the experience of freedom or self-transcendence is both critical of any essential understandings of the self and affirming of at least one essential understanding of the self, that it is free. Niebuhr's claims about human self-transcendence, then, are both essential and essentially deconstructing (though not to the point of rejecting realism). By focusing on human self-transcendence, Niebuhr retains both a substantive definition of human experience that grounds normative and political claims and a dynamic mechanism to criticize internally those claims. Freedom provides both a ground and a critical mechanism. He rejects any claims about the nature of being that would deny this dynamic freedom. His aversion to ontology, then, springs from the paradox of human experience as bound and free.

Niebuhr's ethic starts from experience rather than from explicit questions about ontology or knowledge. Similarly, it does not begin with an inquiry into the nature of God or the requirements of salvation. It is common to note the centrality of anthropology and moral and political concerns in Niebuhr's work.25 James Gustafson claims that theology plays a secondary or derivative role to ethics for Niebuhr. He writes that "it is experience that validates faith and theology; it is for this reason that I claim that in the end, for Niebuhr, theology was in the service of ethics." He continues, "They are dialectically related, but in my judgment the weight is on ethics."26

Gustafson's claim is literally true for Niebuhr. Page for page, pound for pound, the weight *is* on ethics. And clearly, Niebuhr's reflections on human experience *are*, in some procedural way, prior to his inquiries about God. It is important to add, however, that even though Niebuhr *begins* with human experience of boundedness and freedom (and goes on and on about it for half a century and thousands of pages), human experience is clearly not the center, end, or even the ultimate source of his theological ethic.

We are as we are because of a prior work of God. And our seemingly endless transcendence of our selves and our environments prompts us to hope and believe that our freedom can find its true end in its Creator. Thus, while human faith is seen as a "requirement" of human freedom, God's existence is not predicated on our experience or our existence. Finally, the center of Niebuhr's theological ethic is not human experience but God. God's transcendence of and relationship to life as creator, judge, and redeemer makes it possible for humans to live responsibly in relation to self and neighbor. By procedure and structure, Gustafson is surely right; theology is in the service of ethics. But ultimately for Niebuhr, ethics, theology, and all of human life find their true end, center, and source in God. In the final analysis, Niebuhr's is a theocentric ethic.

An Appeal to Human Experience: Bound and Free

Niebuhr claims that there are two aspects of the "essential nature of man."[27] The "facts" of human existence are freedom and boundedness. Niebuhr writes, "He is a 'creature,' which is to say that he is involved in and part of, the temporal-natural process. But he is also made in the 'image of God,' which means that he is not simply involved in the temporal process but has capacities to transcend it and to ask questions about the character of reality in its totality."[28]

This tension between boundedness and freedom is the source of human creativity. The givenness of nature, body, time, and community forms the limits or boundaries within which human life is lived. Through human freedom, the boundaries are often pushed and partially reshaped. History emerges from freedom's constant reshaping of the givenness of its life; but the givenness is never fully overcome. Both boundedness and freedom are inevitable facts of human life. The tension between these elements is the source of human creativity, human sin, and the human need for some source of meaning or center of value outside itself. Niebuhr's understanding of God and human moral and religious experience can be understood only from the perspective of the tension between these two components.

Human Self-Transcendence

As we have seen, human self-transcendence is the unique capacity of the human self to somehow "stand outside" its self, reflecting on and judging its communities, its rational processes, its values, and other aspects of the finite world to which it is bound. Thus, human self-transcendence makes the transformation of that world a possibility: it is the source of human history and creativity. This unique capacity is the part of essential human nature that is made in the image of God. And because of this capacity, humans recognize the limits of their finite existence and are drawn toward faith in a center of value that transcends and unites their finite values.

Niebuhr associates self-transcendence or freedom with various human capacities. He claims that Augustine's focus on human memory as it transcends the present is a recognition of the human capacity for self-transcendence. Niebuhr writes, "The human memory is of particular importance to him as a symbol of man's capacity to transcend time and finally himself."[29] Niebuhr also claims that human conscience and will are two "levels" of self-transcendence.[30] The will refers to the self's transcendence over its "impulses and desires" to achieve some purpose.[31] Conscience refers to the free self's judgment of those "purposes" that results in a sense of obligation.[32] At one level, conscience serves to evaluate the selfish or noble ends to which the will strives. Yet both will and conscience are formed within social structures that bring their own loyalties and prejudices.[33] Moreover, the self's "universal inclination" to use its freedom to further its own purposes and claims taints will and conscience.[34] Human imagination, foresight, memory, conscience, and will are all aspects of self-transcendence.[35]

Niebuhr commonly uses analogy and negative comparison to describe freedom. This style speaks to the character of freedom itself. Because self-transcendence includes the partial transcendence of language and understanding, all conceptions of it are necessarily limited. Niebuhr uses several different images to speak of human self-transcendence. In freedom, the self stands outside its self and other aspects of the finite world.[36] The word *self-transcendence* is itself a spatial image. The self "views" itself, its internal processes and other aspects of the finite world.[37] In freedom, the self "talks" to itself.[38] These spatial, visual, and dialogical images are not to be taken literally, of course, but suggest some partial freedom of the self from those aspects of creation to which it is bound. On the one hand, it is ironic that Niebuhr uses language of our bound life (location, vision, and speech) to make sense of this capacity for freedom from boundedness. On the other hand, it is not so simple. He insists that humans cannot express anything without turning to finite experience and language. This language problem illustrates the dilemma of the human self that is always bound, even in its freedom, to the structures of creation.

Niebuhr often speaks of self-transcendence negatively, by focusing on what it is not. He contrasts his emphasis on self-transcendence with the classical focus on human reason.[39] Human uniqueness is suggested not so much in the ability to reason but in the ability to reflect and to assess reason. He writes, "The very effort to estimate the significance of his rational faculties implies a degree of transcendence over himself which is not fully defined or explained in what is usually connoted by 'reason.'"[40] Reason is a part of the created world that the human partially transcends. It is an expression of our boundedness. Similarly, self-transcendence is not "mind." The mind is also a part of our boundedness.[41] The capacity to make "mind" or "rational process" an object of its reflection and judgment points to the self-transcendent capacity of human life.[42]

Moreover, freedom is found not so much in consciousness as in the capacity to transcend or reflect on consciousness. Niebuhr writes of human self-transcendence "which stands above consciousness as the consciousness of consciousness."[43] Consciousness is shared with the animals and simply emerges from the natural environment. Self-consciousness, by contrast, implies some separation or distinction from the natural.

Similarly, the human proclivity to ask questions about the value of human life suggests some capacity to transcend the life that is observed. Niebuhr claims, "If one turns to the question of the value of human life and asks whether life is worth living, the very character of the question reveals that the questioner must in some sense be able to stand outside of, and to transcend the life which is thus judged and estimated."[44] Even human denials of life's value through suicide point to the self's ability to stand outside the life that is judged and destroyed. Thus, for Niebuhr, human uniqueness lies not in reason or consciousness or even in the moral systems themselves but in our capacity to partially transcend those systems and processes.[45]

The capacity for self-transcendence does not imply that humans have a point of view from which the truth can be seen. Indeed, what self-transcendence provides is a recognition of the limits of all claims about truth. Human freedom, writes Niebuhr, "makes it impossible to accept *our* truth as *the* truth."[46] And yet it is precisely *because* of self-transcendence that we humans often do claim "our truth as the truth." When the self, in its freedom, sees that all human structures are limited, it becomes anxious and pretentiously claims too much for its perspective. Thus, it is out of freedom that humans become dissatisfied with their finite perspective. Niebuhr writes:

> Man is a creature of time and place, whose perspectives and insights are invariably conditioned by his immediate circumstances. But man is not merely the prisoner of time and place. He touches the fringes of the eternal. He is not content to be merely American man, or Chinese man, or bourgeois man, or man of the twentieth century. He wants to be man. He is not content with his truth. He seeks *the* truth.[47]

Niebuhr uses the story of the Tower of Babel to illustrate this tension and the destructiveness of human pretense.[48] Out of the anxiety of freedom, humans often claim too much. These deceitful claims lead to destruction. But at some level, the self-transcendent human knows that its claims are partial. This is why it tries so hard to deceive. Yet, in spite of the deception, it cannot be satisfied with any finite end or perspective. Thus, the free self seeks an end beyond itself. It is out of this longing that humans turn to God.[49]

It is through faith in God that the free self is able to reconcile the tension between its boundedness and its freedom. Through faith in God, the self no longer identifies its own truth with the truth. It no longer denies its finite existence but lives with and creatively transforms it. As we see in Niebuhr's analysis of the story of Babel, human self-transcendence can lead to sin, pretense, deceit, and destruction. At the same time, self-transcendence is also the basis of the beneficial aspects of human creativity, history, religion, and moral systems. Even laughter is an expression of human self-transcendence. It is made possible by the free self's recognition of "the incongruities of its existence" as a free and finite self.[50]

More significantly for feminist discussion, self-transcendence makes history and social transformation possible. Because of its freedom, the self can reflect on, judge, and transform the givenness of its context. Niebuhr writes, "This freedom over natural impulse makes man, who is undoubtedly a creature of nature, into a creator of, and agent in, history."[51] Freedom makes it possible, then, for humans to challenge given social structures and cultural norms. It is the source of revolution. Niebuhr writes, "Any individual who is completely immersed in historical processes is naturally forced to accept the moral, political and religious norms which the caprices of that process make definitive at a given moment. His ability to challenge the victory of a culture or civilization depends upon a measure of freedom over its presuppositions and credos."[52] Thus, Niebuhr's appeal to human self-transcendence is not intended to support the status quo but to account for the possibility of social transformation.[53]

Though I will explore these implications of human freedom more fully later, it is important to make several points about the relation of this account of self-transcendence to feminist criticisms. First, both Niebuhr and many feminists agree that human appeals to transcendence can be expressions of a desire to deny finitude, to underwrite personal power, and to enforce one's truth at the expense of others. But Niebuhr also gives a more positive reading of human self-transcendence. Because of the human capacity for self-transcendence, humans realize that they do not and cannot have the final truth. Because of this capacity, humans turn to a transcendent God who does not underwrite but instead relativizes their truth and power. And because of self-transcendence, humans can radically transform the givenness of their social and even natural environments. I will argue later that these points are crucial for feminist theology.

In spite of some feminist charges, Niebuhr's emphasis on human self-transcendence does not deny human boundedness to the finite. Indeed, any denial of finitude is itself sin. Niebuhr insists throughout his work that human boundedness to social and natural life is not only an inevitable fact of finitude but also a good gift of God's creation. It is to these aspects of human nature that we now turn.

Human Boundedness

The givenness of human life has many aspects for Niebuhr. Humans are partially bound by time and space, by geography and climate, by social context, by the forces of nature, and by the many aspects of bodily life.[54] He writes, "To the essential nature of man belong . . . all his natural endowments, and determinations, his physical and social impulses, his sexual and racial differentiations, in short his character as a creature imbedded in the natural order."[55] Though humans are bound in many ways, I focus here on the relation to society and to body. These aspects are central to Niebuhr's understanding of the self and also provide a helpful context from which to examine feminist criticisms and reflect on the place of boundedness in a feminist Christian realism.

BOUNDEDNESS TO SOCIETY

One locus of this boundedness is the social group in which the human is formed and lives. Niebuhr's self-transcendent human is by no means isolated from natural or social context. Human selves are firmly grounded in human communities, social systems, and ideologies that are not separate from them but form their very identities. This socially formed self can partially transcend community and can even transform it, but the self is always tied to communities by virtue of its formation and continuing existence within them.[56]

Though Niebuhr affirms the positive aspects of human boundedness to community, he is often associated with a more negative spin on social life. Feminists have criticized Niebuhr's focus on the moral capacity of a self-transcendent individual and his suspicion about the selfishness and "inevitable hypocrisy" of human communities.[57] This suspicious, political realist reading of community life was expressed especially strongly in his early work *Moral Man and Immoral Society*, in which Niebuhr writes, "As individuals, men believe that they ought to love and serve each other and establish justice between each other. As racial, economic and national groups they take for themselves, whatever power they can."[58]

Feminist critics of Niebuhr (along with many others) have so emphasized and even exaggerated the distinction between moral man and immoral society that Niebuhr's fuller understanding of the positive role of community has been obscured.[59] Although Niebuhr remained suspicious about human communities (and individuals) throughout his life and continually emphasized the self-transcendent capacity of the individual, he wrote positively about the social nature of human selves.[60] A common theme of his prayers, for example, was thanksgiving for the communities in which humans are formed and live.[61] Moreover, he was critical of the "bourgeois" emphasis on individualism and self-sufficiency.[62] Liberal or bourgeois understandings of individual conscience, Niebuhr wrote, "do not do justice to the fact that the individual is best able to defy a community when his conscience is informed and reinforced by another community."[63] Thus, even acts of conscience are supported by a community that forms and nourishes the self.

Niebuhr rejects the very possibility of an isolated self. Communities are not simply historical artifacts but have a "primordial character."[64] Thus, our social nature is not incidental but a central part of our good created nature.[65] In the early 1930s, Niebuhr wrote, "Man is endowed by nature with organic relations to his fellowmen."[66] The social nature of the self has an even greater role in Niebuhr's later theology. He writes of the self's social formation in family and community. Because human infancy and childhood are so long, human social care is required to train, form, and protect the young.[67] From this natural family unit, humans develop other social groupings that respond to basic human needs. Niebuhr's description of humans' "physical and spiritual need" for permanent relationships with others suggests that the role of community goes beyond the simple provision of care for the young or for protection and order.[68] Niebuhr claims that the self "is not merely dependent upon others for its sustenance and security. It is dependent upon them for the image which it has of itself and for the spiritual security which is as necessary to the self as its social security."[69]

In a later psychological analysis of human social needs for security, Niebuhr locates the source of the capacity for self-giving love within the family and other caring communities. "Self-giving is impossible to the self without resources furnished by the community."[70] Only with the gift of security can the person be freed to love. How is this necessary security formed? Niebuhr draws on psychological theory to explain the possibility of self-giving love. He writes, "The community, chiefly the family in the infancy of the self, is the primary source of the self's security which enables the self to love and relate its life to others. The psychoanalytic study of the child has shown how the security of the self is derived from the love it experienced in childhood from the 'mothering one.' "[71] As the self experiences security through the self-giving of another, it is then able to give itself to others in community, providing security for them. Thus, not only the family but also various human communities offer "the opportunity of self-fulfillment through self-giving."[72] Some human communities not only offer security but also "engage creatively the reason and imagination of the self, thus leading to self-realization by the fulfillment of all its talents."[73] Moreover, "Thus modern psychiatry has validated and given new emphasis to what was defined in orthodox religious thought as 'common grace.' This element of grace may be defined as the 'gift' of security, without which the self is incapable of becoming free of preoccupation with its own security so that it might relate itself to others and achieve true fulfillment of the self."[74]

Grace, security, self-fulfillment, and self-giving love are not separate from or antithetical to community; they are formed within it. The moral capacity for self-giving love, Niebuhr writes, is not a matter of "a robust will" but is instead "a gift of the original security of the self; that is, it is a matter of 'grace.' "[75] Niebuhr's claim that the moral capacity for self-giving love is formed in and nourished by community stands in sharp contrast to some feminist criticisms of his work. As we have seen, many critics charge that Niebuhr promotes an isolated moral individual and a morally bankrupt community. The Niebuhrian individual is "isolated," "monadic," "atomic," "separate," "self-objectifying," and "self-enclosed."[76] The Niebuhrian political community is devoid of morality.[77] Clearly, many of these blanket criticisms do not take into account Niebuhr's positive evaluations of the role of community in the moral formation of highly social selves.

But any analysis of Niebuhr's positive estimation of the social formation of social selves must be balanced by other Niebuhrian emphases. Certainly, Niebuhr's suspicion of communities and of self-transcendent individuals does continue into his later work. The highly positive evaluations of the social nature of human life are always balanced by a suspicion of community selfishness and of human sin.[78] As we have seen, Niebuhr recognizes that injustice and tyranny are even a part of family life. And he insists that families, along with other communities and individuals, tend to hide their selfishness and injustice behind the language of love or loyalty.

As a feminist, I do not find this suspicion troubling. Indeed, a hermeneutic of suspicion about the power dynamics and interests hidden in human communities and human moral claims is an essential aspect of most liberation theologies. Moreover, feminist criticisms of Christian theology and Christian church history assume this hermeneutic of suspicion. This political realism is a benefit to feminist theology.

While noting the social formation of the self, Niebuhr does retain some sense of individuality and individual self-transcendence. This capacity is central to Niebuhr's understanding of the self. It can also be a helpful factor within feminist discourse. If the self is only a social self and lacks individuality or some capacity to transcend community, then the ability to question, criticize, and transform society is weakened. In contrast, some sense of individual self-transcendence allows humans to reflect on, judge, and transform the distortions of society and self.

Though Niebuhr affirmed the centrality of community, he remained ambivalent about the place of the community in human moral life. Although he suggests in later works that the community has a positive role, these ideas are never fully developed.[79] Moreover, he continues to insist that communities lack the capacity for self-transcendence and are, consequently, less responsible morally. Niebuhr fails to consider the profound possibilities for transcendence within the public discourse of a community. Individuals and the community itself can be prodded to higher levels of self and mutually critical reflection. As we will see, a rejection of individual self-transcendence and an emphasis on "horizontal transcendence" within community are central to Sharon Welch's argument and offer a helpful correction to Niebuhr's ambivalence about community interactions.

BOUNDEDNESS TO BODY

Human bodiliness is another crucial aspect of our bound life. For Niebuhr, human self-transcendence over bodily life does not imply a dualism or division of body and mind. In fact, the self's relation to and partial transcendence over body and mind are similar. Niebuhr writes, "The self . . . can take a partially objective view of its body just as it can of its mind. But it has an internal relation to its body as to its consciousness. . . . There is an organic unity in every animal organism which is usually described as its 'soul.' The self is 'soul' insofar as it can think of its body as an object even while it is an inner experience of the bodily organic unity."[80]

So, Niebuhr is not claiming a division of the self. Indeed, drawing on Hebraic tradition, Niebuhr affirms the fundamental unity of the human self.[81] Dualistic understandings of mind and body "stand in sharpest contrast to the Biblical view of man."[82] Niebuhr also notes that the dualism between body and mind often includes the denigration of the body and other aspects of creation.[83] He draws on Hebraic and Christian traditions to affirm the *goodness,* as well as the unity, of all of finite life. All of creation is a good gift of God.[84] Thus, Niebuhr insists, finitude is not evil or the source of sin or evil.[85] Niebuhr writes, "The whole Biblical interpretation of life and history rests upon the assumption that the created world, the world of finite, dependent and contingent existence, is not evil by reason of its finiteness."[86] Sin emerges not from human finitude itself but as an anxious response to the tension between finitude and freedom. It is our denial of our created nature or the exaltation of some aspect of our finitude that is the ground of sin.[87] Thus, Niebuhr affirms the goodness of creation and the full unity of human life. He denies any dualistic divisions of the self and rejects the association of finitude with sin. So far, then, his arguments are similar to those of many feminist theologians.

Some feminist critics maintain, however, that Niebuhr has a negative view of creation in spite of his claims to the contrary. According to Plaskow, human finitude is "an unpleasant fact" for Niebuhr.[88] Indeed, though Niebuhr adamantly affirms the goodness of creation, his language about it often *does* have a negative cast. As creatures, humans are weak, insecure, and insufficient.[89] They must accept this condition "with reverence and humility."[90] In a classic description of the finite side of human nature, Niebuhr writes, "The obvious fact is that man is a child of nature, *subject to* its *vicissitudes, compelled* by its *necessities, driven* by its impulses, and *confined* within the *brevity* of the years which nature permits its varied organic forms, allowing them some, but not too much, latitude."[91] Thus, Niebuhr's human is subject to, driven, confined, and compelled by God's good creation. Clearly, as Plaskow argues, Niebuhr's language *does* express some ambivalence about human creatureliness.

On one level, the ambivalence of Niebuhr's language about creation is somewhat misleading. It is mitigated by the fact that his statements about self-transcendence are not particularly glowing either. Niebuhr describes the self-transcendent person as "anxious" and "homeless."[92] Self-transcendence tempts the person into "megalomania," idolatry, tyranny, and sin.[93]

Moreover, any claims that Niebuhr devalues creation are met with Niebuhr's insistence throughout his work that creation is a good gift of God.[94] This high view of creation is also evident in many of Niebuhr's prayers. One of the constant themes in his published prayers is thanksgiving for creation.[95] Again and again, Niebuhr offers thanks for the "beauty," "wonder," "pleasures," "abundance," and "joy" of the physical creation.[96] He praises God for "the creation of this world, for the wonder of all living things, for the order and harmony in which your creation moves. . . ."[97] He asks God to remind humans of their "kinship with the creatures of the field" who share "our common dependence" on creation.[98] The goodness of creation is a sign of God's love and care. Niebuhr prays:

> We thank you for this good earth and for all the dependable rhythms in this our natural home, which speaks to us of the constancy of your love: for the alternations of day and night, of seed time and harvest; for the fruits of the earth and every miracle of abundance by which our life is sustained; for the daily round of our duties and the discipline of our responsibilities; for the rest which comes after toil at the end of the day and also at the end of our day of life.[99]

Thus, the rhythms of life—day and night, planting and harvest, work and rest and even death—are not devalued or denied. Instead, they are praised as good parts of God's creation and as signs of God's love. These prayers do not portray creation as "an unpleasant fact."

Plaskow overstates Niebuhr's ambivalence about creation. Even so, Niebuhr does give much less time or consideration to the moral implications of our boundedness. Because freedom always transmutes the natural, no pure nature is available. And, in spite of his affirmations of the goodness of creation, his language about creation is often ambivalent, and it is, perhaps, somewhat *more* negative than the language about freedom. Moreover, as we will see later, his ambivalence about human boundedness is mirrored in his ambivalence about natural law. Feminist criticisms of Niebuhr's negative evaluation of creatureliness may be overdrawn. Nevertheless, they do point to a neglected area that invites greater reflection. A feminist Christian realism will need to explore more fully the moral implications of a good creation.

Freedom and the Natural Law

Niebuhr's ambivalence about createdness is mirrored in his ambivalence about the natural law. This ambivalence stems from the tension between human freedom and boundedness. On the one hand, Niebuhr relates his own claims about the requirements of human boundedness to the natural law tradition.[100] Reflection on human creatureliness yields certain laws with "tentative validity."[101] Natural law "defines the proper performance of his functions, the normal harmony of his impulses, the normal social relations between himself and his fellows within the limitations of the natural order."[102]

Yet because of human freedom, any claims about the natural law are profoundly qualified. Human freedom or self-transcendence not only qualifies human boundedness by reflecting on and judging it but also leads to the creative transformation (and sometimes distortion) of that which is given in nature. Because of freedom, there is "no uncorrupted natural law."[103] Consequently, Roman Catholic natural law tradition is troubling to Niebuhr precisely because it fails to account for the dynamic reality and the effects of the other part of human nature (freedom) and overestimates the capacity of reason to discern sure moral norms.

For example, Niebuhr objects to natural law arguments about fixed gender roles because they fail to account for the complexities of human freedom. Though Niebuhr acknowledges briefly the natural demands of pregnancy that somewhat limit a mother's freedom, the whole point of the discussion is to show the limitations of any arguments from nature.[104] Because of human freedom, social forms (even those based in nature) can be creatively transformed. Because of the destructive use of freedom, social forms emerge that support a dominant group who, in turn, claim that those social forms are natural and fixed. Speaking of gender roles, Niebuhr writes: "The freedom, which is the unique capacity of humankind, makes it difficult to set precise standards for all time for any kind of relationship, including the relation between the sexes. The sinfulness of man, on the other hand, makes it inevitable that a dominant class, group, and sex should seek to define a relationship, which guarantees its dominance, as permanently normative."[105] So, Niebuhr is suspicious of natural law arguments because he suspects that they often represent attempts by prideful selves or groups to solidify their position by giving it "natural" justification.

For Niebuhr, then, claims about the natural law are suspect because they are so often interest driven. Moreover, they are also a problem because it is difficult to discern any "original" natural social patterns, given the millennia of social transformations that have taken place since the earliest human civilizations. Humans cannot see nature in pure form. They see nature (including their own) only through the lens of social forms that have been changed over time by the creative and destructive powers of freedom. Their self-transcendence provides the capacity to reflect on nature and society, but it is impossible to see natural and social givenness in pure form.

As we saw previously, however, Niebuhr does have a place for some minimal moral argument based on human creatureliness.[106] Moreover, because human freedom is an essential element of human nature and createdness, his analysis of the requirements of freedom could itself be read as a sort of natural law argument.[107] Niebuhr, however, normally associates the demands of freedom not with natural law but with original righteousness. He writes, "We have suggested that what is usually known as 'natural law' . . . is roughly synonymous with the requirements of man as creature and that the virtues, defined in Catholic thought as 'theological virtues,' that is the virtues faith, hope and love, are the requirements of his freedom and represent the *justitia originalis*."[108]

Thus, freedom, though distorted by human sin, is still available to human life. It is not an extra gift of God but part of the essential nature of all humans. And out of this natural capacity for self-transcendence come the theological virtues of faith, hope, and love. They are the requirements of freedom. Freedom, then, serves both a critical and a constructive role for Niebuhr. It both undermines and overdefines claims of natural law and it carries its own requirement. I now turn to these claims about the demands of freedom.

God and the Requirements of Freedom

Niebuhr's emphasis on freedom is not only a negative or critical principle. The reality of self-transcendence is reflected in certain fundamental human needs or longings in human life; freedom carries positive requirements with it. As Niebuhr lays out the requirements of freedom, he reenvisions the traditional theological virtues. They are not supernatural gifts beyond human nature but are, in fact, a requirement of our essential, natural selves. Niebuhr sets this claim about the theological virtues and original righteousness in contrast to both "Catholic theology" and "Protestant theology."[109] He objects to the "Protestant" assertion that natural justice is lost in the Fall. He objects to the "Catholic" assumptions both that original justice was lost and that natural justice remained undefined. Instead, Niebuhr suggests that humans retain some capacity for natural justice (though significantly tainted by sin). Moreover, original justice also remains after "the Fall" as a "potentiality" of human life that is a requirement of freedom. He writes:

> The real situation is that "original justice" in the sense of a mythical "perfection before the Fall" is never completely lost. It is not a reality in man but always a potentiality. It is always what he ought to be. It is the only goodness completely compatible with his own and his fellow man's freedom—that is, with their ultimate transcendence over all circumstances of nature. Man is neither completely bereft of original righteousness or as completely in possession of "natural justice" as the Catholic theory assumes.[110]

Thus, both natural justice and original righteousness are retained in tainted form after the Fall. The theological virtues are not an extra gift of grace in Christ. Our experiences of faith, hope, and love are "requirements of [the self's] nature as free spirit."[111] And according to Niebuhr, this human experience itself gives witness to the divine reality.[112]

We have seen that the self-transcendent human senses the limitations of all the claims and structures of the world and longs for the ultimate. Niebuhr suggests that these shared human experiences can point toward God. Humans believe that "God is both the ground of our existence and the ultimate pinnacle of perfection toward which existence tends. Therefore, the highest human excellencies are clues to the character of God."[113] How is human nature—particularly its "excellencies"—a "clue" to the nature of God? How does self-transcendence require faith, hope, and love? Human self-transcendence causes humans to look for an end, a norm, or a source of meaning beyond themselves. Humans, sensing the tension between the limits of the finite situation and the seemingly infinite but unreachable possibilities of self-transcendence, become anxious. Human self-transcendence continues in "infinite regression." The free self is distinguished not just by its ability to choose among finite options presented in ordinary life. It is distinguished in its capacity to choose its "total end."[114] As much as the self might try, it cannot find a satisfactory end in any finite thing or self. Yet, because it is self-transcendent, the self still searches for some end beyond itself and the creation to which it is bound. It is not satisfied with partial limited ends but must choose a "total end." It "cannot find the end of life except in God."[115]

Likewise, as free humans see the limitations of their own norms, they long for an unconditioned norm.[116] Niebuhr writes that the self "cannot regard anything in the flux of nature and history as his final norm. Man is a creature who cannot find a true norm short of the nature of ultimate reality."[117] Moreover, the self, because of its transcendent element, is unable to understand itself except in relation to God and as it feels itself to be understood by God.[118] The free self sees the limits of all human understanding and all principles of comprehension. Yet, because it is transcendent, it longs for some ultimate principle of comprehension of the "whole" to make sense of life. Thus, it is unable to understand itself and its world "without a principle of comprehension which is beyond [its] comprehension."[119]

Similarly, attempts by the free self to find meaning and coherence in the finite structures and processes of the world inevitably end with failure.[120] Indeed, Niebuhr writes, "Genuine freedom, with the implied possibility of violating the natural or rational structures of the world, cannot be conceived in any natural or rational scheme of coherence."[121] Though human freedom negates any ultimate reliance on such structures, humans "discern a mystery and meaning above and beyond their rational faculties."[122]

In summary, as the free self recognizes the limits of its norms, its finite ends, its principles of comprehension, and its systems of coherence and meaning, it yearns for the ultimate.[123] Out of this predicament and this longing, faith is born. The self is only transcendent enough to see its need for an ultimate end and unifying principle. No matter how hard the effort or how loud the claims, the self is unable to create or attain such an end. Only through faith in God and an acceptance of its finite condition can the human find peace and reconciliation. Niebuhr writes, "Faith in the providence of God is a necessity of freedom because, without it, the anxiety of freedom tempts man to seek self-sufficiency and self-mastery incompatible with his dependence upon forces which he does not control."[124] Thus, only when the self trusts in God is its freedom made tolerable. Only through faith is self-transcendence transformed from a destructive force into a creative force in human lives and in history.

Similarly, hope is a requirement of freedom that springs from faith. Hope is "faith with regard to the future."[125] When the self faces the reality of human sin and the openness of the future without faith in God, the picture is bleak. Only hope allows the self to live confidently into the future. "Hope . . . deals with the future as a realm where infinite possibilities are realized and which must be a realm of terror if it is not under the providence of God; for in that case it would stand under either a blind fate or pure caprice."[126] Thus, without hope as trust in God's providence, we cannot live responsibly. The radical openness of the future without faith threatens our basic "systems of meaning."[127] It is only through this hope as faith for the future that our paralysis is overcome and we can move forward without succumbing to fear.

The third requirement of freedom is love. Love is both a direct requirement of freedom and (like hope) is also derivative of faith. Humans, though bound together by social relations and natural social impulses, separate themselves from one another because of the anxiety that arises from self-transcendence. It is only through love that they can relate to each other "in terms which will do justice to both the bonds of nature and the freedom of their spirit."[128] In love, the self is delivered from its anxiety to be present as an "I" to the other (and to itself). And in love, this present self can see the other as a "Thou," "a unique center of life and purpose."[129]

Though freedom requires love, faith makes it possible. Faith in God liberates humans from self-preoccupation and frees them to love others as selves and not as things.[130] "Without such trust [in God] man is involved in the vicious circle of anxiety and self-sufficiency which inhibits him from genuine concern for the needs of the neighbor. Love between man and man is thus but one facet of the total *justitia originalis*. It is also the final form of that righteousness."[131]

For Niebuhr, then, faith, hope, and love spring from human freedom. These "theological virtues" are a part of our original righteousness. They are not a *donum supernaturale*, a supernatural gift, but emerge from our created nature. They were not lost in the Fall but form a part of common human experience.[132] This original righteousness finds its "final form" in communities of love.

Revelation: The Witness of Human Experience and Scripture to the Divine

So, if faith in God and God's providence in the future is a requirement of freedom, what is revealed about this God in whom we believe? For Niebuhr, revelation occurs in two interrelated ways: general (or personal-individual) revelation and special (or social historical) revelation.[133] Special revelation is "the record of those events in history in which faith discerns the self-disclosure of God."[134] General revelation is the personal sense that all humans share of being "confronted" by or aware of a reality beyond themselves and the finite world.[135] As we live in the tension between our self-transcendence and our boundedness, we sense that things are not right with us. As we saw, our transcendence finds no true end except in God. Humans experience this "encounter" in a sense of awe, moral obligation, and desire for mercy. Niebuhr writes, "The sense of being confronted with a 'wholly other' at the edge of human consciousness, contains three elements. . . . The first is the sense of reverence for a majesty and of dependence upon an ultimate source of being. The second is the sense of moral obligation laid upon one from beyond oneself and of moral unworthiness before a judge. The third . . . is the longing for forgiveness."[136]

These shared human experiences of dependence and awe, moral obligation and unworthiness, and desire for mercy and forgiveness speak to us about God and are confirmed by the biblical witness. We know God as a creator on whom we depend, a judge before whom we feel morally unworthy, and a redeemer in whom we hope for reconciliation and mercy.[137] Though these aspects of God are known partially through general revelation, they are understood and made clearer in the biblical witness of God's relation to human life.

The biblical conception of God's creation of the world suggests God's transcendence and "His intimate relation to the world."[138] The idea of general revelation makes sense in the context of God's creation. It suggests that the "world in its totality" is revelatory.[139] The world is understood to somehow "point beyond" itself and "to" the Creator. Yet, the biblical idea of God as Creator avoids any simple identification of creation with the Creator. The creation is not the Creator. Thus this "'primitive' concept" of God's creation "preserves and protects the idea of the freedom of God and His transcendence" while affirming the goodness of God's creation.[140] Therefore, in this biblical idea of God as Creator, humans find a limit to the "infinite regression" of their self-transcendence. Moreover, the boundedness of human life and history is unified and given meaning by virtue of its relation to its Creator.[141]

The biblical witness speaks to the general human sense of moral obligation and judgment. The Bible, particularly the writings of the prophets, speaks words of judgment against human idolatry and pretense. The prophets saw the tendency of the human self to deny its limitations, to seek a "power and security" incompatible with its finite existence, and then to pretend that its sin is actually virtue.[142] This prophetic interpretation claims that such human sin will lead to divine judgment and destruction.

The biblical witness speaks not only to the human sense of being judged but also to the general human longing for forgiveness. In Christ, God's mercy and God's judgment are brought together. Niebuhr writes:

> Christian faith sees in the Cross of Christ the assurance that judgment is not the final word of God to man; but it does not regard the mercy of God as a forgiveness which wipes out the distinctions of good and evil in history and makes judgment meaningless. All the difficult Christian theological dogmas of Atonement and justification are efforts to explicate the ultimate mystery of divine wrath and divine mercy in its relation to man.[143]

Though divine mercy and judgment are both emphasized in Scripture, mercy is the "final revelation of the divine personality." While divine judgment is connected to the "structure of reality," divine mercy expresses "God's freedom in the highest reaches of its transcendence."[144] This mercy and judgment make it possible for the free and bound self to live responsibly. Divine judgment stands over and against and relativizes all the idolatrous and pretentious claims of the self. At the same time, divine mercy makes it possible for the self to avoid paralysis in the face of sin. Through divine mercy, the self can accept its condition as free and bound. And through the mercy expressed on the cross, the transcendent is made immanent. The self is given a transcendent norm by which its life is judged and redeemed. This transcendent norm of love stands over all human relationships and communities, judging them, forgiving them, and calling them to a greater fulfillment of love.

Throughout this explanation, we see the overall correlation and tension between the general revelation of human experience and the special revelation of the Bible (the account of "events in history which are discerned by faith to have revelatory power into the ultimate mystery").[145] The common human sense of being judged corresponds to the biblical witness of divine judgment. The biblical witness correlates with human experience but also shows its limitations and pretense.

To describe the relation between God's self-disclosure and human knowledge "about the 'hidden' God," Niebuhr uses the analogy of human knowledge of another person. Before a person speaks, we might know something of the person by observing behavior. But because we do not know the internal processes of the person, our knowledge is profoundly limited. Moreover, because we project our own needs and assumptions onto the other, our knowledge of the other is distorted by our self-concern and self-preoccupation. Only as the other speaks and is self-disclosive do we come to know the other more fully. The self-disclosure completes the partial knowledge we had from observation. It corrects the distortions and uncertainties.[146]

Niebuhr compares this knowledge of the other person to human knowledge of God through experience in the world. Human knowledge is not wholly wrong; it is partial, distorted, and uncertain. Niebuhr writes, "When prophetic Messianism affirms that life and history are under the sovereignty of a hidden God it declares . . . that they can be understood only in terms of a dimension deeper and higher than the system of nature, that there are obscurities and contradictions in the 'behavior' of history which can be clarified only if the unique purpose of God is more fully disclosed."[147] The disclosure will also "correct" the distorted, sinful aspects of human knowledge. (The sin is magnified because it is God, not simply another person, that we are claiming to understand.) This analogy is primarily negative. That is, through God's self-disclosure, we discover the radical partiality and distortion of our previous assumptions. Even so, this analogy and Niebuhr's description suggest that there is some relation between general human knowledge and divine self-disclosure.

This analogy from personhood is common in Niebuhr's work.[148] He frequently draws on the biblical analogy of "divine personality" to talk about God's relation to the world.[149] The biblical witness "clings stubbornly" to the language of divine personality, he insists, because it suggests both God's freedom over and involvement in the structures of the world.[150] Divine transcendence and immanence are described metaphorically from the experience of freedom.[151] Thus, the concept of personality provides a way to think of God as free and in relation to the world.[152] Niebuhr writes, "The thesis of Biblical faith, that the self is in dialogue with a God who must be defined as a 'person' because He embodies both the structure of being and a transcendent freedom, is more valid than the alternative theses which find much greater favor among the sophisticated."[153]

Niebuhr recognizes that the idea of God as "person" is a rational "absurdity" but denies that this admission invalidates the idea.[154] He insists that verification in the "realm of persons" is about faith and love, not rationality. For Niebuhr, any rational conception of God is suspect. He writes that "the God we know purely by our reason is something less than God because he is an impersonal divinity."[155]

Although Niebuhr defends the language of personality to express God's freedom over and intimate relation to the structures of the world, he clearly recognizes its limitation. As humans use the language of divine personality or any other mythical language to talk of God, they are "deceivers yet true."[156] How is this analogy of personhood limited? Clearly, human freedom has finite limits that do not apply to the divine. And the involvement of the divine in the world is not one of finitude and contingency but of free acts of love, justice, and mercy. Likewise, the human tension between freedom and boundedness is clearly not applicable to God. Indeed, the highest expression of God's freedom is to be in relation to the world in love.

In spite of the limitations of this analogy, Niebuhr insists that it is still "serviceable" because "it connotes precisely that height of freedom on the one hand and that relation to organic process on the other which prophetic and Christian faith assumes in understanding God's transcendence over, and his immanent relation to, the world."[157] So, even though the language of divine personality is limited, it expresses a central affirmation of the Christian faith that God is both free from and engaged in the structures of the world.

This understanding is especially helpful when Niebuhr talks of the atonement. The reconciliation of God's mercy and God's judgment in the atonement is made possible because of God's freedom and God's engagement in the world. God's justice expresses God's relation to the structures and processes of the law and God's freedom as judge over and against those structures. God's mercy toward humans expresses God's freedom over those structures (and freedom over God's own judgment), as well as God's love and relation to the world. Out of God's freedom, God gives Godself to the world through Christ in love. In Christ, God expresses God's freedom and transcendence most fully by giving of self. Thus God's engagement in the world is not an expression of God's limitations but of God's freedom.

God's self-disclosure does not invalidate general human experience of awe, judgment, and mercy. The divine self-disclosure in Christ "completes incomplete knowledge;" it "clarifies" and "corrects" human understanding.[158] Through this fully self-giving love, God gives humans a "transhistorical norm." This norm of self-giving love, though not a full possibility in history, helps the self to overcome the anxiety that emerges from its finite and free condition. Through faith in God, humans are freed from anxiety to give themselves in love.

In spite of its obvious limitations, Niebuhr finds the analogy of "divine personality" helpful for several reasons. Divine personality suggests freedom and relation or transcendence and immanence. God's freedom, then, entails a radical "discontinuity" between God and the world.[159] Because of this discontinuity, the self is checked in any claims to *be* God. Because of the discontinuity, the self can be related only by faith to that which is not finite. Because of God's transcendence, God is not identified with the world and thus can fulfill the human need for a unifying end outside itself and the finite world. Yet, because the transcendence of God is ultimately expressed in God's relation to the world, the unifying end beyond the finite, we have a model for a life of engagement with and on behalf of the finite.

We see, then, that divine "freedom," like human freedom, plays both critical and positive roles. God's transcendence stands over and relativizes our finite claims and plans. Any appeals to divine transcendence to underwrite our own power are idolatrous denials of that transcendence. Yet God's transcendence is necessary positively for human moral life. By trusting in that which is greater than all of our systems and theologies and finite desires and plans, we can accept ourselves and be freed for responsible relationships with others and creation. As God's transcendence finds its highest expression in God's relation to the world through Christ, humans are given a transcendent norm that draws their relationships to a higher level of expression.

This reading stands in sharp contrast to many feminist criticisms of divine transcendence in the thought of Niebuhr and others. As we have seen, divine transcendence is thought by some feminists to be a projection of male needs for separation.[160] In an effort to lessen their anxiety or to increase control over their environments, males deny their ultimate dependence and relation to creation and to society. Claims to transcendence over context express male needs for separation. These claims are further sanctioned as many males associate their own transcendent selves with God. Daphne Hampson writes of the "Christian God" who is "transcendent above humankind." Hampson muses, "His power, freedom and self-sufficiency know no bounds. Is He, one wonders, the reflection of what have been many a man's wildest dreams?"[161]

As we saw before, appeals to transcendence support male separation, justify male domination, and encourage the denigration of the created world and human social relationships. Clearly, this is not the role that Niebuhr intends divine transcendence (or self-transcendence) to play. As we have seen, any appeal to divine transcendence to justify human power is understood as sin and idolatry. God's transcendence relativizes *all* human claims.

At the same time, God's freedom has its highest expression not in separation from the world but in acts of concrete, loving engagement with the world. God's transcendence is ultimately in relation. Because many feminists have claimed that Niebuhr's understanding of God and the self are finally isolated, and that a focus on transcendence is an expression of male needs for separation, it is important to note the social aspects of the divine and human in Niebuhr's ethic.

As we have seen, Niebuhr uses the language of social interaction even to speak of transcendence. Niebuhr explains human uniqueness by turning to the dialogues in which it participates.[162] He writes, "The self is a creature which is in constant dialogue with itself, with its neighbors, and with God, according to the

Biblical viewpoint."[163] Niebuhr also uses this social metaphor of dialogue to speak of human likeness to God. According to Niebuhr it is not human reason or consciousness, but the dialogical understanding of the self that "may give more accurate content to the original metaphor 'image of God.'"[164] For Niebuhr, our self-transcendence, the image of God, is described with a profoundly social and interrelational metaphor.

Likewise, Niebuhr's conception of God and of God's interaction with the world is profoundly relational. The self is in "dialogue" with God. Its dialogical nature reflects God's image. The language of "divine personality" is used because it suggests not only God's freedom but also God's engagement in the world. And even God's freedom is made known in God's presence in relation. According to Niebuhr, God's suffering in Christ is the highest expression of God's freedom. Therefore, when Niebuhr is criticized for developing a highly individualistic understanding of the self and a radically individualistic model of God's aseity and transcendence, the social and dialogical language of his later work is not taken seriously enough.

This divine relationality is the key to human fulfillment and responsibility for Niebuhr. If the self is unique in its dialogues and is profoundly social, it is also tempted to focus in on itself or to lose itself in some aspect of the finite world. The dialogue of the self with the self can tempt it to idolatry. Only through God's gift can the self be in right relation with self and others and see others authentically.

Christ: A Transcendent Norm for Historical Life

Throughout Niebuhr's work, there is a sharp tension between the ideal and the actual.[165] Because of our self-transcendence, we see the limits of any human plans and values. We long for an end and a standard that is beyond our reach. Thus, our creation as bound and free is the source of the tension between the ideal and the actual. For Niebuhr, humans are unable to resolve the tension between ideal and actual. Only through a work of God is resolution possible. Through God's suffering for us in Christ, the ideal and the actual come together. According to Paul Lehmann, Christology is the "leitmotiv" of Niebuhr's theology.[166] In the cross, God's mercy and forgiveness are revealed, and humans are reconciled to God and given a norm for life.

Thus, the atonement is crucial to Niebuhr's understanding of God, human history, and nature. Niebuhr writes, "The revelation of the Atonement is precisely a 'final word' [which God has spoken to humans] because it discloses a transcendent mercy which represents the 'freedom' of God in quintessential terms: namely God's freedom over His own law. . . . This is the paradox of the Atonement, of the revelation of the mercy of God in its relation to the justice of God."[167]

Through the atonement, then, God's immanence and transcendence come together; God enacts God's freedom in relation.[168] Even so, the tension between the ideal and the actual is not fully overcome. In the sacrificial love of the cross, humans are given a norm for human life that is beyond the possibilities of finite life. It stands as a goal and a judgment, but it cannot be fully realized within history. In the cross, Christ shows us the reality of divine love and discloses the perfect norm for human life, agape or sacrificial love. Indeed, Christ is that norm.[169] In Christ, the transcendent norm of agape love exists in history. Yet, as a norm for human life, sacrificial love is always beyond history. Sacrificial love gives itself completely to the other without thought of its own interests or self. It is perfectly disinterested. Because of human freedom and all its temptations, such a love cannot be fully enacted in human life. In fact, Niebuhr insists that it is a "violation of natural standards of morals, as limited by human existence."[170] Yet it is not irrelevant to life. It serves both as a goal or incentive and as a judge.

While agape love is beyond full human enactment, mutual love and justice may be partially realized in human life. Mutual love gives freely of itself and normally entails some level of reciprocity. Justice, on the other hand, is the balancing of power and interests. Therefore, they both lack the purity of the transcendent norm of agape love that stands over these less perfect norms, judging them and drawing them toward a greater fulfillment. Mutual love, then, is "the highest possibility of history."[171] While agape love is the "harmony of the soul with God beyond the limitations of sinful and finite history," mutual love is "the harmony of life with life within terms of freedom."[172] Mutual love, though "second best," is not a matter of calculating interests and recording credits and debits. In reciprocal human relationships of mutual love, the lover seeks the good of the beloved. Mutual love can be a genuine expression of affection and "disinterested concern."[173] In mutual love, Niebuhr writes, "the concern of one person for the interests of another prompts and elicits a reciprocal affection."[174] Because of the reciprocity of these relationships and because of human freedom, mutual love can degenerate into calculation. As the free self seeks reciprocity and mutuality, it becomes self-interested and loses the possibility of genuine mutuality. Niebuhr writes, "Mutuality is not a possible achievement if it is made the intention and goal of any action."[175] Mutual love is possible only when the self is drawn forward by the transcendent norm of agape love. Self-giving love both reminds the lover of the limits of finite love and draws the lover toward the "impossible possibility" of agape love. Thus, mutual love is made possible in human life by the longing for that which is ultimately impossible in human life.

Even mutual love, though conditioned and finite, is not perfectly expressed in human life. What passes for love in many families, for example, is partially tainted by expressions of the ego needs of the parents.[176] And even generosity in community life is distorted by self-interest. Niebuhr writes that "the number of people who do not mix a considerable amount of will-to-power with their kindness and philanthropies is extremely rare."[177] As difficult as mutual love is to achieve in family and more intimate communities, it is even more difficult in larger political structures. Niebuhr criticizes the idealists of the social gospel movement who believed that the love ethic of Jesus could be applied directly to social and political structures.[178] As we saw previously, Niebuhr insists that social relations are always tainted because of human sin and pretense. The problem worsens in larger communities, which lack the capacity for self-transcendence and which confuse group selfishness for the virtue of loyalty. Niebuhr's political realism centers around the recognition of these "factors of self-interest and power" in politics.[179]

Niebuhr's criticism of idealists and his "realism" about political life do not leave Niebuhr "pessimistic." Although agape love cannot be directly applied, it can encourage the growth of justice in the political realm. Niebuhr defined mutual love as "the harmony of life with life within terms of freedom."[180] By contrast, justice is demanded because "life is in conflict with life, because of sinful self-interest."[181] These conflicts require "a scheme of justice which prevent one life from taking advantage of another."[182] Because of the complexity that human freedom brings to any age, humans are unable to establish a fixed scheme for themselves but need, instead, the "nicely calculated less and more of justice" that is always being retooled for each situation. Justice demands the balance of power, a calculation of rights, the protection of the interests of the weak and a check on the power of the strong. Coercion and force are necessary within systems of justice. But love is not irrelevant to these systems of calculation and coercion. Agape love, a transcendent norm, stands over all systems of justice, both judging them and drawing them toward a purer form. Because of this relationship, justice is not simply calculation (in which case it would not really be justice at all) but an expression of genuine concern for the other. The relationship between love and justice is multifaceted. Niebuhr writes, "Love is both the fulfillment and the negation of all achievements of love in history. Or expressed from the opposite standpoint, the achievements of justice in history may rise in indeterminate degrees to find their fulfillment in a more perfect love and brotherhood; but each new level of fulfillment also contains elements which stand in contradiction to perfect love."[183] Under the judgment of love, then, no finite system of justice is perfect. And because of the creative power of human freedom, no system of justice is final.

Even though justice is dynamic, its growth is guided by "essentially universal 'principles'" of equality and liberty.[184] Niebuhr claims that political freedom is a requirement of the self's free nature. This freedom is important for both the individual and the community because it allows for the continual creative growth of new structures and systems.[185] Equality is the highest expression of justice because it moves a society toward love's disinterested concern for all. Thus, "equal justice is the approximation of brotherhood under the conditions of sin."[186] Though the approximations never reach perfection, some attempts come closer to the mark than others. By placing themselves under the judgment of love and of the principles of freedom and equality, societies can be drawn toward a higher expression of justice. Thus, both mutual love and justice are judged, improved, and even made possible by the influence of a transcendent norm that is not a "simple possibility" in history. Without the influence of this norm, they degenerate into pure calculation of interest. And even under the influence of love, they are never perfectly realized.

As noted earlier, some feminists suggest that this appeal to a transcendent norm has powerful negative consequences for human life. It sets up an ultimate norm that glorifies self-sacrifice and is finally irrelevant for social transformation. It encourages a pessimism about social change that, in the end, supports the status quo. It paints the public realm as a place of conflicting interests and powers while depriving it of moral norms. And it romanticizes intimate human relations as the locus of love in human life.

Clearly, my description of Niebuhr stands in sharp contrast to many of these criticisms. As we have seen, even though Niebuhr does claim that love is more possible in intimate relationships such as the family, he also insists on the need for justice in intimate relationships and on the place of a love-inspired justice in the public realm. Moreover, Niebuhr does not see the "impossibility" of the transcendent norm as an excuse to support the status quo but as a goad to change it. The transcendent norm has great practical relevance for Niebuhr. Indeed, the transcendent norm of agape love and the human capacity for self-transcendence make social change on behalf of justice possible.

Having examined some of the criticisms in chapter 2, I want to focus here on Niebuhr's norm of the sacrificial love of the cross. As we saw, some feminists have criticized Niebuhr and other Christian theologians for focusing on the cross and sacrificial love as the highest norm for human life. Critics charge that this norm of sacrifice promotes the abuse of women and the worsening of women's self-abnegation.[187] Moreover, some feminists reject theories of the atonement that portray the suffering of the "Son of God" on the cross to satisfy the judgment of the "Father God." This is seen finally as "divine child abuse" that promotes human child abuse.[188] Thus, an appeal to sacrificial love in human life or in Christ's life is said to be dangerous. Many feminist theologies, then, focus on love as mutual empowerment and have either rejected or largely ignored the place of sacrifice.

In contrast to these arguments, I contend that a theological ethic of love would be incomplete without accounting for the place of sacrifice and costly self-giving love in human life and in the divine. Even so, I agree with feminist criticisms of Niebuhr's overemphasis on sacrifice and the cross. Niebuhr's focus on the cross as the highest norm is troubling for several reasons. Because, as Niebuhr loves to remind us, humans *are* finite and not God, is the sacrificial norm of Christ the highest norm for human life? More important, does Niebuhr's focus on the cross and sacrificial love neglect other aspects of love and of God's activity in the world? How might the love of the cross be understood as one manifestation of God's love, which is also made manifest in creation, liberation, incarnation, and community? What implications would a broader focus on God's love have for our understanding of the highest forms of human love?

Sin: Denying Finitude and Freedom

Niebuhr's analysis of sin also begins with human nature as free and finite. As we have seen, these two aspects create a tension within human life that has no finite resolution. Neither finitude nor freedom is sin; both are part of God's good creation. Neither does the tension or "contradiction" between finitude and freedom *cause* sin. This natural human condition, however, becomes the *occasion* for sin when it is "falsely interpreted" by the denial of either finitude or freedom.[189] Niebuhr writes, "This false interpretation is not purely the product of the human imagination. It is suggested to man by a force of evil which precedes his own sin. Perhaps the best description or definition of this mystery is the statement that sin posits itself."[190]

Sin develops inevitably, but not necessarily, from our situation as finite and free beings. The tension between our finite reality and the infinite possibilities that we can imagine, causes anxiety. Niebuhr writes, "In short, man, being both free and bound, both limited and limitless, is anxious. Anxiety is the inevitable concomitant of the paradox of freedom and finiteness in which man is involved. Anxiety is the internal precondition of sin. It is the inevitable spiritual state of man, standing in the paradoxical situation of freedom and finiteness."[191]

Anxiety, then, is the precondition for sin, but it is not itself sin. Neither does it always lead to sin. It can, in fact, encourage creative as well as destructive impulses in human life. If the anxiety that naturally emerges from the tension between human boundedness and freedom is not the direct cause of sin, then what is? For Niebuhr, sin arises not through the tension between our finitude and freedom but because of a refusal to *accept* the tension by denying one part of our nature. Our temptation to sin, writes Niebuhr, "resides in the inclination of man, either to deny the contingent character of his existence (in pride or self-love) or to escape from his freedom (in sensuality)."[192]

Thus, in sin we turn away from our true nature as finite and free. In sin as pride, the self denies its limitations and finitude while trying to make itself the center of existence. In sin as sensuality, the self denies its freedom and loses itself in some finite aspect of existence. Though both pride and sensuality emerge from a denial of the self's true nature, the Christian tradition has usually insisted, according to Niebuhr, that pride is the more basic sin of human life and that sensuality is derivative from it.[193]

Pride: The Denial of Finitude

Out of pride, the self not only exalts itself unduly but also tries to hide its idolatry from others and even from itself. This deception is necessary because the free self knows the finitude of its claims. When we claim that *our* truth is *the* truth, we are at some level unsettled because we know ourselves to be contingent. We then try all the harder to deceive ourselves and others to justify our idolatrous claims. Yet, we are never fully convinced or satisfied in our self-deception, because we have within us, by virtue of our self-transcendence, an awareness of a standard beyond us. Thus, ironically, our uneasiness and our desperate attempts to deceive give witness to our knowledge, through self-transcendence, of our own finitude. The self deceives because "it cannot pursue its own determinate ends without paying tribute to the truth."[194]

Thus, the self's pride, no matter how strong, never fully erases the self's uneasiness. Because of its self-transcendence, it retains some sense, however faint, that its deception *is* deception and not the final truth. This remnant of uneasiness in the prideful self is the basis for Niebuhr's claim that social groups have an even greater problem recognizing their deception or pretense than individuals do. A group is "more arrogant, hypocritical, self-centered and more ruthless in the pursuit of its ends than the individual."[195] Because loyalty to the collective can appear to be self-giving and not self-centered, the collective is free to pursue its own interests under the guise of altruism. Also, because the group is not as self-transcendent as an individual, it lacks that uneasy recognition of its own limitations. Despite this difference between sin in the individual and the group, the similarities are striking. Within groups, the sin of pride is expressed in the tendency toward tyranny, whereas the sin of sensuality is expressed in the tendency toward anarchy.

For Niebuhr, pride has both a religious and a moral aspect. Pride in its religious aspect is idolatry. The self attempts to "usurp the place of God."[196] Pride in its moral aspect is injustice to other humans.[197] When we overextend our own freedom and will, we do so at the expense of other people. For Niebuhr, pride takes three forms in human life—pride of power, pride of knowledge, and pride of virtue or self-righteousness. An additional aspect—spiritual pride—is the culmination of these other forms of pride. It is "pride and self-glorification in its inclusive and quintessential form."[198]

The pride of power expresses itself in two ways. First, some humans, most often those with great social power, refuse to recognize their own contingent and finite nature. Their pretentious claims on behalf of their own power blind them to their true finite nature and situation. Niebuhr also acknowledges that even the powerful may feel insecure and seek to achieve more power still.[199] Pride of power is the root of much human domination.

The pride of power can also emerge out of a deficit of power. The self, anxious that its power is not secure, seeks to further extend its power by taking advantage of others. Where the first pretentious aspect of the pride of power is found in those with greater social positions, this second aspect is more common among those who have less power. Niebuhr writes, "Among those who are less obviously secure, either in terms of social recognition, or economic stability or even physical health, the temptation arises to overcome or obscure insecurity by arrogating a greater degree of power to the self."[200]

Thus, the pride of power can be a sin both of those who have great power and of those who are weak. Whether exercised by the powerful or the weak, this pride is central to the Christian conception of sin. Niebuhr writes, "The will-to-power in short involves the ego in injustice. It seeks a security beyond the limits of human finiteness. . . . The will-to-power is . . . both a direct form and an indirect instrument of the pride which Christianity regards as sin in its quintessential form."[201]

In the second form, the pride of knowledge, the self tries to deny the contingency of its own knowledge. The sin is not the limitation of the knowledge but the pretense that denies those limitations. The self makes too much of its own limited intellect. Both its pretense about the limits of its knowledge and its attempt to use that knowledge in the interests of its own power are a part of intellectual pride. Again, this tension stems from the self's finitude and freedom. Because humans are finite, they cannot have knowledge that does not partake of their own contingency. Because humans are self-transcendent, they imagine and desire a knowledge greater than their own limits. The sin of intellectual pride emerges from the denial of human finitude.

Closely related to intellectual pride is moral pride, which tries to make its own finite virtue into a final or eternal standard. Like the other forms, moral pride also exists both as pretense born of ignorance and as self-righteousness or domination born of insecurity. Out of insecurity, humans judge and even attack others. Thus, moral pride "is responsible for our most serious cruelties, injustices and defamations against our fellowman."[202] In the pride of virtue, the self not only judges others but also fails to see its own lack of virtue and its own need for judgment and for forgiveness.

For Niebuhr, this blindness has striking religious consequences. "The sinner who justifies himself does not know God as judge and does not need God as Saviour."[203] Spiritual pride develops as an expression of moral pride. The self makes its own self and virtue sacred. It replaces God's judgment and mercy with its own judgment and self-righteousness, which it then pretends is God's judgment. This is the sin of religious groups that proclaim their own standards to be underwritten by the almighty. Niebuhr writes:

> Religion . . . is the inevitable fruit of the spiritual stature of man; and religious intolerance and pride is the final expression of his sinfulness. A religion of revelation is grounded in the faith that God speaks to man from beyond the highest pinnacle of the human spirit; and that this voice of God will discover man's highest not only to be short of the highest but involved in the dishonesty of claiming that it is the highest.[204]

Thus, pride of power, knowledge, and virtue reach their highest and most disturbing level in their identification of human categories with God. Human self-transcendence propels itself into a denial of the divine transcendence in which it finds its source. In the sin of pride, the self is unjust as it judges and uses others for its own benefit, and it is idolatrous as it vainly attempts to take the place of God.

Sensuality: The Denial of Freedom

If the sin of pride is the denial of finitude, the sin of sensuality is the denial of freedom. Out of its anxiety in the face of the openness and indefiniteness of its freedom, the self may lose itself in some finite thing or person or activity outside itself. Niebuhr writes, "Sensuality represents an effort to escape from the freedom and the infinite possibilities of spirit by becoming lost in the detailed processes, activities and interests of existence, an effort which results inevitably in unlimited devotion to limited values."[205]

In this definition, sensuality is understood to be the counterpart to pride's denial of finitude. They are mirror images of each other. In other citations, sensuality is secondary to pride. Much of Niebuhr's analysis and the source of subsequent feminist criticism centers on how sensuality and pride, relate. As we saw in chapter 2, feminists criticize Niebuhr for making sensuality derivative of or secondary to pride. Is sensuality an overextension of the self or a denial of the self? Is sensuality derivative of pride, or is it a different sort of sin altogether? Niebuhr's response is muddled. In his general analysis of sin, Niebuhr seems to suggest that sensuality, in strong contrast to pride, is a *loss* of self or freedom for another finite thing or person. He writes:

When anxiety has conceived it brings forth both pride and sensuality. Man falls into pride, when he seeks to raise his contingent existence to unconditioned significance; he falls into sensuality, when he seeks to escape from his unlimited possibilities of freedom from the perils and responsibilities of self-determination, by immersing himself into a "mutable good," by losing himself in some natural vitality.[206]

But when Niebuhr explores the sin of sensuality more fully, he initially seems to claim that it is a manifestation of self-love or pride.[207] In sensuality, the self overidentifies with "particular drives and impulses within itself."[208] The context of Niebuhr's discussion of the derivative nature of sensuality shapes his initial hesitation to label sensuality as a separate sin. He is responding to the parts of the "Hellenistic" and "rationalist" parts of the Christian tradition that have focused on a separate sin of sensuality. These arguments, he notes, tend to view our embodied natures negatively.[209] Sin becomes the indulgence in the created pleasures of the world. Thus, the Augustinian, Thomist, and Lutheran discussions of the secondary relation of sensuality to pride serve as a counter to the anticreation bent of the "Hellenistic" or "rationalist" traditions. Within this counterargument, sensuality is "the inordinate love for all creaturely and mutable values which results from the primal love of self, rather than the love of God."[210] Thus, sensuality is not love or involvement of the self in the world; sensuality is that "inordinate love" that emerges from love of self.

While Niebuhr is sympathetic with the reasons behind this countermove (i.e., as a rejection of the "Hellenistic" association of sin with bodily pleasure), he hardly offers an enthusiastic endorsement of it. He writes, "While we accept this general analysis it must be pointed out that the explanations of the relation of sensuality to self-love are *unsatisfactory*, partly because they are too vague and partly because they are contradictory."[211]

Thus, Niebuhr claims that this Christian analysis of the derivative nature of sensuality is finally "unsatisfactory" and "contradictory." Why would one lose *oneself* as an act of *self-love* or gratification? Niebuhr then returns to the original question. "Is sensuality . . . a form of idolatry which makes the self god; or is it an alternative idolatry in which the self, conscious of the inadequacy of its self-worship, seeks escape by finding some other god?"[212]

Niebuhr confuses the matter further when he answers that "there is a little of both in sensuality."[213] In sexuality, for example, both self-centeredness and self-loss are present. Sex involves "both the assertion of the ego and the flight of the ego into another." There is a temptation toward the "domination of one life over the desires of another and the self-abnegation of the same life in favour of another."[214] In sexuality, the temptations to self-centeredness *and* to self-loss are present for both men and women.[215] He writes, "While the more active part of the male and the more passive part of the female in relation of the sexes may seem to point to self-deification as the particular sin of the male and the idolatry of the other as the particular temptation of the woman in the sexual act, yet both elements of sin are undoubtedly involved in both sexes."[216]

Niebuhr muddles the discussion further by claiming that sensuality has a third aspect. It may involve more than worship of the self or the loss of the self in the worship of another. According to Niebuhr, sensuality also may entail a "flight not to a false god but to nothingness."[217]

Thus, Niebuhr's analysis of sensuality is more complex than it seems at first. Sensuality is not simply derivative of pride. Indeed, the traditional Christian arguments for the derivative nature of sensuality are "unsatisfactory" and "contradictory." Sensuality, instead, is multifaceted. Moreover, all three facets are *always* involved in sensuality: "Sensuality is *always:* 1) an extension of self-love to the point where it defeats its own ends; 2) an effort to escape the prison house of self by finding a god in a process or person outside the self; and 3) finally an effort to escape from the confusion which sin has created into some form of subconscious existence."[218] Thus, sensuality involves a further development of pride toward the loss of self into another finite thing or person and a disenchantment with the other that prompts a flight into nothingness.

There are several interesting points about this analysis that relate to the feminist criticisms of chapter 2. I have summarized this argument to show the complexity of Niebuhr's understanding of the sin of sensuality. While some feminists have criticized Niebuhr for his insistence on the derivative nature of sensuality, Niebuhr himself does not seem wholly convinced by these "unsatisfactory" or "contradictory" arguments that it is indeed derivative. He is convinced *primarily* of sensuality's complexity. Interestingly, he traces the Christian arguments about the derivative nature of sensuality back to an original intention that most feminists would find praiseworthy—an affirmation of human embodiedness. This is especially noteworthy because Judith Plaskow suggests that Niebuhr insists on the derivative nature of sensuality precisely *because* of his negative feelings about the body. Whatever Niebuhr's personal ambivalence about human creatureliness, that is clearly *not* the reason that he gives in the text for thinking of sensuality as derivative of pride. Moreover, Niebuhr's suggestion that sensuality points to a loss of the self in "a process or person outside the self" or into an escape or "nothingness" fits remarkably well with feminist analyses of "women's sin."

My reflections here do not dispute several important feminist arguments. First, for all his ambivalence, qualifications, additions, and "worthy" reasons, Niebuhr *does* partially "accept" the derivative nature of sensuality. Moreover, Niebuhr gives much less attention to the sin of sensuality than to pride. As we saw in chapter 2, this is troubling for many feminists because it does not fully account for the experience of sin as the loss of self and loss of freedom.

In fact, it does not fully account for one part of Niebuhr's own two-part understanding of human experience. Niebuhr's argument would be more consistent if he *had* given equal status and emphasis to sin as loss of freedom. Such an argument would need to fill out the content of sensuality beyond Niebuhr's typical references to the excess of some bodily pleasure. An argument that gave equal status to the denial of freedom and that developed it in a more complex and nuanced way could be more consistently Niebuhrian than Niebuhr.

I will also suggest later that Niebuhr's understanding of sin as pride and sensuality could fit well with feminist analysis. Clearly, feminist criticisms of patriarchy are reminiscent of Niebuhr's descriptions of the pride of the powerful, who extend their own wills at the expense of others. They not only use others for their own ends but also deceitfully justify their domination with the language of religion and virtue. They "usurp" God's place and claim their finite knowledge for eternal knowledge, their virtues for the ultimate norm, and *their* truth for *the* truth. Given the similarities between Niebuhr's analysis of pride and feminist criticisms of patriarchy, Niebuhr's categories would be helpful in feminist analysis.

In addition, Niebuhr's analysis of the sin of pride among those people with less power could also be applicable to feminist analysis. As we saw, Niebuhr saw that those with less power were also subject to prideful assumptions about the superiority of their own knowledge or virtue. These "weaker" people may exercise their power in relation to others with still less power. This dynamic relates to feminist analyses of lateral or horizontal violence and discrimination. Many feminists have noted the historical complicity of women of higher status in various forms of domination of those of lesser status.[219] Some womanists and feminists have charged that many middle-class white feminist theologians have been oppressive in their assumption that their own perspective was women's perspective universally.[220] Indeed, British feminist Mary Grey is suspicious of middle-class feminists who claim that woman's sin is the loss of self. Given their role in structures that dominate others, Grey suggests that this claim is a pretentious cover for their own complicity. She asks, "Was it the sin of passivity which was responsible for racism within the feminist movement?"[221] Thus, perhaps the pride of power, knowledge, and virtue is applicable to feminists and other women.

Finally, feminists have given much attention to the sin of loss of self or of freedom in women.[222] These analyses offer an important resource for developing a feminist realist model of sin. In addition, these feminist analyses of sin as the loss of self could be more broadly applied not only to women but also to other groups or to other aspects of our culture. Moreover, feminist definitions of women's sin as loss of self or passivity must themselves be subject to the critical gaze of the political realist. If Mary Grey is correct, feminists must critically examine the focus on women's sin of passivity as a possible cover for complicity in domination.

Niebuhr as a Resource for a Feminist Christian Realism

Feminist Criticisms: Summary and Reflection

I have explored Niebuhr's Christian realism as a resource for feminist theology. This examination of Niebuhr has been informed by several conversations. First, this exploration grows out of my claim that freedom and some minimal moral grounding are conditions for the possibility of feminist moral experience. Niebuhr is a resource because his focus on human experience as bound and free provides a way to respond to these conditions of feminist moral experience.

Second, this study of Niebuhr is a response to and a participant in feminist discussions about the place of human freedom and boundedness and divine transcendence and immanence within feminist theology, reviewed in chapters 1, 4, and 5. Because I argue that transcendence is crucial to a feminist argument, the common feminist move away from transcendence is troubling. Thus, my turn to

Niebuhr is a response to the concerns raised in chapter 1 and an anticipation of similar issues that will be addressed in the following chapters.

Third, this analysis is a direct reply to feminist criticisms of Niebuhr. I structured my explication of Niebuhr's theological ethic as a response to and partial refutation of feminist criticisms. The point is not to defend him, however, but to show that a model that develops out of the tension between freedom and boundedness can *do* the sorts of things that feminists want to *do* and *make* the sorts of arguments that feminists want to *make*. Moreover, the discussions about fixed gender roles and parenthood reveal the need within feminism for a model by which to understand both our boundedness to and freedom over social and natural givenness.

Fourth, these feminist reflections on Niebuhr are also in conversation with Rosemary Ruether and Sharon Welch, who will be the focus of the next chapters. Welch and Ruether pose problems for feminist theology to which a Niebuhrian understanding of the self as bound and free can respond. And Ruether and Welch offer models for exploring the moral significance of nature and community that are neglected in Niebuhr.

Feminist Realist Response

Both my criticisms and appropriations of Niebuhr center on his understanding of human boundedness and freedom and divine transcendence and immanence. The points of difference and appropriation can be best summarized by drawing on the categories of political realism, moral realism, and theological realism. For Niebuhr, political realism is "the disposition to take all factors . . . into account, particularly the factors of self-interest and power."[223] This aspect of political realism is often present—explicitly or implicitly—in feminist theologies. Many feminist theologians are political realists in the sense that a similar lens of suspicion drives the analysis and criticism of the ideologies of patriarchy. Indeed, the feminist criticisms of Niebuhr are classic examples of political realist arguments. Niebuhr's ideas about sin, nature, society, human self-transcendence, and divine transcendence are seen as extensions and justifications of male interests and preoccupations. Recently, feminists have also begun to be more critical about the self-interestedness of some feminist arguments.[224] This self-critical turn is crucial for the integrity of feminist theology. A feminist Christian realism would attempt to further this analysis.

Throughout his work, Niebuhr attends not only to the distortions of self-interest but also to the human potential for moral responsibility. Thus, Niebuhr's turn to what Robin Lovin calls naturalist moral realism is an extension of the attentiveness of political realism. The focus on human experience as bound and free is at the center of Niebuhr's moral realism. Several aspects are particularly helpful to feminist theology. The focus on human freedom allows us to make sense of two factors crucial to feminist experience: the judgment of social forms and theologies and the possibility for radical historical transformation. At the same time, freedom carries with it certain positive political and ethical requirements that could support feminist affirmations of political voice and self-determination for women.

Moreover, Niebuhr's focus on human boundedness offers minimal grounding for additional moral claims. Yet, Niebuhr's emphasis on the critical aspects of freedom always stands as a check against claiming too much about the moral claims of nature. This critical mechanism allows realism to help account for the internal problems within other systems and to modify itself in the face of external criticism. Although a feminist Christian realism would retain the critical mechanism of freedom, it would also want to explore more fully the moral implications of human boundedness to community, to body, and to nature.

Though Niebuhr neglected these areas, they have been a focus of much feminist exploration. Ruether and Welch, for example, offer models for understanding the moral significance of human boundedness to nature and to community. An examination of these models in the next chapters will help to correct some of the limitations noted in Niebuhr's realism.

Niebuhr's theological realism is also a resource and a problem for feminism. I will continue to argue that Niebuhr's emphasis on divine transcendence is important for feminist theology. God's transcendence relativizes and judges all human claims and systems while also providing a center of unity, meaning, and value beyond them. Because the highest expression of divine freedom is in divine presence, this understanding of God is ultimately relational. While these aspects of Niebuhr's theology are useful for feminists, his focus on the cross as the primary locus of the transcendent and as the revelation of the highest norm is troubling. As we saw, feminists have claimed that the focus on sacrificial love as the highest norm is dangerous for those whose sin is loss of self. This focus on the cross also narrows the witness of the Bible and human life. A feminist Christian realism would include, along with a focus on the cross and sacrificial love, a further exploration of the love expressed in creation, liberation, incarnation, and community. Ruether and Welch offer models of creative, liberative, incarnational, and community love that are helpful in this exploration.

Thus, Niebuhr's Christian realism is both a resource and a problem for feminist theology. A feminist Christian realism would draw on Niebuhr's understanding of God and the self. At the same time, Ruether and Welch provide models by which we can take more seriously those aspects that Niebuhr has neglected, such as the positive normative significance of human boundedness to nature and to community.

FOUR

The Evolution of Cooperation and Consciousness

Rosemary Ruether's Naturalist Moral Realism

THIS chapter examines Ruether's naturalist moral realism as both a resource and a problem for a feminist Christian realism.[1] Focusing on Ruether's understanding of human boundedness to and divine presence within the natural evolutionary process, I contend that her exploration of the moral norms expressed in the evolving natural environment and human nature offers a resource for the grounding of moral claims. This chapter also looks at Ruether's criticisms of Christian understandings of divine transcendence and human self-transcendence as ideological tools to support elite male domination. Her alternative emphasis on divine immanence within and human boundedness to the created world is an expression of a cosmic evolutionary theory that she has drawn from ecofeminists, Teilhard de Chardin, and other process perspectives. I argue that her move away from transcendence and radical freedom and toward immanence and boundedness undercuts a critical perspective that is crucial for the judgment of patriarchal domination and the transformation of society that are the goal of her work. Without some capacity to radically transcend our social and natural boundedness, it is difficult to account for the sort of transformation that Ruether promotes. Thus, I maintain that her attempt to turn away from domination and toward empowerment prompts her to deny the very concepts that support empowerment and check domination. Moreover, I argue that because of the confidence of her moral naturalism, she lacks a consistent "political realism."

Ruether's Task: A Summary

Ruether likens herself to a "great cultural recycler" who stands in an "enormous toxic waste dump of ideas and images, sifting through, trying to find some usable material to create a new world."[2] We must create this new world, claims Ruether, because our old ways of domination and exploitation have pushed us to the brink of environmental and social destruction. Many aspects of Western culture and classical Christian theology (particularly the appeal to a transcendent realm or transcendent experience) sanctify and maintain these relationships of domination.

If we are to save ourselves and the earth, Ruether insists, we must reenvision our patterns of living and thinking. To survive, we must form a new consciousness or a new psyche, characterized not by domination and competition but by "biophilic mutuality," a recognition of our mutual interdependence with and responsibility to each other and the earth. Ruether claims that the new consciousness is already emerging. Indeed, she hopes that her work will play a "part in that new consciousness and social vision."[3] To this end, Ruether, fulfilling her vocation as "cultural recycler," sifts through Western culture and science, eclectically choosing that which promotes biophilic mutuality or empowered interdependence and discarding that which encourages domination. The goal of her labors is the formation of a "new humanity," a "new soul," and even a "new religion" for a "new earth."[4]

Ruether's descriptions of the two choices—the mode of domination or the mode of biophilic mutuality—are similar to common feminist distinctions between power over and power with.[5] She rejects both dominating, coercive power and the abdication of power, while promoting a community-based, mutual empowerment. Her theological criticism and reconstruction, including her criticisms of transcendence and her movement toward immanence, grow out of this root concern about power and domination.

What is the source of human domination? According to Ruether, humans and other animals have natural internal powers or "life drives." When used rightly, according to its natural interdependency, the life drive can work for the benefit of human life and of the earth. But when humans (especially elite males) become anxious, their exercise of this natural power becomes competitive. They "maximize [their life force] at the expense of others."[6] This distorted power is always insecure. To safeguard their own power, those with overextended life drives appeal to the transcendent for legitimation. In their anxiety, they deny the finitude and interrelatedness that is the reality of their embodied existence. Ruether criticizes those aspects of theology that support domination, such as an appeal to a transcendent realm or to a powerful, male God.[7] She claims that such models of God are projections of the desire of elite males to legitimate their power by associating themselves with a transcendent God. These males then associate women and other less powerful people with nature. This theological hierarchy underwrites unhealthy domination.

Human domination, or the overextension of human life drives and the denial of natural interdependence, then, is the cause of our current environmental crisis, as well as many other problems in human history. Throughout her work, Ruether's analyses of racism, anti-Semitism, sexism, environmental misuse, and other problems stem from her rejection of domination and exploitation and her affirmation of responsible interdependence and mutual empowerment. This norm drives her reevaluation of Christian theology, including transcendence, and her proposals for new, biophilic theology and ethics. Ruether's reevaluation and new proposals draw on a broad range of textual resources. She combines some parts of the Bible with other ancient stories, recent social and political theory, the ecological sciences, ecofeminist theory, and other diverse resources to develop "a working paradigm of some main trends in our consciousness."[8]

The primary source of theological reflection is experience. In a 1967 letter to Thomas Merton, Ruether wrote that she "distrust[s] all academic theology. Only theology bred in the crucible of experience is any good."[9] While experience is the "starting and ending point" of all theology, feminist theology draws especially on women's experience and works for the full humanity of women.[10] At the same time, Ruether's theology draws heavily on the experience of the whole ecosystem and works from a broader norm of biophilic mutuality.

Ruether's theological ethic, including her alternative understanding of power as biophilic mutuality, is grounded in her model of natural evolutionary development. Drawing on Teilhard de Chardin (modified by recent process and ecofeminist perspectives), Ruether describes a process of cosmic growth in which energy becomes organized in increasingly complex ways.[11] The creative energy within this process will occasionally reach a boiling point and cause a leap in the complexity of organization. Human consciousness and altruism represent the growing edge and greatest complexity of this evolution. In human life, this natural process reflects on itself. Humans thus have a unique role in creation. They are bound to and dependent upon creation. And through consciousness and altruism, they can reflect on and transform some aspects of creation. This capacity is not separate from nature; it is, instead, a part of natural evolutionary development. Consciousness and altruism reflect and emerge from the natural interdependency of this process. Thus, when Ruether speaks of nature, she refers to all of life, including history. The divine is also in this process. Ruether speaks of God as the "primal matrix" of energy that grounds this process and draws it forward. Thus, both God and human moral life find their locus in this process.

Ruether's theological ethic is also dependent on recent ecological theories that emphasize the cooperative interdependence and interrelationality basic to healthy ecosystems.[12] Human failure to live within this natural interdependence will lead to the destruction of the environment and human life.

Thus, Ruether's theological ethic emerges from her model of nature. The locus of human moral reflection is natural evolutionary development. Humans reflect on this process to discover the norms by which to live responsibly. The laws of cooperative interdependence and interrelationality are visible throughout the created world. Moreover, human altruism and consciousness also provide laws for human life that can further the natural development. A responsible moral actor lives within and accepts these two parts of human reality: human boundedness to natural process and the human ability to reflect on and change the process through consciousness (which is also a part of the natural process). The good is that which furthers this natural process of mutual, interdependent cooperation or biophilic mutuality. By contrast, those acts and systems that undermine interdependence by encouraging competitiveness and domination distort the values inherent in the evolutionary process and authentic human nature.

Ruether's use and understanding of religious language is informed by her model of creation. She insists that all language about the divine is analogical.[13] Because of her model of nature (of which the divine is the ground), she is able to claim that some analogies are better than others. As we will see, she criticizes patriarchal understandings of a transcendent, monotheistic God as a projection of elite male desire to have ultimate control over nature and women. These projections represent distortions of the natural order of biophilic mutuality. By contrast, she suggests that an understanding of the divine as the primal matrix or ground of this creative evolutionary process is an expression of a more authentic way of being or a "fuller" divinity.[14] Although all human language is limited, Ruether suggests that we can know something of the divine. Because the whole of life is profoundly interrelated and because God is the ground of this process, the divine is somehow reflected in the process. Thus, patriarchal God language is described as distorted projection, while the model of the divine as primal matrix is more reflective of reality.

In summary, Ruether's ethic centers on her model of nature. A cosmic natural-historical evolutionary process is the locus of the divine and of human moral reflection and action. Moral responsibility entails the attentiveness to and furthering of the laws that are a part of nature, including human nature. A human social, psychic conversion from domination to biophilic mutuality demands new social structures and new theologies. Without these changes, humans may destroy themselves and nature.

Problems and Causes: Global Crisis of Domination

The presenting issue for much of Ruether's work is a global crisis of domination. Ruether has continually linked many social, economic, and environmental problems to domination by male elites. In an influential early essay, "New Woman and New Earth," Ruether insists that the environmental crisis cannot be resolved "within a society whose fundamental model for relationships continues to be one of domination."[15] Connecting the domination of women, the poor, African Americans, and nature, Ruether goes on to call for an "alternative value system" that moves away from "drives toward possession, conquest, and accumulation to the values of reciprocity and acceptance of mutual limitation."[16] She repeatedly links the domination of women to that of other oppressed groups and proposes a "mutually supportive . . . cooperative model of fellowship of life systems."[17]

Ruether's warnings about the devastating consequences of domination have become increasingly dire. She describes the " 'four horsemen' of destruction," human population growth, environmental devastation, global militarism, and massive poverty, which bear down on us and threaten "irreparable destruction."[18] Because of these interconnected problems, human life, as well as the life of all plants and animals, is at ultimate risk.

An Etiology of Domination: Mothers and Transcendence

Sin: Life Drives Gone Wrong

If a mentality of domination is responsible for many of the world's ills, then what is the origin of domination? For Ruether, our life drives are not necessarily destructive. So, what causes them to become distorted? Ruether points to a mix of social and ideological roots of this distortion. The life force becomes "evil," according to Ruether, when it pursues its own good at the cost of others and thereby ignores its natural interrelationship with all of life. She writes, "There is a tendency in the life drive itself in each species to maximize its own existence and hence to proliferate in a cancerous way that destroys its own biotic support."[19] Because of the human ability to manipulate its environment, the overreaching of the life drives is especially dangerous.

The proper direction and management of this drive are central both to a healthy ecosystem and to responsible moral life. The "good," then, "lies in . . . a balancing of our own drive for life with the life drives of all the others in which we are in community, so that the whole remains in life-sustaining harmony. The wisdom of nature lies in the development of built-in limits through a diversity of being in interrelation, so that none outruns its own 'niche.' "[20] Let no one doubt which segment of the ecosystem is the most guilty of overreaching "its own niche." Ruether points the finger at elite males who "have learned to maximize their own lives, both for leisure and consumption over against other humans." And the overextension of power is sin. Ruether writes:

> The central issue of sin . . . is the misuse of freedom to exploit other humans and the earth and thus to violate the basic relations that sustain life. Life is sustained by biotic relationality in which the whole attains a plenitude through mutual limits in interdependency. When one part of the life community exalts itself at the expense of the other parts, life is diminished for the exploited. Ultimately, exploiters subvert the bases of their own lives as well. An expanding cycle of poisonous hostility and violence is generated.[21]

So, sin is the exaltation of one's own power and freedom at the expense of another's. Ruether also describes the opposite problem as sin.[22] Some people (especially women) do not express this life drive actively enough. They passively give in to the selfish life forces of others and fail to take responsibility for their own lives and for the ecosystem. They lose themselves and fail to enact their own agency. Thus, sin, writes Ruether, is not only "competitive hate" but also "passive acquiescence to needless victimization."[23]

Many feminist theologians have made similar claims about women's sin.[24] They have criticized traditional theology for its focus on the "male" problem of sin as pride or selfishness as a universal human experience and its insufficient attention to the "female" sin as lack of self-identity. It is ironic, then, that Ruether gives much greater attention to the sin of domination or the overextension of the life force than to sin as abdication of the life force. This sin of domination is, however, the primary cause of our current plight according to Ruether. But why does the life force go bad? If biophilic mutuality is one of the laws of nature, why is it so often broken?

Mothering and Male Anxiety: The Creation of Domination

Ruether suggests that one of the causes for the corruption of the life drive is the social structure of many human families and communities. The argument that many gender differences arise out of matricentric parenting is common to much feminist theory.[25] Because girls are raised primarily by a caretaker of their own gender, they experience the world differently than boys, who are raised primarily by a caretaker of a different gender. Girls see themselves in continuity with the mother-caretaker. Their identities, then, are formed in connection with their environment and their primary relationship. Conversely, boys find their identity as males in discontinuity with and even in opposition to their mother-caretaker. Male animosity and social domination of women and others, claim many feminists, is related to their place within matricentric family structure. Ruether describes this process as "the basic insecurity of the mother-parented male who makes his way to adult male status through mother-negation."[26] The mother's power is threatening to the male. In the ensuing anxiety, he overemphasizes his own life power to find security. This "pattern is itself the breeding ground for male resentment and violence, rooted in male strategies of exploitative subversion of women's power."[27]

Ruether does not simply focus on the psychological implications of female parenting for gender formation. She also emphasizes the social implication for women's power. Because women are often tied to more menial, child-rearing responsibilities, they are excluded from other activities—often those with the greatest power and prestige. The double workload of women in most societies is a significant problem for the formation of just communities.[28]

Ruether claims that the pattern of male domination of females is the model for other domination.[29] A hierarchical dualism is set up in service of elite males and transferred onto other relationships. "This view of women as inherently inferior, servile, and 'carnal' beings creates a symbol system which is also applied to the relations of masters and slaves, ruling and subjugated classes."[30] Consequently, an examination of the domination of women by elite men sheds light on the broader problems of domination through society and our ecosystem. If one could identify the ideological underpinnings of the domination of women, one would also find the justification for a larger web of social and environmental domination that threatens our survival.

Transcendence and the Sacralization of Male Power

A primary ideological support for elite male privilege is an appeal to a transcendent realm or experience. Elite males justify and sanctify their privilege and power by associating themselves with a higher realm. This justification carries wide-ranging social consequences. For Ruether, domination is not, of course, limited to family and individual relationships described previously, but emerges from and is built into the broader social structure. Moreover, it is supported and "sacralized" by historical narratives, cultural myths, and theological categories. These larger cultural patterns thus cause and promote the distortion of the life drives. Just as individual males were threatened by the power of their mothers, males in society were threatened by the power of female reproduction and the power of nature. They establish their own power by identifying themselves with a transcendent, non-natural realm. Sexism emerges, then, from this distortion. Ruether writes,

"Sexism is rooted in the 'war against the mother,' the struggle of the transcendent ego to free itself from bondage to nature . . . making one half of humanity . . . the symbol of the sphere to be transcended and dominated."[31] The God of patriarchal religions, such as Christianity, underwrites this sexist dualism. Indeed, this dualism finds its "ultimate theological rationale," according to Ruether, in the image of God as transcendent father.[32] Thus, many traditional understandings of God are projections of male need.

Unlike some feminists who explore the origins of the oppression of women, Ruether does not posit an original matriarchy that was overthrown by patriarchy.[33] Instead, Ruether traces the increasing sacralization of the domination of women through the development of complex social organization—especially in the growth of urban civilization. Elite males, fearing the power of nature and women's natural creativity and wanting to secure their own power, posit a higher transcendent realm with which they associate themselves. Within this development, Ruether recognizes "the roots of evil." Evil lies, she writes,

> in patterns of domination, whereby male elites in power deny their interdependency with women, exploiting human labor and the biotic community around them. They seek to exalt their own power infinitely, by draining the lives of these other humans and non-human sources of life on which they depend. They create cultures of deceit which justify this exploitation by negating the value of those they use, while denying their own dependence on them.[34]

The primary concept within this culture of deceit is transcendence. Elite males in the West have justified their own power by the creation and maintenance of the idea of a supernatural or spiritual realm transcending nature and body to which they have special access. Divine transcendence is the supreme projection of male anxiety and male desire to secure and extend power.

Ruether sees several stages in the development of this "culture of deceit" that rely on a hierarchical division between the transcendent and the finite to underwrite elite male power over women.[35] Ruether claims that primitive agricultural and village cultures exhibited greater equality between men and women, as well as greater connectedness between humans and the rest of the natural world.[36] Though Ruether is not looking back to an original matriarchy, she does point to the importance of female nature deities in many ancient Near Eastern cultures. She suggests that the Goddess represented the profound sense of connection that these people felt with nature and each other. In describing this ancient understanding of the Goddess, she writes, "We can speak of the root human image of the divine as the Primal Matrix, the great womb within which all things, Gods and humans, sky and earth, human and non-human beings, are generated. Here the divine is not abstracted into some other world beyond this earth but is the encompassing source of new life that surrounds the present world and assures its continuance."[37]

In contrast to this model of continuity, a further stage is characterized by the partial conquest of the mother. When the male God overcomes the mother Goddess (as Marduk overcomes Tiamat), he derives his power from her. His power is distinct from but still dependent on the female power and the power of nature. A still further stage of the sacralization of male power is centered on the "negation of the mother." With the development of urban civilization, ruling males needed to justify their own control because, as Ruether writes, their "power was no longer based on physical prowess of the hunter or warrior, but on the inherited monopoly of political power and knowledge. . . . The cultural spokesmen for ruling-class males began to develop ideologies of both class and female inferiority to justify their position."[38]

These justifying ideologies centered on the negation of the power of women and nature and the extension of male power into a transcendent or spiritual realm. In this stage of development, the mother's power or the Goddess's power is seen to be demonic, and male power is separated from nature and the body into a spiritual level. The male thus denies his dependence on women and nature, which are associated with a lower realm. Within Judaism, monotheism emerges out of this negation of the mother and nature. Ruether writes, "Male monotheism becomes the vehicle of a psychocultural revolution of the male ruling class in its relationship to surrounding reality. . . . [It] begins to split reality into a dualism of transcendent Spirit (mind, ego) and inferior and dependent physical nature."[39]

According to Ruether, the negation of the mother and of nature is seen in many genesis stories, including the one found in the Hebrew Bible. The power of creation is taken away from nature and women and given over to a spiritual male realm. She writes:

> Nature, which once encompassed all reality, is now subjugated and made into the lower side of a new dualism. . . . A struggle ensues against the old nature and mother religions by prophets or philosophers who portray it as immoral or irrational. Consciousness is abstracted into a sphere beyond visible reality. . . . This higher realm is the world of divinity. . . . Matter is created by an ego-fiat from a transcendent spiritual power.[40]

Taken to its extreme, this hierarchical dualism finally denies the power of nature completely. In modern capitalist society, nature is valued only for its role in production. "There is an effort to sterilize the power of nature altogether, imagining it as dead stuff totally malleable in the hands of men in power."[41]

Thus, the powerful, transcendent God of Western monotheism is, for Ruether, a legacy of this negation of female power and a denial of the finite world. Elite males gain control over women and nature by

> linking their essential selves with a transcendent principle beyond nature which is pictured as intellectual and male. This image of transcendent, male, spiritual deity is a projection of the ego or consciousness of ruling-class males, who envision a reality, beyond the physical processes that gave them birth, as the true source of their being. Men locate their true origins and natures in this transcendent sphere, which thereby also gives them power over the lower sphere of "female" nature.[42]

Traditional claims about transcendence are, in the end, projections of this dominating mentality. Ruether writes of the "will to transcend and dominate the natural and social world. The exclusively male God . . . transcending nature and dominating history . . . is the theological self-image and guilty conscience of this self-infinitizing spirit."[43] A comprehensive cultural and theological system to support elite male power over women and nature develops out of this sacralization of male power. Larger patterns of cultural assumptions about women and men grow out of these early structures of domination. Males come to be associated with rationality, autonomy, volition, transcendence, and fortitude. Women are linked with passivity, bodiliness, irrationality, weakness, and dependency.[44]

These "female" traits are devalued and come to be associated with nature and many other marginalized groups. In an intriguing article on the striking similarities of Christian elite's portrayals of both female witches and Jews, Ruether offers one of many examples of the linkages between the devaluation and control of women and that of other less powerful groups.[45] These broad systems of hierarchical dualisms are supported by the dominant mentality, including Christian theology. The mentality that has developed from these patterns of domination distorts and threatens the natural evolutionary process. The "linear," "left brain," "dualistic," "dichotomized" thinking found in "dominant white Western male rationality" must be transformed.[46] Ruether claims that "ecological thinking," which "integrates left-brain linear thought and right-brain spatial and relational thought," expresses and furthers the natural evolutionary process.[47]

In summary, this theologically supported system of domination is destructive not only for women but also for the whole ecosystem. The belief in a transcendent, all-powerful God undergirds elite male structures of domination by setting up hierarchical dualisms. These dualisms ultimately devalue the finite and encourage the abdication of power and human responsibility for the world. What is needed, then, is an understanding of God that is radically immanent in natural processes and gives value to those processes.[48]

Much theology promotes and sustains a cycle of violence and domination. In our generation, this cycle has so accelerated the potential for devastation that even the most powerful cannot hide from it. Ruether's graphic and detailed depiction of the coming environmental and social destruction is tendered not as an apocalyptic prophecy of unavoidable doom but as a goad to action. Likewise, an account of the human history of domination (including its theological components) is offered not only as an indictment of elite males but as a catalyst for social transformation. Transformation requires the recognition of past mistakes. Ruether writes that "a search for a truthful account of one's history is the collective analog of psychoanalysis. The resolution of neurotic habits in the present is related to the discovery and acceptance of a true account of one's past."[49] To find such a resolution or healing for humanity, human beings must see themselves and their pasts clearly and recognize the massive patterns of deceit out of which they have lived and been formed. Only then may one begin to establish a new consciousness, a new ethic, and a new theology.

Solutions: From Domination to Biophilic Mutuality

Ruether's theological ethic goes beyond the criticism and analysis of the problems of domination. She proposes practical solutions to create a more mutually loving society that lives in greater cooperation with the natural environment. Her suggestions for creating this new humanity, new consciousness, and new earth reflect a striking confidence in human nature, the natural environment, and large-scale social organization. This confidence is grounded in her understanding of nature. As we saw, Ruether claims that human consciousness is the most complex expression of natural evolutionary growth. Through greater attentiveness to this process, humans can further evolution through social manipulation.

A New Humanity

Ruether charges that the dangerous patterns of exploitation are caused by human denials of their natural interdependency with each other and nature. Humans are not only the primary *cause* of ecological destruction but also, as responsible co-creators, the sole hope for renewal and healing. A new vision of co-creation calls for a recognition of our biophilic mutuality. Humans would recognize their interdependence with and responsibility for each other and all the world. Such a turn toward biophilic mutuality would lead not only to new social structures and better environmental conditions but also to "a new type of social personality, a 'new humanity' appropriate to a 'new earth' . . . even a new religion."[50]

A New Prophet: The Scientist

How is this new humanity known? Ruether turns to the natural world itself as the primary source for her ecofeminist ethic. She insists that the patterns of interrelation and cooperation visible in healthy ecosystems should be the model for human interactions with each other and the biosphere. Those who study these systems, the ecological scientists (particularly those not necessarily mainstream scientists who support an ecofeminist reading of the natural world), are the new ethical guides or visionaries. "We need scientist-poets who can retell the story . . . in a way that can call us to wonder, to reverence for life, and to the vision of humanity living in community with all its sister and brother beings."[51] In her turn to the ecological sciences as the primary source for her ecofeminist naturalism, she proposes "some restoration of the classical role of science as normative or as ethically prescriptive."[52] What, then, do Ruether's ecological scientists tell us about the ethics of nature?

Solutions: A New Ethic

A Summary

Ruether's naturalist ethic has two linked components.[53] First, the "laws of Gaia" are those patterns discernible within the ecosphere that promote its health and sustainability. Cooperative interdependence of the life drives is the key factor. Second, the "laws of consciousness and kindness" are those unique capacities of human nature that allow us to reflect on and improve our world and our condition. These characteristics are very much of nature and Gaia because they embody its "evolutionary edge." In them, the cooperative interdependence or biophilic mutuality of the ecosystem is made reflective or conscious of itself. Humans are "the 'mind' of the universe."[54] She suggests that God is the source of this capacity or the process from which it emerges. Ecological ethics is, she writes, "an uneasy synthesis of both these 'laws': the law of consciousness and kindness, which causes us to strain beyond what 'is,' and laws of Gaia, which regulate what kinds of changes in 'nature' are sustainable in the life system of which we are an inextricable part."[55]

This tension between the givenness of the natural laws of the earth and the freedom (the "straining beyond what 'is' ") involved in the laws of consciousness and kindness is reminiscent of Niebuhr. As we will see later, Ruether's interpretation of human "boundedness and freedom" is very different from that of Niebuhr. She is much more confident both that humans can know the laws of nature and that the laws of nature are good. Another difference is her understanding of human uniqueness not as self-transcendence but as consciousness (or the thinking impulse) and altruism. Moreover, Ruether sees these capacities as much more closely connected with the natural process than does Niebuhr. These capacities grow out of and reflect the natural evolutionary process. By contrast, Niebuhr's human self-transcendence, though a part of human nature, suggests a greater discontinuity with the natural and social worlds. These differences will be explored more fully in the concluding chapter.

The Laws of Gaia: Relationality and Interdependence

For Ruether, "Gaia" refers to the "living and sacred earth."[56] In her use of this term, she follows the lead of many who envision new models for ecojustice.[57] For some ecofeminists, though not for Ruether, Gaia is the radically immanent Mother Goddess replacing the transcendent Father God. But Ruether uses the word "Gaia" to represent the natural processes of the earth whose voice is interpreted by ecological scientists.

The role of the ecological scientist is prophetic and visionary in this age because humans are not accustomed to listening to the voice of nature. Ruether writes throughout her works of the silencing of this voice within Western thought. The classical division of nature and body from soul and intellect, which she traces in its Greek and Christian developments and its rootedness in the male domination of females, is a source of the destructive disengagement of humans from environmental responsibility; nature and body are denied in favor of a transcendent realm. To become responsible again, humans must turn away from these patterns of domination and transcendent hierarchical dualism toward a new model of mutuality. Humans must affirm their ultimate dependence on, relationship to, and unity with their good bodies and all of the natural world.[58] The study of nature is an ethical guide for survival. Thereby, we may learn "the laws by which nature, unaided by humans, has generated and sustained life."[59] These laws are not merely descriptive but also prescriptive, suggesting "guidelines for how humans must learn to live as a sustaining . . . member" of the world community.[60]

What laws, then, are revealed through the long-silenced voice of nature? The primary relationships of healthy, sustainable ecological systems, claims Ruether, are those of interrelation and cooperative interdependence. Humans must realize, as the first lesson of Gaia, that all is interrelated. "Recognition of this profound kinship must bridge the arrogant barriers that humans have erected to wall themselves off."[61] The second lesson from the study of the natural world is "coevolutionary interdependency."[62] As members of the ecosystem evolve together, patterns of interdependence are created. Any human destruction of one part of the system leads to dramatic changes in another. Harmony and balance of the web of interrelated life drives in the ecosystem are necessary for the good of the whole and the parts.

This cooperative interdependence as normative nature is both a fact of the ecosystem and a positive moral good. Ruether relies on recent studies that refute the common Darwinian assumption that competition is the primary relationship within nature.[63] In fact, within such an interdependent system, "any absolutization of competition that causes one side to be wiped out means that the other sides of the relation thereby destroy themselves as well."[64] By focusing on competition, on power as domination or control, humans are alienated from the very creatures and systems on which they depend for their survival.[65] The laws of Gaia emphasize both the factual reality of interrelation and the moral necessity of cooperative interdependence. These natural laws offer clear moral guidelines for human life. They are good parts of the natural world.

The Laws of Consciousness and Kindness

Ruether claims that even these crucial laws are not sufficient for human life. Nature, she claims, is "not capable of completely fulfilling human hopes for the good."[66] Humans have a second set of laws that are a part of *human* nature, the human capacities for consciousness and kindness. While these "laws" of consciousness and kindness distinguish humans from other creatures, they are also the development or the growing edge of the natural evolutionary process itself. They are not separate from the rest of nature but reflect the biophilic mutuality found throughout the ecosystem. Through consciousness and kindness, humans are able to further the natural laws of cooperative dependence and live in biophilic mutuality with nature. Human altruism is a further expression of the cooperative dependence of nature. "Human ethics should be a more refined and conscious version of this natural interdependency, mandating humans to imagine and feel the suffering of others, and to find ways in which interrelation becomes cooperative and mutually life-enhancing."[67]

Thus, the laws not only reflect the values of the natural process but also allow humans to further develop those values. At the same time, consciousness and kindness allow humans to "strain beyond what 'is.'"[68] Through consciousness, humans are able to reflect on their condition and that of the world and to imagine that it might be other than it is. Through altruism, humans have compassion on and want the best for their fellow creatures. These two factors are the sources of ethical reflection. Ruether writes:

> Fundamental to human experience is a basic sense that things are not as they should be. Self consciousness allows humans to stand out from the environment and image better alternatives, in relation to which both the natural world and human society are judged as lacking. It would be better not to be cold, hungry, in danger of injury and death . . . or subjected to strife within one's own community. The categories of good and evil are absolutized extrapolations from these more concrete experiences of negativity and preferred alternatives.[69]

Conscious human life, then, is able to "stand out from" the environment, reflecting on it and imagining better ways of being. This capacity for thinking and imagining is the source of human ethical reflection. Because human consciousness emerges within and should further the natural process of development, the conscious self can look to the cooperative values of nature as a guide.[70] When humans use these unique faculties to further cooperation and to enhance the life drives or energy of all of life, they are acting for the good. But when humans use this same capacity to imagine alternatives for the advancement of their own life drives in competition with and at the expense of others, they are acting for ill.

These human capacities are not only "of nature" in the sense that they reflect and may further the biophilic mutuality of the ecosystem. They also "arise from natural evolution" and are even "the 'growing edge' of nature itself."[71] Humans are the conscious part of the natural world process in which the energy matrix becomes organized and aware of itself. Ruether writes that "*humans alone*, amid all the earth creatures and on all the planets of these vast galaxies, are capable of reflective *consciousness*. We are," she insists, "*the 'mind' of the universe*, the place where the *universe becomes conscious* of itself."[72]

Ruether's description of human consciousness as an expression and development of the natural process is drawn in part from Teilhard de Chardin's model of nature.[73] Ruether describes creation as a dynamic organic process. The world is made up of patterns of energy that grow into more and more complex forms. Human consciousness is the most complex level of this development. Ruether writes, "Consciousness comes to be seen as the most intense and complex form of the inwardness of material energy itself as it bursts forth at that evolutionary level where matter is organized in the most complex and intensive way—the central nervous system and cortex of the human brain."[74]

Thus, for Ruether, the human consciousness or thinking dimension is a natural development of an evolutionary process in which that process becomes conscious of and reflects on itself. Consciousness is "where this dance of energy organizes itself in increasingly unified ways, until it reflects back on itself in self-awareness."[75] Thus, because of this consciousness and altruism, humans have a unique role within creation. For both Teilhard and Ruether, these capacities are related to the divine. Ruether writes that human consciousness and kindness "point to an aspect of the source of life that is also an impulse to consciousness and increased kindness that is still imperfectly realized. We humans are the evolutionary growing edge of this imperfectly realized impulse to consciousness and kindness."[76] Thus, the growth of these capacities in human life points to something beyond human life that is the source of the process. The development "expresses this deeper source of life 'beyond' the biological."[77] For Ruether, "to believe in divine being means to believe that those qualities in ourselves are rooted in and respond to the life power from which the universe itself arises."[78] Thus, human nature and the evolutionary process are somehow reflective of the ground of that process. Humans are the growing edge in the process of which God is the ground. We will examine Ruether's understanding of God more fully later.

Though Ruether's model of nature is very similar to Teilhard's, she does distance herself from some aspects of his thought. The relation of the conscious self to the material is a point of difference. Ruether rejects his suggestion that the complexity of the process will eventually develop to the point where matter disappears and energy is organized only as divine consciousness. Ruether affirms, instead, the goodness of the material and the ultimate relation of consciousness and the divine to it. Moreover, Ruether rejects the "hierarchicalism of [Teilhard's] evolutionary theory." Human consciousness is distinctive but should not separate or raise humans above the rest of creation. Human intelligence is the "'thinking dimension' of the radial energy of matter." Though consciousness is a "critical breakthrough" in the process, it is still ultimately dependent on the process and responsible to it. "The privilege of intelligence," she writes, "is the responsibility to become the caretaker and cultivator of the welfare of the whole ecological community."[79]

This responsibility to care for the community is contrasted with the destruction and domination that Ruether links with "dysfunctional" patriarchal thinking. "White western male rationality" has distorted these natural cooperative patterns, turning instead to domination and hierarchical dualism.[80] Ruether suggests that the new emerging consciousness or intelligence is more reflective of the natural world but is also transforming of the natural. The conversion of "our minds to nature's logic of ecological harmony . . . will necessarily be a new synthesis, a new creation in which human nature and nonhuman nature become friends."[81] Both the destructive and creative possibilities of the human relationship with the rest of nature stem from its unique capacity to reflect on and change the environment. "Humans alone perpetuate their evolutionary advances primarily through cultural-social means."[82] Because of this capacity, humans have the potential either to further the creativity of the natural process or to destroy the natural process. Ruether attempts to articulate a vision for a new consciousness so that humans will turn away from domination and destruction and toward cooperative interdependence with nature.

Human consciousness, then, is both an expression of and responsible to the natural evolutionary process. Responsible moral actions are those that are attentive to the laws of nature and of consciousness and kindness and that further the natural development of cooperative interdependence. Irresponsible moral actions are those that distort nature and human nature by turning away from biophilic mutuality and toward domination. These options are supported by different theologies. Thus, to save the world from environmental and social devastation, Ruether criticizes patriarchal theologies and works to develop a new theology for this new consciousness.

104   *The Bonds of Freedom*

Solutions: A New Theology

Norms and Sources

If some aspects of classical Christian theology are complicit in the construction and maintenance of systems of domination, then that theology needs to be reconsidered. Ruether's sweeping and systematic reworking of Christian theology operates primarily out of the norm drawn from the laws of Gaia and of human consciousness and kindness. That which encourages biophilic mutuality or cooperative, empowering interdependence is good. That which promotes domination and competitiveness is bad. The norm of biophilic mutuality, though explicitly delineated only in her most recent work, is implicit in many of her theological arguments. Even when she focuses on the norm of the full humanity of women, her arguments suggests a broader concern. In *Sexism and God-Talk*, Ruether writes:

> Whatever denies, diminishes, or distorts the full humanity of women is, therefore, appraised as not redemptive. Theologically speaking, whatever diminishes or denies the full humanity of women must be presumed not to reflect the divine or an authentic relation to the divine, or to reflect the authentic nature of things. . . . This negative principle also implies the positive principle: what does promote the full humanity of women is of the Holy, it does reflect true relation to the divine, it is the true nature of things.[83]

Though Ruether focuses here on the norm of the full humanity of women, it is important to note that her arguments themselves suggest a broader norm, explicit in more recent works, that includes but is not limited to the full humanity of women. The arguments are driven by the assumptions that those things that promote biophilic mutuality or the balancing of life drives for the benefit of creation are good and holy. In contrast, structures or ideas (such as divine transcendence) that promote domination and passivity are bad.[84]

The idea of transcendence is one of the primary theological culprits in this dangerous structure of domination and submission. As we have seen, Ruether contends that the human appeal to divine transcendence and its own transcendent capacity is a ruse to cover or justify its own domination of "others" who are seen to be less transcendent and more bound to the material. This division sets into motion the hierarchical dualisms that are at the root of our current social and economic crises. Christian theology has been a leading promoter of this ideology of domination. Christianity and other traditions of the West, while in many ways responsible for the ideologies and structures of domination, also offer resources for criticizing and undermining domination. Ruether writes that they "have not only created domination and cultures of deceit that justified domination. They have also created critical cultures designed to unmask deceit and spiritualities that awakened compassion for others, thus rebuilding culturally the balances of self-limitation and respect for the lives of others that make for good community."[85]

One of the primary Judeo-Christian traditions on which Ruether draws is the "prophetic liberating strand" of Scripture that provides an internal principle "by which Biblical faith constantly criticizes and renews itself."[86] The prophetic strand criticizes "dominant systems of power" and speaks of God's activity on behalf of the oppressed.[87] This principle is normative for Ruether because it corresponds to her natural ethic of biophilic mutual empowerment.

Ruether's whole theology is built around this model of a mutually empowering ecosystem. Consequently, the test for an appropriate theological resource is not its honored place in the canon. The final judge of a theological symbol or formula is not whether it is confirmed by revelation or validated within the vast web of Church tradition or verified by human reason or established in Scripture. The first and last judge of any theological resource is the extent to which it creates persons, communities, and social policies that support mutually empowered interrelatedness and discourage domination within the ecosystem.

Given this norm, Ruether insists that "feminist theology cannot be done from the existing base of the Christian Bible."[88] Because the Bible "sacralizes patriarchy," women must turn to a broader range of texts in order to "develop . . . a new canon."[89] To that end, Ruether offers a collection of texts "as a working handbook from which such a new canon might emerge."[90] Selections from traditional Christian sources, other ancient myths, new feminist rituals, recent political and feminist theory, and ancient Greek philosophy are all examined together on equal footing.[91] These resources are judged according to their promotion of domination or biophilic mutuality. She claims that her exploration of different traditions is an attempt to develop "a working paradigm of some main trends of our consciousness."[92] Keeping in mind her comprehensive norm and eclectic canon, I now turn to several categories of Ruether's theology.

Dualism, Domination, and Transcendence

Kathryn Rabuzzi claims that for Ruether dualism is the root of human error.[93] And, indeed, throughout Ruether's work, one of the primary criticisms leveled at Christianity and other Western traditions is that they are profoundly dualistic. But Ruether's arguments about dualism appear to be grounded in a deeper human error, that of domination. Within Ruether's examination of theological categories, that which promotes hierarchical, dualistic systems of domination is rejected and that which promotes a more egalitarian, mutual empowerment is promoted. The link between dualism and domination is transcendence.[94]

The domination by elites is supported by a division of the world into a hierarchical dualism of transcendent spirit and finite matter. Gender divisions are the primary model for this social domination. Ruether writes, "Whereas the male is seen essentially as the image of the male transcendent ego or God, woman is seen as the image of the lower, material nature. . . . Gender becomes a primary symbol for the dualism of transcendence and immanence, spirit and matter."[95] These patterns of gender division are carried into other forms of social domination. The elites associate themselves with a transcendent realm and their subjects with a lower earthly existence. For Ruether, this hierarchical dualism is dangerous because of the way it is used by dominant groups to make weaker groups into "the other." Ruether claims that a dominant group tries to cement its power by associating positive characteristics with itself and negative characteristics with the group to be dominated. The dominant group asserts its natural rights to domination on the basis of characteristics it confers on its own group. Thereby, its own life drive is extended at the expense of others. Those in power associate themselves with the transcendent, the rational, the active, the good, the wise, and the spiritual. And they associate slaves, women, or other devalued groups with negative attributes of passivity, weakness, irrationality, and moral and bodily impurity. Ruether claims that the dualistic objectification of women by men was the model for all other hierarchical, dominating dualisms,[96] and a transcendent God is its primary justification. She writes, "The ultimate theological rationale for the hierarchical symbolism of masculinity and femininity is the image of God as transcendent Father."[97]

Many feminist theologians have joined Ruether's criticism of patriarchy for its production of hierarchical dualisms.[98] These dualisms, the argument runs, are created by the dominant class to support their own power and further their overreaching life drives. The model of hierarchical dualism is central to the Christian tradition, claims Ruether, and it places in jeopardy the sustenance of a healthy, mutually empowering world community. Again, the chief theological support for these hierarchical dualisms is the appeal to a transcendent God.

Clericalism

Ruether's examinations and criticisms of ordained ministry run throughout many of her works.[99] For years, she has called not only for the inclusion of women into the given structure of clericalism but also for the total revamping of the system itself. Her primary criticism of the hierarchical division between lay and clergy is that it is disempowering to the laypeople, especially to women. This hierarchical dualism encourages the unhealthy system of domination in which we now live. Male elites, including clergy, overreach their own life drives in the name and under the supposed authority of God; less dominant people are encouraged to abdicate their own power and responsibility. Clericalism is suspect, then, not only for its traditional association of the minister and maleness with God but also because it promotes domination and disempowerment. More recently, Ruether has called for the complete "dismantling" of clericalism because of its thoroughly patriarchal character. New, mutually empowering forms of community should be created. Ruether's promotion of "women-church" is a response to this call.[100]

The elimination of clericalism calls for more than a change in polity. According to Ruether, male clericalism is supported by the appeal to a transcendent power. Ruether writes:

> I have already shown that the ultimate theological rationale for the *hierarchical symbolism* of *masculinity and femininity* is the image of *God* as *transcendent Father*. . . . This image allows the king and patriarchal class to relate to their women, children, and servants through the same model of domination and dependency. . . . This image of [clerical] leadership splits the Church into two groups, a *clerical caste* who represent the *transcendent* "male" principle hierarchically related to a "female" or

"passive" principle. Both clericalism and the pacification of the laity operate out of this symbolic psychology. . . . *The people assume the prone, passive position before the raised altars and pulpits of the "fathers."*[101]

Thus, to alter the polity that sets the people "prone" before the "pulpits of the fathers," its theological underpinnings must also be transformed. Ruether argues throughout these systematic categories that the appeal to a transcendent realm must be rejected as a cover for male power.

Evil

The criticism of hierarchical dualisms extends to Ruether's understanding of evil. Ruether rejects simple good and evil dualisms.[102] She claims that humans, especially dominant humans, tend to deny the evil within themselves by projecting it onto other people and especially onto less powerful groups. A primary justification for abuse and domination is the association of the "other" with evil by virtue of their supposed link to the carnal and the concurrent association of the male elite with a pure, transcendent realm. Thus, an appeal to transcendence allows the dominant to justify their oppression of another as evil. The labeling of a particular group or person as evil is an illusion. There are no evil people or evil powers, claims Ruether. There are simply evil relationships, that is, relationships in which the life drives of the participants in the relationship are not balanced. Ruether writes:

> Evil comes about precisely by the distortion of the self-other relationship into the good-evil, superior-inferior dualism. The good potential of human nature then is to be sought primarily in conversion to relationality. This means a *metanoia* . . . into mutual interdependence. . . . Sin, therefore, has to be seen both in the capacity to set up prideful, antagonistic relations to others and in the passivity of men and women who acquiesce to the group ego.[103]

Sinful relationships and distorted life drives are to be overcome, finally, in a holy conversion from competitive domination to relationality or empowering biophilic mutuality. By building new social structures and designing new ideologies, humans may grow toward greater altruism and consciousness and away from distorted relationships.

Jesus

Ruether's examinations of Christology follow a similar line of argument.[104] Those Christologies that emphasize Jesus' maleness as normative necessarily encourage the domination of women by men and are, consequently, not acceptable. Jesus' liberating qualities, not his maleness, are normative for Ruether. Moreover, exclusivist Christologies that emphasize Jesus as the divine Logos are unacceptable because they promote hierarchy. "Christology becomes the apex of a system of control over all those who in one way or another are 'other.'"[105] So, if understandings of Jesus' power and/or maleness encourage hierarchical domination on the one hand and female or lay obedience and disempowerment on the other, then they are unhealthy. Acceptable Christologies emphasize Jesus as normatively liberating, not normatively male. Moreover, Christ is not limited to the Jesus of history but is disclosed again and again. Indeed, we can find Christ "in the form of our sister. Christ, the liberated humanity, is not confined to a static perfection. . . . Rather, redemptive humanity goes ahead of us, calling us to yet incompleted dimensions of human liberation."[106]

Mary

These themes are also evident in Ruether's examination of the place of Mary in Christian theology.[107] She asks if the veneration of Mary is healthy and good for the world and for the promotion of biophilic mutuality. If Mary is portrayed as a model for women's obedience and as a passive natural instrument or recipient of the dominating power of a transcendent God, then the answer, of course, is no. According to Ruether, this view is supported by the elite male desire to protect its own power. "Mariology has its appeal for males because it enshrines the dominant ego and active principle as masculine in relation to women, who become the symbol of passive dependency upon the male."[108] The veneration of Mary is appropriate only if she is portrayed as actively "choosing" pregnancy and faithfulness.[109] Mary, properly understood, is shown to be a model for a responsible "new humanity freed from hierarchical power relations, including that of God and humanity."[110] Mariology, then, can be a force for the promotion of mutual empowerment and connectedness. However, if Mary is presented as passive matter through which an active transcendent power moves, then Mariology is a tool for domination. Thus, Ruether again draws the connection between domination, transcendence, and dualism.

God

Ruether's arguments about God and God language follow a similar tack. As we have seen, she is not merely proposing the use of inclusive, gender-free names for God but a radical reshaping of our traditional understandings of God. She claims that traditional Christian appeals to a powerful and transcendent male God undergird a theology of domination that creates and sustains dualisms that are oppressive for women and others. Such a transcendent God, especially when tied to male language and images, instead of relativizing all human power, gives legitimacy to the powerful and perpetuates elite male subjugation of women, nature, and less powerful males. Moreover, divine transcendence, by placing ultimate value outside the world, encourages the devaluation of nature, body, and finite existence.

Ruether's understanding of God, then, attempts to overcome the dualism that associates a transcendent, powerful God with the good, the spiritual, and the masculine, and the natural world with the evil and the feminine. This dualism encourages and even excuses the overreaching of the life drives of the powerful and discourages the enactment of power and responsibility in the less powerful. Responsibility is discouraged when passivity is affirmed as a human value. Even parental language for God is questioned because it suggests that humans are in the position of children, and so have little power or responsibility. Ruether writes, "God becomes a neurotic parent who does not want us to grow up. To become autonomous and responsible . . . is the gravest sin against God."[111] The concern, then, is that many traditional ideas and much language about God promote disempowered dependency and justify human domination. Whatever images and language are to be used for God, they should not encourage humans either to overreach or to abdicate their power.

Ruether turns to the language of "God/ess" to refer to the "primal matrix" of life. This "sign" "point[s] toward that yet unnamable understanding of the divine that would transcend patriarchal limitations and signal redemptive experience for women as well as men."[112] She claims that she is not simply opting for a radically immanent earth Goddess. "Ecofeminist theology and spirituality has tended to assume that the 'Goddess' we need for ecological well-being is the reverse of the God we have had in the Semitic monotheistic tradition; immanent rather than transcendent, female rather than male identified, relational and interactive rather than dominating, pluriform and multicentered rather than uniform and monocentered."[113]

Ruether suggests that we need not a reversal but a more "imaginative solution" that does not fall into the spirit-matter dichotomy. In a discussion of the ultimate unity of matter and energy on a subatomic level, Ruether writes, "Thus what we have traditionally called 'God,' the 'mind,' or rational pattern holding all things together, and what we have called 'matter,' the 'ground' of physical objects, come together."[114] Thus divinity includes and unifies these aspects of life.

This conception is drawn from Ruether's process model of natural evolutionary development, which was previously described. The divine is the ground or source of that dynamic organic process of which humans are the growing edge. Ruether uses many names to refer to God/ess. The divine is called "the great womb," the "primal" or "empowering matrix," "the World egg," "the encompassing source of new life," "the ground of being," "Divine Wisdom," "the Great Self" and "the ongoing creative matrix of the whole."[115] These names point toward the divine as the source, power, and unity of the evolutionary organism.

We saw that Ruether's understanding of God is linked to human consciousness. In the human mind, the energy of the universe or the primal matrix is organized. Human consciousness is the "growing edge" of the evolutionary process.[116] Our consciousness "reflects back on" this process. Ruether writes, "*humans alone*, amid all the earth creatures and on all the planets of these vast galaxies, are capable of reflective *consciousness*. We are . . . *the 'mind' of the universe,* the place where the *universe becomes conscious* of itself."[117] Human consciousness and altruism point toward the matrix of the evolutionary process. Ruether claims that that which "has flowered in us as consciousness must also be reflected in that universe as well, in the ongoing creative Matrix of the whole"[118] Our unique human capacities express "this deeper source of life 'beyond' the biological. . . . To believe in divine being means to believe that those qualities in ourselves are rooted in and respond to the life power from which the universe itself arises."[119]

Thus, our unique human capacities reflect something beyond us. They point to "the source of life," which is "also an impulse to consciousness and increased kindness that is still imperfectly realized. We humans are the evolutionary growing edge of this imperfectly realized impulse to consciousness and kindness."[120] For Ruether, then, the divine is not separate from, but one with, the entire cosmic process. This natural process includes both matter and consciousness. Therefore, God/ess is not subject to the divisions of matter and spirit or immanence and transcendence, because the whole process is a unified, dynamic pattern of energy that expresses itself in both matter and consciousness. In human consciousness, "the mind of the universe" reflects this "impulse" to consciousness and kindness that is the source of life.

Thus, Ruether's model of nature (including humans and the divine) is a unified, growing process of mutuality. In contrast, the characteristics that she finds in patriarchal theology (dualism, domination, and transcendence) are a distortion of authentic nature and the divine. Patriarchal theology is a "dysfunctional" and "distorted" system that is "imposed" to underwrite domination. God/ess theology, by contrast, reflects authentic reality.[121] She writes of patriarchy:

> This world arises in revolt against God/ess and in alienation from nature. It erects a false system of alienated dualisms modeled on distorted and oppressive relationships. God/ess liberates us from this false and alienated world . . . as a constant breakthrough that points us to new possibilities that are at the same time, the re-grounding of ourselves in the primordial matrix, the original harmony. The liberation encounter with the God/ess is always an encounter with our authentic selves resurrected from underneath the alienated self.[122]

Ruether suggests that this new theology and way of being reflect the true nature of reality and the divine. By living out of this cooperative interdependence, humans will uncover their authentic selves and a truer understanding of the divine. Humans are called to live out this new vision not only in the creation of new theologies and psyches but also in the transformation of social structures. Ruether's optimism about fundamental social, theological, and psychological transformation is rooted in her model of the natural world.

New Social Structures

The recognition of human capacities for cooperative mutuality and the formation of new theologies are not enough for Ruether. Real change requires "a fundamental restructuring of all these relations from systems of domination/exploitation to ones of biophilic mutuality."[123] To transform ourselves and our worlds, then, we must imagine new social structures. Within these structures, humans are formed—either for good, for biophilic mutuality, or for ill, for domination or submission. Ruether's call for radical social change is found throughout her work. These proposals show a profound optimism about the potential for social change and about the impact of social change on the production of new psyches.

New Families

If matricentric child-rearing practices are among the causes of the male tendency to domination and the female tendency to passive acquiescence, then those practices must change for the health of the individuals and the ecosystem. For deeper social change to come about, men need to partake in the normal routines of childcare and housework.[124] Ruether writes, "They need to do regularly what they have hardly ever done. . . . : feed, clothe, wash, and hug children from infancy, cook food, and clean up wastes. Only when men are fully integrated into the culture of daily sustenance of life can men and women together begin to reshape the larger systems of economic, social, and political life."[125]

These changes would do more than simply free up the time and energy of the many women who spend themselves in the maintenance of the home. The participation of males in child rearing and homemaking would also alter the formation of gender identity. If the psychological need for a transcendent realm develops, in part, out of male insecurity and overindividuation, then a change of gender formation and gender identity will undermine the need for a transcendent realm to sacralize domination. These proposals for new families suggest that social conditioning is the cause of the "crisis of domination" and can be the locus of new ways of being. They reflect Ruether's optimism about the capacity of humans and their social structures for profound transformation.

New Communities

The locus of human healing and reformation is not limited to the family. Local communities that share in worship and social action can also participate in the change of human psyche and soul.[126] These small communities are not to neglect international issues but are encouraged to think and act both "locally" and "globally."[127] These "base communities" have several tasks. They are to encourage the creation of "personal therapies, spiritualities and corporate liturgies by which we nurture and symbolize a new biophilic consciousness." These liturgical communities are reminiscent of the women's groups called for in Ruether's *Women-Church*.[128] The communities use local institutions as "pilot projects of ecological living." Ruether's works are replete with recommendations for the day-to-day function of such "pilot projects." They also build networks for interacting with other communities and with national and international systems in order to overcome global social and environmental domination.[129] Although the community structure is small in scale, the intended impact is massive and widespread. Transformation not only of social structures but also of the human souls is the intended result.

Militarism

Ruether does not stop with these changes in family and local community life. She also turns to broader political systems that were created to meet the sick needs of distorted human psyches. One of the primary "systems of political life" in need of reshaping is militarism. Ruether connects the dominating mentality of militarism to the matricentric family structure. She writes, "I have suggested that the isolated male ego that demands invulnerable and dominating power over others is shaped developmentally through negation of interdependency with women, in the context of woman-exploited child raising. But this type of masculine ego finds its most global manifestation in militarism."[130]

Thus, militarism is the most threatening expression of men's isolation and competitive life drives. The achievement of true biophilic mutuality is not possible simply through the transformation of life drives in families or local communities. "Genuine demilitarization across the board . . ." she writes, is "the *sine qua non* of any genuine, ecologically sustainable, biospheric economy."[131] The power drives of the elites keep this "system of destructive power" in place. Ruether calls for a "conversion . . . or change of heart . . . that recognizes that real 'security' lies not in dominating power and the impossible quest for total invulnerability, but rather in the acceptance of vulnerability, limits, and interdependency."[132] Militarism is crucial for Rosemary Ruether because it represents the epitome of the dominating male mentality that she opposes and that her new humanity and theology would transform.

New Government Policies

Ruether offers sweeping proposals for concrete policy changes that she contends would discourage systems of dominating power and promote biophilic mutual empowerment.[133] She calls for a dramatic decrease in fossil fuel use. She promotes the complete revamping of transportation systems, including the "phasing out" of private automobiles. These changes would require the creation of new living, working, and recreational communities that decrease the use of private transportation. She suggests that we should "return to seasonal patterns of food, produced and distributed" regionally.[134] Her lists of proposed changes are comprehensive and detailed. The transformation of the human psyche away from a hierarchical dualism that supports domination by appeals to a transcendent realm thus requires widespread social change. Clearly, these proposals reflect her optimism about the possibilities of radical social change and about the subsequent transformation of human values and psyches.

Summary

Ruether's continual reference to concrete suggestions for social change reflects her confidence in human nature and communities. Through the examination of the laws of nature and the expression of these laws in the capacities for consciousness and altruism, humans can know and do the good. Moreover, humans can create better social structures for the production of healthier psyches. Thus, social conditioning is both a part of the problem and a part of the solution.

A Feminist Christian Realist Response

A Summary

As we have seen, Ruether's theological ethic develops from her model of nature. The locus of moral reflection and the divine is the natural evolutionary process. Human consciousness emerges within this process and has the capacity to further it through social change. To guide this change, moral norms can be known from nature, including human nature. Because humans have ignored these natural laws, the natural world (including human civilization) is on the brink of destruction. To save the world, humans need to develop social structures, psyches, and theologies in keeping with these natural laws. Ruether sees her theology and ethic as a part of this evolutionary transformation. She criticizes and hopes to transform the dominating mentality of elite males and the submissive mentality of women and other subordinate peoples. According to Ruether, the powerful justify their domination by associating themselves with the transcendent and the "other" with nature. The hierarchical dualism set in motion by this appeal leads to the cycle of domination and violence that is at the heart of the present social and ecological crises. Ruether's wide-ranging theological revisions and social strategies are designed, then, to lessen domination, to ease the pain of subjugated peoples and the environment, and to promote "biophilic mutuality." To this end, she proposes that we attend to and follow the laws of nature and the evolutionary development of consciousness and kindness. We can move beyond our difficulties by furthering the true nature of ourselves and the whole evolutionary process of which the divine is the ground. My primary question is simple. Given this analysis, will Ruether's naturalist moral and theological realism support her goal to undercut dominating power and promote mutual empowerment?

Analysis and Appropriation: Ruether's Naturalist Realism

When Ruether speaks of nature, she refers to the whole evolutionary process that includes nonhuman creation, human nature, human social forms, and the divine. Consequently, all of her ethic (including her theological realism) emerges from a naturalist realism. Next, I examine different aspects of this ethic.

NATURE, ETHICS, AND DOMINATION

Ruether's ethic and her hope are based on her assumptions about the cooperativeness of life forms in the natural world and the evolutionary growth of altruism and consciousness. Just as the natural world exhibits mutual dependency, so humans may further this natural tendency as they act altruistically in the world. This assumption raises several obvious questions. Given the brutalities of nature—including human nature—described in her work, is her hope firmly grounded? Is nature fundamentally cooperative? Do human beings have a growing capacity for altruism? If so, how do we *account* for the tenacity of sin, evil, and domination? Given her optimism about nature, Ruether has difficulty making sense of the persistence of evil in human life and the violence in nature.

Moreover, Ruether's argument assumes that cooperativeness and interdependence are normative because they are the patterns that are said to exist in nature. This raises several questions. First, does the existence of a pattern in nature make it good for human life? Does the *is* justify the *ought*? If competition and survival were the laws of nature, including human nature, would those laws be normative? This question is made more serious by the fact that Ruether's ecological theories about the extent of cooperative mutuality in nature are by no means universally accepted. It is not difficult to imagine that some scientists would (and do) find less palatable laws and patterns in nature. If the male domination of the female is common among most animal groups, is it normative? This is not, of course, an idle question. Scientists have made that claim. Moreover, Christian natural law arguments have often turned to nature to justify male domination. If a feminist Christian realism were to draw substantive moral claims from human boundedness, it would have to account for and build in checks against these dangers of arguments from nature. It would also have to counter the tendency of ecologically based ethics to look out more for the interests of the whole than the interests of the individual.

SOCIAL TRANSFORMATION: COERCION, FREEDOM, AND BIOPHILIC MUTUALITY

Ruether's naturalist ethic leaves her with a clear mandate and plan for the good life and good human communities. Her detailed political and social recommendations stem from her confidence in nature, human nature, and human communities. We can know the good; we can enact social changes to transform human psyches. If we educate and socialize properly, humans can move away from domination and toward biophilic mutuality. We can further the natural evolutionary process by social means.

Thus, Ruether's ethic leaves her confident about the possibility of creating a "new humanity" through social changes. The problem of how the world is converted from the old humanity to the new humanity, from domination to empowerment, raises troubling questions. Though our natures have a deep potential for goodness, according to Ruether, the radical distortion of our consciousness and the danger we present to each other and to the whole creation could hardly be more grimly painted. As we saw, Ruether compares her task to the "great cultural recycler" who stands in an "enormous toxic waste dump of ideas and images, sifting through, trying to find some usable material to create a new world."[135] Though Ruether produces scores of plans and blueprints for this social transformation, it is unclear, given her picture of the radical extent of our distortion, how we get to her new world from our present location in the toxic garbage heap. Moreover, given the reality of human domination, it is unclear what we do to maintain both some semblance of order and the protection of freedom in the meantime. Ruether generally rejects domination and hierarchical authority without explaining how we maintain some protection from life drives run amok, short of the coercive rule of law. On a few occasions, however, she affirms coercive authority without delineating its limits. She is open to the possibility of extreme government control, not for basic protection or order but for the actual forced creation of "healthy psyches." In a partial defense of communist China from Western criticism, she writes:

> The drive for full equality for women in China shows no signs of stopping with a formal equality before the law . . . the Chinese have engaged in a prolonged cultural revolution intended to tear down and overthrow the psychological structures of hierarchicalism and elitism. The traditional elites of society have been forced to rub their noses in the dirt of peasant labor, while the traditionally subordinate groups have been encouraged to criticize tendencies to elitism in the former mandarins. Students criticize teachers; peasants, city folk; nurses, doctors; children, parents. This is intended to create a revolution in consciousness which destroys the traditional orders of authority and creates direct participation at the base. *Women, the oldest subordinate in every hierarchy, find ample encouragement to struggle against every manifestation of chauvinism. . . . Emancipation is seen as a continual struggle to create a new culture, a new psychology, as well as a new social order . . . this authoritarianism gives women an immense advantage. It would be the male who would have to acknowledge his incorrectness if he were to be convicted of chauvinist ways of thinking.*[136]

This quotation points to a crucial tension—even a contradiction—in Ruether's work. On the one hand, she denounces coercive hierarchies throughout her work. On the other hand, she defends in this quotation the use of extreme coercion and control to create a new, nonpatriarchal mentality. And, it *is* difficult to imagine that the radically distorted life drives and social structures that she describes so vividly for us could be changed significantly without substantial coercion. Moreover, the radical nature of Ruether's own suggestions for social change would seem to require some political force. But given Ruether's consistent rejection of domination and her affirmation of mutuality, she does not have a structure to justify this move. Even so, she seems to claim in this quotation that domination is justified in the name of the creation of new psyches. But how could one be forcefully coerced into a mentality of biophilic mutuality and empowerment?

Perhaps Ruether's partial acceptance of Chinese authoritarianism is itself an odd sort of evidence of her confidence in human nature and particularly in social groups. Because of her faith in social planning for the creation of a new psyche, she is more open to stringent government control. In the interest of promoting mutual empowerment or furthering the evolutionary process, authoritarian restrictions are justified. If some feminists argue that Niebuhr is too optimistic about the moral capacities of the self and too pessimistic about social groups and governments, perhaps Ruether represents the opposite problem. In this quotation, she justifies extreme social control for the sake of creating mutually cooperative societies and individuals.

In addition, Ruether's support of extreme government coercion for the sake of the "good" suggests that she may give a relatively low status to human freedom. The development of a certain type of human psyche that is consistent with natural evolution is more important than the maintenance of freedom of the self to redefine and transform itself and its societies in radically new ways. In this evaluation of Chinese communism (admittedly an exception in Ruether's broader affirmations of socialist democracies), we see a greater emphasis on order and control than on freedom. Although this quotation is unusual in Ruether, it does reflect issues in her socialist plans for transforming cultures and psyches. To initiate Ruether's vision, our government would have to have much broader power and greater control than it now has. Again, this seems to point to a relatively higher value placed on order and community good and a lower value placed on freedom and individual rights. This tension is not strange for a natural law thinker, but it *does* present problems for feminists and others engaged in struggles for liberation. Given the profound limits that have been placed on women's freedoms by coercive governments and social structures, most feminists tend to be wary of any claims for extreme government coercion.

This position stands in contrast, of course, to Niebuhr, who advocates social coercion and control not so much for the creation of healthy psyches but to protect the interests of the weak and to constrain the powerful. Moreover, though he sees the necessity of government, he is always a political realist in his evaluation of it. And he supports forms of government (such as democracy) that place checks on the political powers. Of course, in his early years, he, like Ruether, affirmed the positive place for government in large-scale social planning.[137] But Niebuhr's political realism dampens his expectations for overwhelmingly positive transformation and heightens his suspicion of all political power in a way that contrasts sharply with Ruether. He might (and did) justify strong government coercion in some cases but for very different (politically realist) reasons.

In summary, Ruether's optimism about human capacities to further evolutionary development through broad social transformation sets up an internal tension in her work. In the interest of transforming old mentalities of domination and control to new mentalities of mutual, interdependent cooperation, she sometimes seems to justify extreme control and coercion. In her broader theory, however, systems of domination and coercion are rejected. The relation between Ruether's ethic and her understanding of power should be thought through more clearly. A feminist Christian realism would need to account for the place of government coercion in protecting the weak and promoting justice and flourishing while also defining the limits of that coercion.

CONSCIOUSNESS, NATURE, AND FREEDOM

Though Ruether's model of nature does make room for human freedom, she is critical of many appeals to human self-transcendence. Ruether's criticisms of traditional formulations of human self-transcendence center around their use to justify domination and hierarchical dualism and to devalue the finite. Ruether's focus on human consciousness offers an alternative understanding of transcendence or freedom. Humans are able through consciousness to "stand out from" their context, reflecting on it and transforming it. Ruether's model differs from Niebuhr's in several related ways. Ruether equates consciousness with mind, rationality, and thinking dimensions or impulses. This is quite different from

Niebuhr's insistence that self-transcendence involves the self's further capacity to reflect on its own rational processes and consciousness. In all fairness, Ruether does suggest that consciousness *includes* self-consciousness and a capacity to "stand out from" one's environment. And, as we saw in chapter 3, Niebuhr later *included* reason as one part of the experience of self-transcendence. Even *with* these nuances, one still sees a difference between Ruether and Niebuhr.

For Ruether, consciousness is ultimately a further expression of nature and the natural evolutionary process. It is continuous with this process. For Niebuhr, human self-transcendence or freedom is certainly a part of our nature, but it is more discontinuous with the created world than it is in Ruether. For Niebuhr, self-transcendence is a distinctive part of human nature that he associates with the "imago dei." Of course, for Ruether, human consciousness could also be called the "imago dei" in the sense that human consciousness is said to come from and reflect the process of which God/ess is the ground. But because their understandings of God are *also* so different, the comparison loses its force. The point here is that Niebuhr's self-transcendence is somewhat more discontinuous with the created natural world. Ruether, of course, would not talk about the world in that way because she has one process in which everything is included. Even with all these nuances, Ruether's understanding of consciousness as freedom is more continuous with the natural, and thus more bound, than Niebuhr's self-transcendence.[138]

Thus, both thinkers offer models of human life as bound and free. Niebuhr outlines the moral implications of our freedom in great detail, but he neglects the positive moral implications of boundedness. In contrast, Ruether draws substantial moral claims from our boundedness but neglects the implications of human freedom. This is because Ruether's freedom is properly understood and enacted in continuity with boundedness. For Niebuhr, however, boundedness is transformed, distorted, denied, and/or limited by human freedom. Thus, the roles played by consciousness in Ruether and self-transcendence in Niebuhr are overlapping but significantly different.

Given this analysis, what does Ruether's understanding of consciousness offer to a feminist Christian realism? It does leave room for some human freedom to reflect on and further the natural evolutionary developments. Moreover, the continuity between her understanding of consciousness and boundedness avoids the partial tendency we saw in Niebuhr to discount or neglect boundedness as a ground for moral claims.

Ruether's understanding of consciousness also presents several problems. First, in an attempt to undermine hierarchy, Ruether has offered a model in which human consciousness and altruism represent the most advanced level of the natural evolutionary process. Though she has modified Teilhard's hierarchy, her model is still hierarchical. Second, does Ruether's optimism about human consciousness take into account the embeddedness of domination in our thinking processes? If we are relational, contextual selves, how is our evolving consciousness made free of the distortions of ideology? Perhaps it is not our consciousness but our capacity to transcend and reflect on consciousness and its distortions that offers greater potential to see that distortion. In traditional Christian language, how does Ruether's failure to take seriously the universal nature of human sin affect the coherence of her larger Christian theological reflection on the future?

Finally, does Ruether's focus on human boundedness to natural evolution and her emphasis on the continuity between consciousness and other aspects of boundedness allow for the radical freedom that I argue is so central to feminism? To make sense of the feminist experience of standing outside and reflecting on cultural ideology and even the distortion of one's own consciousness, I argue that an adequate feminist ethic and theology must account for the experience of radical human freedom or self-transcendence.[139]

NATURE AND THE DIVINE

For Ruether, God/ess is in continuity with the natural evolutionary process as its "empowering matrix." Within Ruether's theological realism, God/ess gives unity to diverse human moral claims. Its radical immanence also encourages the valuing of the natural. This continuity raises several questions. By rejecting traditional conceptions of God as somehow radically other than natural and human processes, Ruether gives up a function of God that has been central to many Christian and Jewish theologies. God's transcendence and otherness have served as a crucial foil to idolatry and tyranny, relativizing all human powers under the power of God. Ruether appeals to the prophetic liberating strand of Scripture as ethically normative. Yet to draw on the prophets while denying the greatness and otherness of the God whose judgment they proclaimed is an odd sort of revisionism. God's judgment of human life and human social patterns (including those of domination and passivity) reminds us that there are standards and judgments beyond our own sickness and distortion. If God is this evolutionary process of which we are the consciousness or the mind, where is the point of judgment on human consciousness and on nature?[140] Contra Ruether's version of history, appeals to transcendence have often been used in the history of Christianity to provide the possibility of that judgment.

SUMMARY

We turned from Niebuhr in search of a realist who grounded moral claims in human boundedness.[141] In Ruether, we found a fully developed naturalist moral realism. Ruether combines an ecofeminist understanding of nature and a process Catholic natural law position with a liberal confidence in human nature and the possibilities for radical social transformation. In many ways, this model stands in sharp contrast to Niebuhr's realism. Ruether's naturalist moral realism makes much stronger claims about what humans can know about the good from observation of creation, including their own natures, and about what humans can do to further the good through the transformation of social structures, theologies, and their own psyches. Her understanding of human consciousness is much more continuous with the natural process than is Niebuhr's model of self-transcendence.

Moreover, Ruether looks to the natural evolutionary process not only for moral norms but also for the divine. Within Ruether's theological realism, the divine is the source and the unity of life. Because the divine is in continuity with the world, it lacks the relativizing role that it has in Niebuhr (for whom even God's "presence" is understood as an expression of God's "transcendence"). In many ways, Ruether's focus on the continuity of nature with ethics and God is an important resource for feminism. Within this project, it is a helpful corrective to Niebuhr's neglect of human boundedness as a source for moral norms. With Ruether and other natural law thinkers, the creation reflects the Creator and the Creator's intent for morally responsible human life. The difficulty in Ruether is not the moral realist turn to nature. The difficulty is her lack of political realism. Ruether's confident moral and theological realism are accompanied by only a partial political realism. She makes politically realist arguments about patriarchy, but tends to drop the "hermeneutic of suspicion" when she turns to some feminist assumptions and her own model. This inconsistency of her political realism may stem from the absence in her model of more traditional Christian arguments about the universal and radical nature of human sin.

As we have seen, Ruether lacks a thorough political realism, and Niebuhr neglects the normative implications of human boundedness within his moral realism. These contrasts should not obscure the fact that Niebuhr and Ruether share much in common. They both are moral and theological realists. They begin from human experience and emphasize (though to different degrees) the moral implications of human boundedness and freedom. They both are suspicious of the claims of the powerful. The similarities between the two seem even stronger when we compare them to our next figure, Sharon Welch. We will return to these comparisons and contrasts in the conclusion of this study.

FIVE

Battling for Truth in the Beloved Community

Sharon Welch's Relativist Political Realism

In this chapter, we look to Sharon Welch's political realism as a resource for exploring the moral implications of human boundedness to community. Welch's ethic offers a strong contrast to Niebuhr and Ruether in that she locates moral reflection and the divine within finite, mutually critical communities.[1] For Welch, there are no universal or shared human experiences or capacities to ground our moral claims. Instead, all moral claims are relative to one's own context. Human boundedness to community plays a crucial role within Welch's thought, because within these interactions across communities our ideas are relativized. In addition, the divine is a quality of these community interactions. Her "horizontal transcendence" stands in sharp contrast to Niebuhr's claim that societies lack an organ for transcendence. At the same time, Welch's thoroughly relativist political realism is strikingly different from Ruether's confidence in the grounding of moral claims in nature.

Welch is a resource for a feminist Christian realism. She provides a resource for understanding the critical role of the community. Her idea of horizontal transcendence in community is a helpful counter to Niebuhr's focus on individual self-transcendence. Moreover, unlike Ruether, she extends the suspicion of her political realism beyond the criticism of patriarchy to include feminist discourse itself, though not her own relativist theory.

Welch is also a problem for a feminist Christian realism. I contend here that her ethical framework and theological claims undercut both the ethical assumptions on which feminism and other liberation movements rest and the ethical model she herself wishes to support. Welch's relativist political realism prevents her from finding sufficient grounding to make sense of her moral "choices," her model of moral discourse, her political engagement, and even the moral agent who chooses, talks, and acts. A primary reason for this failure is that Welch, unlike Ruether and Niebuhr, has no moral realism or theological realism.

Welch's Theological Ethic: A Summary

Sharon Welch accuses Christian theology and the dominant ethic of the West with complicity in the "barbarities of the twentieth century."[2] She believes that our culture is undergoing a radical change or "epistemic shift," in which the old forms of rationality will be overcome by new forms in a "battle for the truth." In opposition to the dominant theology and ethic, Welch develops a relativist feminist alternative that she hopes will be more conducive to human liberation. Her work comes out of her own experience within structures of oppression. As a "white, middle-class and American" woman, she has a "double identity—oppressor and oppressed."[3] Out of her context, she enters the epistemic struggle hoping that her new ethic and her "choice" for liberation will be made "true" by their triumph in this battle.

Welch's theological ethic is developed in two primary phases. In her early works, Welch lays out the philosophical and methodological assumptions of her ethic.[4] In *Communities of Resistance and Solidarity*, Welch draws on liberation theology and the French philosopher Michel Foucault as primary resources. She begins with liberation commitments and concerns but turns to Foucault's categories and relativist assumptions to analyze the state of contemporary theology, politics, and liberation movements. She then tries to make sense of her liberation commitments from the perspective of her Foucauldian relativist framework. Out of this curious blend, Welch forms a theological ethic with a radically "relativist" epistemology and a strong, though relative, commitment to liberation.[5] This combination is at the heart of her argument and her difficulties.

In her more recent work, Welch moves from the theoretical model developed in her earlier writings to a critical analysis of Christian theology and "dominant" Western ethics and to a constructive proposal for an alternate theology and ethic.[6] *A Feminist Ethic of Risk* begins with an analysis of the ethic and the theology of control that support a nuclear deterrence mentality. She then looks to African American women's literature and some feminist communities as models for a new theological ethic. This alternative ethic, an ethic of risk, redefines the end, locus, and strategies of morally responsible action.[7]

Out of these resources, Welch charges that appeals to divine transcendence and human self-transcendence support the ethic of control. In contrast, she emphasizes the radical location or boundedness of the divine and of human moral reflection in finite, particular communities. All human norms are tied to particular claims of an age and culture. In contrast to many feminist theological realists (including Ruether), Welch is much less confident about the correspondence of our claims about God and moral truth to something beyond human construction or something grounded in human nature. The postmodern feminist combination of strong political commitments and a tendency toward ethical relativism or, in Welch's case, "qualified nihilism," makes it difficult to explain basic feminist ethical assumptions and feminist judgments about patriarchy.

For Welch, humans have no capacity to transcend the relative truths of their own context except in horizontal interactions with those of other contexts. This "horizontal transcendence" in cross-cultural dialogue does not offer hope for the revelation of less relative truths about human life or morality. There are no less relative or nonrelative moral truths. There is no essential human nature or universal experience that will be discovered. Truth is created by the power relations within a given culture.[8] Cross-cultural interactions show us the relative nature of our own truths. We transcend our own perspective as we see the finitude of our own claims through an encounter with another perspective. The truth (with a lowercase *t*) that we can discover through our openness to others is that our truth is not the only truth. Human moral reflection, then, is radically bound to the existing truths of an age.

Thus, like many other feminists, Welch turns to experience as the source of moral reflection and focuses on experience within community. Unlike many other feminists, however, human experience does not have positive moral content. There are no shared experiences or values on which to ground moral claims or to establish procedures. Our experience in community serves a critical role to relativize each other's claims. Although, as we shall see, Welch finally wants to make broader claims for community, those claims are not credible, given her moral epistemology. Thus, her turn to experience contrasts with that of many feminists.

Welch's understanding of the divine also moves further than many feminist models of divine immanence. For Welch, God is not just radically present in human communities; God is the power within those relationships.[9] God is not the source or ground of the finite; God is the power of the finite. She writes that "divinity is not a mark of that which is other than the finite. . . . Divinity, or grace, is the resilient, fragile, healing power of finitude itself."[10]

These comments about God must be understood within the context of Welch's understanding of religious language. Welch insists that a primary theological crisis of twentieth century theology was the loss of certainty about the "referent" of theological language.[11] For Welch, language about God is a completely human construction. It is an expression of finite human values. The model of a liberating God, for example, affirms the value of liberation. She contrasts her understanding of God with the focus of many theologians on "an ontological structure . . . or . . . that which grounds ontology."[12] She "rejects" any attempts to "correlate" theological language with ontology. For Welch, "the referent of the phrase 'liberating God' is not primarily *God* but *liberation*."[13] Moreover, this language is judged not according to the values expressed but by the practical effects. The phrase *liberating God* is "true not because it corresponds with something in the divine nature but because it leads to actual liberation in history."[14] Welch compares her understanding of God to Feuerbach's. With Feuerbach, she claims that language about God expresses central qualities or attributes within human life.[15] Though she rejects his ambivalence about human finitude, she agrees with his understanding of religious language as projection.

Thus, within Welch's theological ethic, moral reflection and action have their locus in finite, particular communities. There are no shared human natures or universal experiences, revealed Scriptures, divine commands, or shared rational capacities that will ground truth claims or even procedures for discourse. Within mutually critical, struggling communities, we realize the limitations of our own perspectives. Humans, having "chosen" from among the perspectives, enter the battle of truth. That which wins is the "truth." These finite, mutually critical communities are the locus not only of moral activity but also of the divine, which is the "relational power" of those communities. I will argue that her rejection of moral and theological realism and her turn to a relativist political realism have troubling ethical implications for feminism and other radical politics.

Welch's Problems: Crises and Transformation

Moral and Linguistic Crises

Welch's theology and ethic are formed in response to several problems of twentieth-century Western ethics, theology, and culture. Welch claims that Christianity is in the midst of a crisis. First, as we saw before, Christian theologians are no longer sure of the referent of their language about God or the correspondence of truth claims to an objective reality. Is their language pure human construction, or does it refer to a reality beyond themselves? Liberal theologians, charges Welch, "have failed to lay to rest the ghost of Feuerbach" and "have not yet discovered the type of evidence and style of argument that can establish with sufficient certainty the reality of God."[16]

The primary crisis, however, is moral. Christian failure is one both of belief and of practice. Welch lays the blame for the inhumanity of the twentieth century at the door of Christianity. The moral atrocities to which Christians have been party call into question not only Christianity's moral effectiveness but also "the truth of Christian faith and theology—the existence or reality of its referent."[17] The place of Christianity in the nuclear arms race, for example, becomes a "test of the substance of [Christian] faith."[18] Welch claims, then, that the evil that Christianity produces and supports falsifies not only Christian *doctrine* about God but also the very "*existence* and *reality* of its referent."[19]

According to Welch, the moral corruption promoted by Christianity is widespread. Some of its beliefs and practices not only fail to stop oppression but also "have served to perpetuate various forms of oppression."[20] She notes that the Christian turn to a transcendent realm and "escape" from finitude leads Mary Daly to charge it with denying life and supporting "necrophilia."[21] Welch's development of a "theology of immanence" stems from her assessment that ethics of "resignation and despair" and the devaluing of the finite world are accompanied by theologies of transcendence.[22] Welch also argues that conceptions of absolute divine power underwrite human power, even when that is not their intention. Welch writes, "Although rituals and doctrines that affirm the absolute power of God also claim that such a power is had only by God, they also reinforce a human desire for absolute power."[23] These problems cause Welch to doubt the "fundamental morality of Christian faith and Christian theology."[24] Her criticisms of Christian theology—particularly Christian understandings of divine transcendence and power—will be examined more fully later.

Likewise, Welch criticizes Western culture for producing and maintaining an "ethic of control." According to Welch, this ethic is morally culpable for the nuclear crisis, Western imperialism, and much of the violence and domination of our culture.[25] The dominant ethic of control insists that responsible moral action should lead to guaranteed success and complete control and security. Because control is rarely complete and because the stakes of complete control and success are so high, the use of coercive and dominating power is justified. Moreover, this illusory goal of complete success discourages strategies of compromise and openness. Elsewhere, Welch criticizes the dominant ethic for its appeal to universal moral categories and its reliance on the individual moral actor. Her delineation and criticisms of this ethic are examined more fully later.

As we saw before, Christian theology bears a large share of the responsibility for promoting the ethic of control. By emphasizing God's greatness and absolute power, Christians encourage a dangerous pattern of domination and submission. Following this model, humans either dominate or submit. The concept of divine transcendence or radical otherness furthers the dualism while negating the value of this world. The stakes are high in theological debates because theology has powerful, concrete effects in the world.

An Epistemic Shift to Liberation

The current crisis in theology and ethics is no routine in-house struggle but is, instead, a part of a broad historical transformation. According to Welch, contemporary theology is undergoing an "epistemic" shift. The old way is full of conceptual and moral contradictions. Welch claims that liberation theology is "a way out of" the moral and theological crises.[26] Welch writes, "Examining liberation theology and my work in feminist theology of liberation through the lens of Foucault . . . it becomes apparent that such theologies are not merely variants within theology but may represent a new episteme."[27] Thus, Welch claims here that liberation theology, including her own relativist version, may be the emerging perspective that will prod Christianity and the West into a new age. Indeed, she writes that liberation theology "*is* the manifestation of a new episteme."[28] Within this new episteme, the criterion for the truth of Christianity is its enactment of human liberation. In the end, this criterion is itself brought into question because of the underlying relativism that Welch draws from Michel Foucault. To understand Welch's interpretation of these shifts, we must examine her alliance with Foucault and liberation theology.

Welch's Commitments: Relativism and Liberation

Summary

Welch's proposals center around her startling juxtaposition of and commitments to the strong normative claims of liberation theology and the extreme relativism of Foucault.[29] Her relativism makes it difficult for her to make sense of her choice for liberation and the communities' choices for solidarity.

Foucault and Relativism

Drawing from Foucault, Welch insists that each age produces its own understanding of what counts as true or rational or normatively human.[30] Power produces knowledge and truth.[31] And appeals of the powerful to any transcendent authorities or universal experience in order to ground their truth are simply masks to disguise the finitude and self-interestedness of their own positions. There are no essential human experiences or natures or authoritative standards of truth outside or spanning different epistemes by which to judge them.[32] These epistemes, or "fields of knowledge," make themselves true by having enough power to define truth. Likewise, within any particular theological grid, understandings of truth or God do not refer to something existing outside that age. They make sense (or are judged as "true") by their utility within the framework of that age. When different grids come into conflict, the "truth" is determined by which grid comes to be dominant. The truth is that which wins. And the conflict has the properties of warfare.[33] Welch repeatedly uses the words *conflict, struggle, contest*, and *battle* to describe the relationship between conflicting theories or paradigms.[34] Even her "feminist theology of liberation" is itself described only as "a particular option taken in the battle for truth."[35]

Though Welch embraces radical relativism, she does not give up on the possibility of resistance and change. The antidote or critical response to the entrenched truth or truths of an age is to remember or imagine alternative ways of understanding truth. These "subjugated knowledges" are, claims Welch, "a type of knowing or being that challenges the entire apparatus, the system of rationality and sociality."[36] By recalling these "subjugated knowledges" or "dangerous memories" (the losers in past battles for power and truth), one questions the universality of the dominant truths.[37] Welch, like Foucault, encourages the hearing of many voices, not to discover standards of health or rationality or the normatively human but to reveal the limitations of the entrenched power-truth system. Modest internal criticism and creativity can emerge, then, through the hearing of the voices of resistance.

Liberation Theology and Liberation Struggle

Who are the bearers of these "dangerous memories" that challenge the dominant assumptions of truth within the setting of conflictive discourse? For Welch, the voices of the oppressed are examples of such knowledges. These partial attempts to resist oppression provide glimpses of hope in the struggle against the power and truth of any given episteme.[38] Through discourse that is open to these voices and that sees its own limitations, Welch hopes that active solidarity with the oppressed will emerge. In such discourse, truth is liberating power. Claims for truth as liberation or for a privileged voice for the poor are grounded, however, not in arguments about what it means to be human but in a prior commitment to the oppressed.[39] While her criteria are liberation and resistance, Welch's inheritance from Foucault leaves her unable to ground her standards in anything more than contingent—and finally inexplicable—human choice.[40]

Through this contingent choice, then, she turns to liberation theology as the hope for a new theological episteme and to the voices of African American women's literature as a source for a new ethic. Welch's liberation theology is unusual because of her philosophical assumptions. Welch's theology attempts to combine Foucault's radical relativism with strong liberation commitments. This blend leaves Welch with a very different understanding of moral truth than that of most liberation theologians. Welch writes:

> I maintain this [liberation] perspective but do so with a note of skepticism. I agree that it is important to identify one's perspective and to choose to *enter the "battle for truth" on the side of the oppressed*, yet I do so for reasons different from those given by some liberation theologians. Rather than grounding this choice in some atemporal or noncontingent structure—tradition, revelation, the person and work of Jesus—*I understand this choice to be a moral one, a choice not free from the concomitant element of risk*. . . . I believe that this option is chosen, not imposed. To be a feminist theologian of liberation is to recognize the constitutive role of one's matrix—participation in resistance struggles—and to choose to continue to think and act from this perspective, recognizing the *contingency of that choice*, the possibility of that perspective being superseded.[41]

For Welch, then, involvement in liberation struggles is a "contingent choice" that is not justified by an appeal to any truths outside the context. Identification with the poor or commitment to some struggle on their behalf is not supported, as it is in many liberation theologies, by an appeal to divine presence or Scripture or some normative understanding of what it means to be human, but by a "*pre-theoretical*" *choice* for which no reasons are given.[42] The choice cannot be said to be more "true," ultimately, than a choice to be in solidarity with the rich or powerful. This claim, or any other, becomes "true" as it is enacted in history.

Though Welch's understanding of truth and grounding of moral claims contrasts with most liberation thinkers, her "choice" to ally herself with liberation theology makes an odd sort of sense within her relativist framework. For Welch, the crucial role of liberation theology is that by giving priority to the perspectives of marginalized, less dominant groups, it reminds Christian theologians of the contingent and relative nature of their own positions and of the power structures in which their theology is entrenched. A relativist welcomes challenges to the dominant model of truth. Moreover, because of her "pre-theoretical" commitment to liberation, Welch intuitively agrees with their struggle. From Welch's juxtaposition of Foucault and liberation theology, she develops a "theology of resistance."[43] This position includes a commitment to liberation that is self-critical. It questions its own commitments and insists that perspectives that claim to be liberating may actually be oppressive.[44] Welch's theology of resistance recognizes that one's struggles for liberation could fail (and thus be made untrue).[45] Welch also proposes the formation of open communities of discourse that choose to give priority to voices of the oppressed.[46] Finally, she takes from liberation theology an emphasis on "practice as the primary criterion for theological reflection."[47] She claims that the liberation focus on the practical liberating effects of truth does not rely on "ontological or metaphysical" questions but on what works in history.[48]

Political and Social Implications

Although Welch calls for conversion to a liberation perspective, it is difficult, given her radical relativism, to understand what would compel one to turn to the poor or how one could explain one's choices among traditions and political programs. What would constitute a responsible moral choice? Who is the self that chooses? How does it choose? This curious blend of liberation theology and Foucault, of "strong normative claims" and a "qualified nihilism," both shapes Welch's theological ethic and raises serious internal tensions.

As we have seen, Welch tries to skirt the issue of moral truth and theory by focusing on practice. She moves from a relativist rejection of broad truth claims and her suspicion of theory to the focus on the practice or "effects" of truth. It does not matter that a cause cannot be proven to be true, she claims; what matters is its effects. For example, Welch explains that her "choice" for liberation is "practical"; she denies that such a choice needs verification by "correlation with some objective reality."[49] Instead, she writes, "the value of the choice is demonstrated only in its implementation, in the creation of a politics of truth that defines the truth as that which liberates."[50] Thus, drawing on the "criterion of truth" as practice, Welch insists that the "truth" of Christianity or liberation "faith" is its enactment of liberation.[51] As we saw, Welch claims that what is true is what wins, or what exists. So, as she says, liberation is made true "in its implementation, in the creation of a politics of truth that defines the true as that which liberates."[52] Ultimately, then, liberation is true when it exists and has sufficient power to define the truth as liberation. Likewise (though she does not say this), fascism (or racism or slave holding) would be true when it existed and had sufficient power to define the truth as fascism (or racism or slave holding). Thus, the move to practice does not solve the ethical issue for Welch. She still lacks any explanation for her own choice of liberation. She fails to take seriously the ways that practices are fully formed by theory. And, more important, she is left without resources to mount an argument to convince others that liberation is better than fascism or that they should join the struggle for liberation or leave the struggle for fascism.

The skepticism or relativism that Welch proposes for Christian theology is her antidote to an easy certainty about one's theology and political program. Her experience of liberation faith itself, she notes, has led her to relativism. She insists that relativism is not an enemy of faith. Indeed, she claims, faith is this capacity to live "within the fragile balance of absolute commitment and infinite suspicion."[53] Welch's desire to acknowledge the finitude of all human political and theological perspectives is not new to Christian theology. Many other religious thinkers have decried the idolatry of facile political or theological certainty.[54] Her relativism goes further, however, than a recognition of the finitude of human claims. She writes:

> The most pressing reason for the maintenance of a tensive use of the ideals of freedom and solidarity is a tendency in liberation faith itself that impels me toward nihilism. This is the recognition of the possibility that *my own experience of liberation* within some particular forms of ecclesia is nothing but a *fluke*. That is, liberation

and redemption do not reflect something that can be universalized, but reflect contingent configurations of human existence.[55]

Thus even liberation, redemption, freedom, and solidarity are true only as they are made true. If they are eradicated, then they are no longer true.

Welch's use of Foucault is especially troubling when she tries to make sense of moral judgments across traditions or cultures. She denounces as imperialistic any attempts of the West to impose its own moral truths upon others (or conversely, I suppose, any attempts by other cultures to impose their moral truths on the West). She prefers that subjugated groups—and by extension all groups—speak for themselves. "It is," claims Welch, "oppressive to 'free' people if their own history and culture do not serve as the primary sources of the definition of their freedom."[56] The radical implications of Welch's link with Foucault become clear in her discussion of the appropriate responses of U.S citizens to political torture in Chile. Appeals to some abstract, common humanity or to laws or standards of political conduct mask the radically relative nature of all human standards. If U.S. citizens (including, I assume, diplomats or political leaders or members of Amnesty International) have evidence of political torture in Chile, they cannot simply speak out against it or use diplomatic or economic pressure to lessen its severity. Welch claims that to object to political torture in Chile (or "abuses" in any other culture) one must look for and support local resistance efforts against that power. If one does not find such resistance, then she claims, "I have to acknowledge that in this situation humanity as I know it has been obliterated."[57] Denunciations of such a society may assuage our guilt or persuade us that we are doing something substantive when we really are not. And these denunciations deny the fact that this system has created another conception of moral truth or human being. These cross-cultural moral judgments "are a dangerous evasion of the relationship of power/knowledge, of the fragility of discourse."[58]

Even her own and other women's inclusion within an academic realm from which women were previously excluded is not in itself an absolute or universal good. In a passage that reveals the personal extent and costs of Welch's relativism, she writes:

> To acknowledge and to accept this particular [relativist] basis for resistance and critique is frightening. It is tempting to seek solace in the realm of universal values and in certain determinations of the nature of human being. But such refuge is an illusion. It is a denial that the ability to be aware of universal categories is accidental and fortuitous. Born twenty years ago or one hundred years ago (maybe even ten years in the future), such concerns might not be mine; they were not the concerns of most women in the past. I am aware of the oddity of my participation in the academy. Academic participation has not been the birthright of intellectual women. The inclusion of women in the worlds of academia, politics, and business may be a brief anomaly. Our gains could be as easily erased . . . Decisions that women participate in universal structures of human being will not protect or enable that participation.[59]

Thus, Welch claims that women's gains might be lost and that theory is no sure protection. Moreover, given her philosophical assumptions, if these gains are lost, then they are no longer true, because truth is that which wins or exists. In a later essay addressing a similar issue, Welch warns that no particular theory will ensure women's social freedom. "We forget that what defeats us [women] is not incorrect theory per se but brute force, coercion and social control."[60] Clearly, for Welch the "battle for truth" is won not by presenting the most compelling arguments. (Indeed, it is difficult to imagine what would constitute a compelling argument within Welch's system.) Instead, the battle for truth is won by the triumph of one's position in real, political struggle.

Welch contends that this fundamental suspicion of theory offers a certain freedom for feminists. If feminists come to realize that any theory can be used against them, they can take greater creative risks in the development of new theories. Welch suggests that feminists continue to do theory, "holding it lightly, valuing the human connections it serves more than the cerebral connections it makes."[61] As women see the wrongheadedness of "misplaced theoretical fervor," they "can freely experiment with different thought and action."[62] The focus is not so much on the assent to correct theory as on the engagement in community struggle. Welch seems to assume that communities and practices can be separated from theory. But without theoretical understanding or minimal common assumptions (like agreement on basic minimal norms, values, processes, or rules for discussion), how can feminists act or struggle together successfully?

For Welch, the lack of theoretical foundation does not mean that struggle—even successful struggle—is impossible. Feminists can "lessen the chances of defeat" by participating in community, where our theories and actions may be criticized and new theories and strategies are born.[63] Welch rejects as illusory any attempts to find final theories or strategic solutions. Instead, feminists work pragmatically within these communities of solidarity. We are left with the "local figuring and working out, as well as we . . . can, of what seems to work better than worse."[64] The difficulty is in determining how one decides what is better and worse, particularly when the group includes people of diverse backgrounds and when dialogue is finally mutual criticism.

In her more recent work, it is evident that Welch *does* want to make judgments that extend across cultures. She proposes new models of power and responsibility that would be more appropriate in a nuclear age.[65] Certainly, her long experience as an activist in the nuclear disarmament movement and in initiatives for women's health and rights suggest that she has strong normative commitments. And she is sometimes critical of the ethical standards of those of other cultures. For example, she criticizes African American novelist Paule Marshall for the homophobia and sexism of the characters in one of her novels. Welch writes, "It is revealing that Marshall's treatment of structural oppression is marred by her unwitting repetition of two other abuses of power: homophobia and sexism. I find two serious difficulties with Marshall's analysis of power—her negative portrayal of gay and lesbian life and her blame of white women for the power of white men."[66]

Moreover, Welch also suggests that Euro-American feminists can criticize "Indian suttee and African genital mutilation" as long as the Euro-American feminists will accept criticism from those of another culture.[67] While I am sympathetic with Welch's criticism, it is difficult to see the grounds or reasons for cross-cultural judgment within her system. Given Welch's radical understanding of truth as created by and relative to the powers within a particular context and community, on what basis does she criticize Marshall's novels or Indian suttee? Given the "contingent" and relative nature of her "pre-theoretical choice" for liberation, how does she ground her judgments of or offer reasons to those who "choose" another option? What sort of criticism is Welch suggesting? Given the limits of her relativist assumptions, she may simply be suggesting that a discussion among women about suttee, genital mutilation, and homophobia would help us all realize that our positions are not universal. But surely a call for such a pluralistic, open engagement and mutual criticism around moral issues is itself an expression of liberal, Western values.

Clearly, Welch's proposals are quite different from those of most liberation theologians. Many liberation theologians not only make cross-cultural judgments but also ground these commitments in the value of human liberation and human dignity across cultures and generations.[68] Radical relativism (or "qualified nihilism") is not a standard feature of most liberation theologies. Though most liberation theologians are contextualists, they tend to have modified realist understandings of their theological and moral claims. Generally speaking, God not only exists but also suffers, empowers, and judges. And moral judgments are true or false not simply by their failure or success in the "battle for truth" but by their faithfulness to God's will, including the broad norms of human liberation and justice. Thus, while Welch's political commitments are similar to those of many liberation theologians, her alliance with Foucault leaves her with a radically different ethic.

Causes of Domination: Welch's Adversaries in the "Battle for Truth"

An Ethic of Control

Welch uses her liberation commitments and relativist epistemology to criticize Christian theology and "the dominant ethic" of the West. This ethic or worldview, she claims, is responsible for many problems of the twentieth century, from the nuclear arms race to the holocaust. Her analysis of this pervasive "ethic of control" is a response to the intransigence she saw on all sides of the nuclear armaments issue.[69] Welch found that her colleagues in the peace movement, as well as in other political organizations, were faced with repeated defeat in their struggle for nuclear disarmament or social equality for women. In response to this defeat, many surrendered to despair.[70] She asks what ethic and theology lead both to despair and domination.

Welch criticizes Western culture and Christian theology for producing and maintaining an ethic of control. The ethic of control, evident among nuclear strategists, nuclear policy makers, and antinuclear activists alike, insists that responsible moral action must lead to guaranteed success and complete control and security. Because the stakes of complete control and success are so high, the use of coercive and dominating power is justified. Given the high goals of the ethic of control, its practitioners are uninterested in compromises or strategies that lead to only partial success. Moreover, because control is rarely complete and success seldom guaranteed, these groups too easily give in to frustration, cynicism, and despair. The illusory goal of complete certainty and security discourages compromise and openness. Welch claims that the despair and resignation that is sometimes prompted by the ethic of control is the luxury of privileged people insulated from social problems. The ethic of control is not limited to the nuclear issue, of course. Welch claims that all of patriarchy carries "the aim of total control from fear of finitude and vulnerability and relatedness."[71] She explicitly links her criticism of the patriarchal ethic of control with feminist criticisms of dominating models of power as "power-over."[72] As we saw in chapter 1, these feminists contend that a move from a model of power as domination and control (power-over) or submission and selflessness (powerlessness) to a model of power as the internal capacity to act and to empower (power-with) is both normatively and descriptively preferable. Such a model would encourage healthier relationships.[73]

In addition to criticizing the ethic of control, Welch also challenges Western ethics for making universal claims about human rights or values. These sorts of claims are impossible within Welch's system because of the radically relative nature of moral truth. Universal appeals are simply denials of the perspectival nature of all human judgments. Welch's most *positive* statement about universal moral claims comes in a discussion of the norms of liberation theology. She writes, "Affirmations of the worth of all persons, concepts of universal human dignity, are *not totally oppressive*. . . . Their liberating function lies in the concern they express for other people. This concern is, ironically, distorted by the very concepts that express it."[74] Her recognition of the valid concern for others expressed in these universals does not challenge Welch's continual insistence that "the ideal of universal or absolute truth is intrinsically correlated with oppression."[75]

She also criticizes the individualism of dominant Western ethics. Welch claims that moral decisions that are not formed in and responsible to community are subject to greater distortion and deceit. Indeed, Welch goes so far as to claim that "a single actor cannot be moral."[76] Only in community, through horizontal transcendence, is moral reflection possible. In community, we see the limits of our claims. The individual self has no capacity to stand outside and reflect on its self and culture. In the end, our boundedness to history and culture radically limits our capacities for self-transcendence.

A Theology of Domination: Transcendence and Power

Classical Christian theology, argues Welch, supports this ethic of control. She claims that traditional understandings of divine power and transcendence emerge out of and encourage hierarchical patterns of domination within society. Sexism itself is supported by Christian theology. She writes, "We find oppression at the heart of the Christian tradition: in the exclusively masculine symbolism for the divine; in a dualism that devalues the body and the historical; in a hierarchical understanding of power and the order of creation; in an imperial concept of divine power."[77] Christian theology, then, is productive of and furthers patriarchy. Welch writes, "As a feminist theologian, I criticize the patriarchal concept of God not because it falsifies the essence of deity but because of its effects of truth, the type of human subjectivity and society that it produces: the domination of women by men and the self-deprecation of women."[78]

What sort of humans and societies, then, does patriarchal theology produce? Welch argues that an appeal to absolute, transcendent divine power within Christian theology promotes patterns of domination and submission that underwrite elite male control.[79] By understanding God's power as absolute, humans value and "reinforce a human desire for" absolute power that is always dangerous. Welch writes, "The idea of an omnipotent and sovereign God, however, assumes that absolute power can be a good. In the Christian tradition, one does not attribute demonic or destructive traits to Deity. And yet absolute power *is* a destructive trait."[80]

The appeal to absolute divine power is destructive because it sanctions human power. According to Welch, human hierarchies are often justified by appealing to divine authority as their source and by emphasizing their own obedience to this powerful God. Welch describes this process as the "erotics of domination."[81] She writes:

> In fact, the claim of . . . submission to the greatest power, legitimates the domination of others. . . . A powerful group claims that its primary, essential activity is submission and obedience to a higher power. . . . The result of willed abdication [to God] is not passivity, however, but the legitimation of total power. . . . Critique and accountability are displaced: the powerful regard themselves as merely the agents of a higher power.[82]

Thus, according to Welch, an appeal to divine power does not limit human power but abets it. In a critical response to Paul Tillich and H. R. Niebuhr, Welch writes, "While intended to relativize all human claims to power, the valorization of domination and submission leads to the legitimation of imperial power."[83] The metaphor of the "sovereignty of God" is an expression of Christian triumphalism and an "obsession" with absolute security.[84] Welch also notes that appeals to divine transcendence justify the ethic of control and patriarchal power.[85] The division between God and humans that is set up by an emphasis on divine transcendence mirrors and supports human hierarchical dualisms. Moreover, such an appeal leads to the devaluing of our finite life. As we saw before, Welch cites Mary Daly's charge that Christianity, with its affirmation of divine transcendence, denies finite life and thus is a type of "necrophilia."[86]

Welch also claims that the ethic of resignation and despair that she is fighting against is supported by a theology of transcendence.[87] In contrast, she proposes a theology of immanence that "does not attempt to escape from the finite into the realm of the spirit or the transcendent."[88] In a discussion of the "eschatological reservation," Welch argues that transcendent limits do not relativize human claims for power. Instead, they promote the devaluation of the finite world and undermine our will to change our present political situation.[89] Thus, for Welch, such claims encourage resignation to the status quo.[90]

Because of the negative effects of traditional understandings of transcendence on social structures and on the evaluation of the body and the environment, Welch calls for a redefinition of transcendence as "the bonds of solidarity that extend beyond individual existence, rather than in more traditional categories, such as the transcendence of spirit over history and nature or of the divine over the finite."[91] A theological ethic built around this redefinition of transcendence rejects absolute power, exclusivity, hierarchy, and divine otherness while valuing "finitude, interdependence, change, and particularity."[92] This redefinition of transcendence as "the bonds of solidarity" will be examined more closely later.

In summary, Welch charges that traditional affirmations of God's transcendence and absolute power are dangerous for life in several ways. A focus on divine power and control is used both to validate human hierarchies of domination and to promote childlike abdication of responsibility. An emphasis on divine transcendence maintains these hierarchies by associating the powerful with the transcendent. Moreover, this transcendent emphasis devalues the finite, discouraging humans from its care. In response to this theology of domination, Welch proposes an alternative theology that she says will sustain her ethic of risk. Within her theology of immanence, humans find God in community and solidarity with each other. God is the power within or quality of those communities.[93]

Solutions: Welch's Rival Paradigm

An Ethic of Risk

Welch attempts to formulate an ethic that would discourage domination, encourage responsibility, and promote continued struggle in the face of defeat.[94] To develop this alternative ethic, Welch turns to the novels of several African American women. Welch privileges their voices not because of any inherent moral superiority but because they challenge her own perspective and the dominant ethic of control. They represent dangerous memories or subjugated knowledges. Welch writes, "I have listened to the voices of African-American women, not because theirs is the only 'true' voice (replacing the vantage point of the proletariat in the nineteenth century), but because these voices disclose a knowledge of gender and race oppression, of ethical responses and strategies, that is critical of my social location."[95]

The African American novels that Welch explores describe how communities survive in the midst of and continue to struggle against racism, poverty, and sexism. From common themes in these novels, Welch outlines a feminist ethic of risk that she claims is more able to envision strategic, communal responses to entrenched social problems. Within this ethic, moral responsibility is defined not by the ability to coercively get one's way in a situation. Instead, it involves creating empowered communities of responsibility that take pragmatic, strategic risks for the achievement of modest, strategic goals. The ethic of risk is a survivalist ethic that values life and takes risks from, and on behalf of, the community. Though Welch has been criticized for the manner in which she has appropriated African

American women's literature, I have focused not on the appropriateness of her use of this material but on the ethic that she draws from it.[96]

Welch describes her ethic of risk as having three primary foci.[97] It redefines the end, locus, and strategy of responsible moral action. First, to be responsible an action does not have to produce complete success. Welch's ethic of risk is in no way utopian. It is realistic about the difficulties of accomplishing comprehensive social change. A responsible person does not despair over the unlikelihood of completely achieving her goals. Responsible actions aim not for total victory but for the creation of the conditions for later action.[98]

Second, the locus of responsible action within the ethics of risk is the community.[99] If the end of responsible action is the creation of the possibilities for further change, the best way to create those possibilities is through the creation of strong communities. Community-based action is not only more effective strategically. Welch claims that it is also the only locus of *true* moral activity. One cannot act morally as an individual. She writes, "A single actor cannot be moral."[100] It is only within the critical give-and-take of community that one can see the partiality of one's own position. Community is mutually self-criticizing, according to Welch. Third, responsible moral action demands strategic risks. Welch calls for neither martyrdom nor cowardice. Real risks are appropriate only when judged pragmatically effective for the whole community. While the risk of one's life is sometimes called for, Welch's ethic does not focus on self-sacrifice.

In short, responsible moral action—emerging from decisions by and on behalf of a struggling community—does not guarantee total success and most often will lead to only partial success and modest change. Even so, these partial successes will create the conditions for the possibility of further action. Because those who operate out of an ethic of risk do not expect complete success, they are more able to take pragmatically effective, strategic risks.

Though these three components are primary to Welch's definition of the ethic of risk, she also has delineated other components in various writings. For example, central to this ethic is a redefinition of power. Welch links her understanding of mutual empowerment through strategic risk taking in community with other feminist models that reject power as domination (power-over) and affirm an understanding of "power with" as mutual empowering agency.[101] Power in the ethic of risk is not controlling. It is "persuasive, enabling and reciprocal."[102]

Elsewhere, in a criticism of the ethic of control expressed in U.S. nuclear arms policy, Welch delineates a "feminist ethic" as an alternative. This ethic is based on mutuality, openness, and interdependence. It "affirms life and its risks, accepts the power and danger of life as symbolized in the female and does not attempt to escape from the finite into the realm of the spirit or the transcendent."[103] According to her feminist ethic, our fundamental boundedness to the earth and to each other is good. She values not only all of creation but also our unbreakable bonds to it. Even the boundedness and contextual nature of our systems and ideologies, including our ethical claims, is a good part of creation. Within the bounds of creation, we have all we need.

This theme is expressed not only throughout Welch's ethic and theology but also in her own religious life. In an interview for a publication of her church,

Welch makes a revealing comment about a favorite Unitarian Universalist hymn—"Earth Is Enough."[104] "Every time I sing it I just thrill. It talks about how whatever materials the gods would take to build a celestial home are here. This is the mortar: our dreams, our flesh, these trees. There is that sense of 'Who could want more?' "[105] "This is the mortar: our dreams, our flesh, these trees." This is the heart of Welch's theological ethic. The only catch is that Welch contends that the earth, nature, and our human experiences—that is, "our dreams, our flesh"—are radically particular and, thus, relative to context. To ground her ethic, the earth is *not* enough.

A Theology of Immanence

Welch criticizes traditional Christian theology for its promotion of structures of domination and an ethic of control. In contrast, Welch claims that her "theology of immanence" would empower humans for responsible action, discourage human desire for domination and control, and encourage the valuing of the finite. For Welch, God does not simply give value to the finite. She writes that "divinity is not a mark of that which is other than the finite. . . . Divinity, or grace, is the resilient, fragile, healing power of finitude itself."[106] Likewise, God is not just immanent in finite human relationships; God is the quality or power of those relationships.

Welch contrasts her theology to that of Carter Heyward. Where Heyward understands God to be the source of the power of human relationships, Welch claims that "the divine is that relational power. . . . [It is not] necessary or liberating to posit a substance or ground that exists outside of relational power."[107] Divinity, writes Welch, refers not so much to a noun or even a verb but to "an adjective or adverb." "Divinity then connotes a quality of relationships, lives, events, and natural processes."[108] Clearly, the feminist emphasis on divine immanence has moved to a more radical level in Welch.

For Welch, these human relationships are not only *divine* but *also* the locus of moral reflection. Because there is no universal or shared human nature to which one may point or any moment of human self-transcendence that allows for reflection on one's experience and culture, the only source of critical reflection is the encounter in relationship or in community. In community, especially in interaction with those of other cultures or perspectives, one sees the partiality of one's own perspective. One transcends one's own viewpoint through community interaction. Welch claims that her "theology of immanence" offers "the benefits of a theology of transcendence without the social costs."[109]

Welch argues that this relational transcendence is preferable to classical understandings of divine transcendence for several reasons.[110] Horizontal transcendence, she claims, helps us see, celebrate, and love our finitude and the complexity of all of life. In contrast, what Welch calls "vertical transcendence" causes humans to devalue finitude, dominate others, and abdicate moral responsibility. Her concept of finite transcendence also offers hope in difficult, oppressive situations. It "is the transcending of conditions of oppression through loving life, self, and others despite social forces that deny the value of all of these."[111] Finally, Welch hopes that

136   The Bonds of Freedom

transcendence in community will offer the possibility of social transformation. Indeed, movements for political change and for social transformation such as "the labor movement, the civil rights movement, the peace movement, and the women's movement" are "holy." "They are manifestations of transcendence, of the love of life and self leading to work for social change."[112] Human transcendence is possible, then, only in diverse communities. There one realizes the limitations of one's own perspective and comes to value life and to work for social transformation.

Theology and Ethics in the Beloved Community

Because community relationships are the locus of the divine *and* of human moral judgment and action, it is not surprising that Welch devotes considerable space to the analysis of theologies of community. Welch criticizes the "Kingdom of God" model because it promotes a mentality of domination. Welch's model for appropriate social interaction is not the Kingdom of God but the beloved community. Citing Martin Luther King Jr., Welch describes the beloved community as an open fellowship in which people learn to love and accept themselves and to love, accept, and listen to others.[113] Welch explains her preference for the beloved community model. "The kingdom of God implies conquest, control, and final victory over the elements of nature as well as over the structures of injustice. The 'beloved community' names the matrix within which life is celebrated, love is worshipped, and partial victories over injustice lay the groundwork for further acts of criticism."[114] Thus, the community finds its focus not in shared moral values, stories, or decisions but in a spirit of love and "solidarity."

Welch draws on the idea of "jouissance" in the writings of French feminist Luce Irigaray to describe the character of this loving community.[115] Welch's reading of Irigaray emphasizes the fluidity, plenitude, openness, and joy of love and life. She relates this "jouissance" to her reading of Audre Lorde who emphasizes the "power of the erotic" as an embodied, relational, life-affirming joy. From these resources, Welch describes the love of the beloved community as an erotic, open, abundant, joyous love of all things. Welch writes of an

> alternative understanding of communion articulated by feminists [which] provides deep joy and the strength required for sustained resistance to oppression. It is possible to combine skepticism about the likelihood of certain, total victory over injustice, and persistent, energetic, work for justice. The key is a complex, fluid, concrete love: love for the earth, for oneself, for those who are oppressed, and for those who work against oppression.[116]

Welch speaks here of the full openness of the loving community that includes the love for the oppressed and those fighting oppression. She does not explain how a fully open community responds to oppressors or protects the oppressed from them.

Welch's open community is the locus of moral reflection and action. Within this model, openness to multiple, particular perspectives (especially those that are least often heard) is primary. She does not provide boundaries for the community, rules for judgment, procedures for establishing any guidelines, or an understanding of shared discourse or rationality or nature or the self that might ground discourse. If this community is the locus of moral discourse and activity, what sort of moral discourse is possible within it? As we saw previously, the discourse and resistance of an open community can serve to relativize finite human opinion. Welch contrasts the mutual criticism possible within her ethic with the relativizing role of the eschatological reservation. She writes that her ethic of love "can provide self-critique and social critique without the enervating cynicism of the eschatological reservation."[117] Welch is unable to explain how the community might move beyond mutual critique toward positive models for a healthy and just society. She clearly *wants* the community to do just that.

Welch leaves us with many questions about how we make moral decisions from within these diverse communities. If there is no common human experience, if reason and truth are completely relative to a particular episteme and if humans share no essential nature, how might moral decisions be made within and among the communities? Moreover, the call for mutually critical, open communities of reflection and solidarity is itself a broad ethical claim that carries theoretical assumptions.

Welch considers and finds deficient several contemporary models of community moral reflection. As we have seen, the primary characteristic of Welch's beloved community is its openness to other perspectives. Not surprisingly, Welch criticizes ethical proposals that emphasize community identity around shared traditions and stories. Welch contrasts her ethic of risk to the communal ethic of Stanley Hauerwas and Alasdair MacIntyre. Like Hauerwas and MacIntyre, Welch denies the existence of an unencumbered reason or universal human nature to which one may appeal for moral judgment. Welch's proposal stands in sharp contrast, however, to their models of moral community. According to Welch, Hauerwas and MacIntyre insist that moral reasoning presupposes a "cohesive community with a shared set of principles, norms and mores."[118] Welch argues that cohesive communities, such as the communites offered by Hauerwas and MacIntyre, encourage not the best moral reasoning but communities that are blind to their own injustice and uncritical in their exclusion of other points of view. She writes, "In contrast to MacIntyre, I argue that the 'moral calamity' of our day lies not in the lack of shared moral criteria but in the inability of most communities to engender or accept a thorough critique of their 'own purposes.'"[119]

In opposition to MacIntyre and Hauerwas's "tribalism," Welch proposes a "communicative ethic" that is open to many perspectives. An individual ethic is impossible from this perspective. Welch writes, as we saw before, that "we cannot be moral alone."[120] Instead of reflecting privately or immersing oneself in one culture, one opens oneself to many cultures. Welch contrasts her communicative ethic with MacIntyre's communitarian ethic:

> Communicative ethics . . . avoids the danger of isolation and self-justifying ethical systems by its involvement in political coalitions and its openness to political conflict. . . . We can see foundational flaws in systems of ethics only from the outside, from the perspective of another system. . . . In order to determine which interests or positions are more just, pluralism is required, not for its own sake, but for the sake of enlarging our moral vision.[121]

It is not clear, given her alliance with Foucault, how one may judge between the many perspectives or finally allow them to authentically criticize each other or to improve one's own position or any position. Welch clearly wants to create communities of moral discourse that can develop norms and judge policies. Can her fundamental philosophical assumptions account for the possibility of such a community?

Welch's reflections on George Lindbeck are similar to her comments about Hauerwas and MacIntyre. In her analysis of liberalism, Welch agrees with Lindbeck that the universal human experience to which liberals appeal is "vacuous." She refuses, however, to follow Lindbeck in his turn to a particular "grammar of faith" or to a particular linguistic community. Instead of immersing oneself in one's own grammar or language, the ideal is to expose oneself to many languages and grammars. She insists on an openness to many concrete experiences.[122] And she is optimistic about the outcome of these interactions. Pluralism, she claims, not only allows us to see the limits of our perspectives but also helps us "determine which interests or positions are more just."[123] She gives little clue, however, about how one would judge which position is better or worse. And, as we have seen, in many places she denies that such broad judgments are even possible. Welch rejects the communitarian turn of Hauerwas, MacIntyre, and Lindbeck to the stories and models of a particular tradition. Yet her proposal for multiple, open, mutually critical communities makes sense primarily within the liberal democratic tradition. Her communities are not tradition-neutral.

Although Welch draws on Martin Luther King's language for the beloved community, her definitions of that community are quite different. Katie Cannon, a womanist ethicist, also draws on both African American women's literature and the work of King.[124] She claims that King's model of community was not characterized simply by open love. He made, Cannon insists, a place within the beloved community for justice and strong claims about the necessity of coercive power to control evil. Whereas King's beloved community included a mechanism for boundary setting and the exclusion or control of those who promote or commit evil acts that are destructive of individuals and communities, it is not clear how Welch would justify such exclusion or control.

Welch notes that she is drawing on King's understanding of the beloved community described in *A Testament of Hope*.[125] But the contrasts between Welch's and King's models are striking. King's model of the beloved community includes not only the possibility of coercion, as Cannon notes, but also the assumption that individuals in the community are held together by shared human experiences, common rational processes, creation in the image of God, and the mysterious power of God's love. Furthermore, the King article that Welch cites as the *source* of her model for the beloved community focuses on agape love and claims that both God and "the universe [are] on the side of justice."[126] Moreover, for King the moral truth is not simply what wins or what exists and has sufficient power to define itself as true. Working from natural law traditions, King insists that all humans can know what is morally good and just. King's theological ethic (including the very article on which Welch draws) sharply contrasts to Welch's relativist ethic. Thus, she uses some of the language and commitments of King's beloved community, while stripping them of the underlying theological and moral assumptions.

Without these assumptions, it is not clear what the beloved community is. In Welch's terminology, what "effects" does the community have beyond mutual criticism and relative (and finally inexplicable) choices for action? Welch is still left with questions about how communities might set rules for discussion and come to some consensus of opinion *or* solidarity in action. Welch's use of Jürgen Habermas seems initially to provide hope for moral grounding. Welch says that she turns to Habermas because he provides what she finds lacking in Foucault: "*the possibility of significant social transformation and emancipation.*"[127] From Habermas, she hopes to develop a model for conversation that would promote the fair hearing of a plurality of voices.[128] She insists, however, that her use of Habermas's categories does not extend to Habermas's hope for the achievement of some consensus or to his broader claims about the nature of human speech. Indeed, the goal of consensus in community discourse is itself oppressive.[129] Welch proposes, instead, the importance of "solidarity" within discourse. Welch writes, "The intention of solidarity is potentially more inclusive and more transformative than is the goal of consensus. Many liberation ethicists argue that the search for consensus is a continuation of the dream of domination."[130]

Welch's use of Habermas sets up a false expectation for the possibilities of discourse. In the end, she appropriates Habermas's language as a tool within her Foucauldian relativist framework.[131] She writes that she is similar to Habermas in valuing conversation but that she values it for "Foucault's reasons."[132] As she explains it, she is only grafting Habermas's language onto her relativist framework.[133] Thus, she tries to appropriate Habermas's language while rejecting his fundamental argument. Her alliance with Foucault's relativism will not permit her to do what she wants to do—ground moral claims for liberation. And, again, we see that the primary moral function or "effect" of discursive communities is to show us the relative nature of our own perspectives.[134]

In this analysis of Welch's model of the beloved community, we see the conflict between her relativist ethical epistemology, her liberation commitments and desire for change, and her implicit liberal assumptions about human communities. Many questions about the task and nature of Welch's inclusive community remain unanswered. I argue that Welch's understanding of the formation of truth makes it difficult for her to make sense of loving, tolerant, pluralistic communities that act in solidarity, as well as the self that chooses one perspective or another.

A Feminist Christian Realist Response

Summary

Welch outlines a radically relative understanding of moral experience and attempts to hold it in tension with her relatively radical commitment to liberation. For Welch, human moral experience is made of moments of horizontal transcen-

140   The Bonds of Freedom

dence or mutually critical interaction. We transcend our social condition and truth by seeing that they are not the same as someone else's social condition and truth. Somehow, we choose one way or another of understanding the world. And in community, we struggle for the victory of this perspective in "battles for truth." Transcendence is radically "located" in community interactions. And within these communal relationships and mutually critical human interactions is the divine. We humans are radically bound to social and community structures; God is likewise bound. We are many and conflicted; the divine is us.

Analysis and Criticisms

My criticisms and questions center around Welch's juxtaposition of radical moral relativism, strong liberation commitments, and unacknowledged liberal assumptions. Welch's relativist assumptions about moral truth leave her unable to justify her hopes for the formation of open and loving communities of solidarity on behalf of justice and liberation.[135]

THE NON-COERCIVE BATTLE AGAINST COERCION

One of the most troubling aspects of Welch's work is the inconsistency between her description of the formation of truth and her model of noncoercive power and open, loving communities. Welch contends that truths are made by forces of power within a "bloody" and "lethal" "battle."[136] The truth is that which has sufficient power to be made true. She joins the battle on behalf of her own liberation and feminist perspectives. And she also reminds feminists that "what defeats us is not incorrect theory per se but brute force, coercion and social control."[137] Welch's ethical criticisms and alternate proposals also center around power. She rejects ethics of control and theologies of divine power because they are destructive. She proposes models of noncoercive power and fully open, loving communities.

Can Welch maintain both her "battle" epistemology and her noncoercive ethical model consistently and coherently? It is difficult to understand how, in a system built around the coercive production of truth, one might expect a new, noncoercive understanding of power to be victorious. Within Welch's original framework, a "battle for truth" will surely favor the strong and not the weak, the powerful and not the powerless, the coercive and not the mutually empowering. Ironically, in an attempt to avoid an ethic of domination and despair, Welch leaves us with the very thing she set out to avoid: domination and despair.

THEORY AND PRACTICE

Having established a relativist framework, Welch attempts to skirt the problems of truth and theory by focusing on practice or effects. What matters is not the theory that supports a community but whether it has liberating effects. Though we do not share theories or truths, she insists, we must enter into acts of solidarity in community. Feminists should recognize, she says, that any theory can be oppressive and should, instead, focus primarily on political struggles. But Welch's attempt to move away from theory by focusing on practice underestimates the ways that theories *inform* practice. Feminists and other liberation theologians focus so much on theory *because* theory matters; it has effects. Theories and models of truth are behind practices, political struggles, and solidarity; they make communities of resistance and solidarity possible. A focus on practice or solidarity must take the theories and truths that inform them more seriously.[138]

Welch's suspicion of theory is an aspect of her political realism. Almost any theory can become a tool for domination. This relativist political realism extends much further in Welch than in many feminists. She questions the ultimate "truth" of feminism and liberation. She is not, however, completely consistent in her political realism. Her suspicion of theory does not extend so far as to question her own theory. Welch is finally uncritical about her relativism and her "choice" of Foucault. Given her suspicion of theory, it is puzzling that she continually insists on the "truth" of her own relativist theory from Foucault. Why is relativism the one truth left unrelativized?

CHOOSING LIBERATION

A cluster of problems center around Welch's understanding of the "choice" for liberation. She writes of her "pre-theoretical" commitment or contingent choice of liberation. Because of her radical relativism, she cannot explain her commitments and choices by appealing to human nature, reason, shared experience, or revealed truth. Moreover, she rejects community-focused narrativist arguments. What sort of claim, then, is Welch making when she points to a "pre-theoretical" commitment? Cornel West argues that Welch's position amounts to an "unacknowledged intuitionism" or "ideological fideism." He writes, "Her intuitionism is almost an a priori allegiance to a political form of confessionalism, to the belief that fundamental convictions are less than authentic if they are the result of or motivated by rational argument. But since Welch's intuitionist/confessionalist political commitment is neither self-evident nor singular, she must give good reasons for it."[139]

It is not surprising that Welch does not give reasons but simply opts for a sort of "ideological fideism." Given the tension she has set up with her affirmation of radical relativism, her concern for liberation, her rejection of shared community-centered ethics (like Hauerwas or even a more pragmatic version), her suspicion of theory, her exclusion of rules for discourse, her denial of any appeals to common human nature or experience, her rejection of the ethic of control, her repudiation of cynical despair and resignation, her condemnation of the goal of consensus, and her desire to make moral claims and judgments, she has painted herself into a corner.

This unexplained "choice" raises several other questions. If we are formed by the truths of an age and have no essential human nature, how do any "pre-theoretical commitments" avoid the distortions of the age? Welch insists that we are formed in structures of violence and terror. She speaks of the "erotics of domination" that draw us into these patterns of violence. Given this account, where do "pre-theoretical" commitments come from? Because we are formed in social structures, what sort of self could have "pre-theoretical" commitments? And given Welch's focus on the violence of our culture, how would our "gut" commitments avoid the distortion of our age? Welch would probably say that they do not. But given that answer, it is difficult to account for our moral choices or our moral solidarity in community. What is a "choice" in this radically relativist framework where we are formed by the truths and powers of our episteme? *Is* Welch finally an "ideological fideist"?

SELF, COMMUNITY, AND DISCOURSE

These issues raise additional questions for Welch's understanding of the self, communities, and discourse. What is the self that chooses liberation? Welch denies that individual selves are moral actors. The appropriate locus of moral reflection is always community. And she claims that "truths" are made "true" by their enactment. Yet, she speaks of her own "choice" for liberation. Ironically, Welch seems implicitly to suggest a liberal model in which the separate, agential, choosing self has some control over its own destiny and makes its own choices about political and social allegiances. Yet, she denies the possibility of such a self within her broader framework.

Moreover, what sort of community and discourse is possible within Welch's system? In *A Feminist Ethic of Risk*, Welch promotes a joyous, loving community that is in solidarity. But given her earlier descriptions of the formation of truths in "battles," it is difficult to understand how this joyous, open community of discourse is possible. Having rejected the ethic of control, how would Welch deal with violence in the beloved community? Moreover, how is solidarity to be formed in a diverse community, short of some minimal prior agreement about common ends or similar needs or established procedure? Indeed, her call for solidarity on behalf of a cause implies at least some minimal agreement about that cause. Finally, is her model of pluralistic, open communities more substantive than her basic theoretical assumptions will allow? Even openness and inclusivity are guidelines. Ironically, though she begins with radical relativism, she ends with a model of pluralistic, tolerant communities that are the staple of liberalism.

Within Welch's relativist framework, what sort of discourse is possible? Welch calls for the inclusion of all voices in the discourse of her beloved community. She especially emphasizes the importance of hearing those with less power. But if perspectives are relative, how do we justify giving priority to one group over another? Indeed, how do we justify listening to each other at all? Given this framework, does one have the grounds for respectful regard and genuine listening? If all voices are included in order to remind one of one's own limitations, is that any real solace to a struggling community? Is open listening without a call for some boundaries of justice, order, and exclusion necessarily good for those in society who have the least power and hence the least protection from the worst abuses of human brutality? One wonders if a relativist call for the formation of a pluralistic, mutually critical community is in the interests of those with little power. Finally, if our conversations are primarily exercises in mutual criticism, what hope have we for the development of Welch's new societies, new ethics, and new theologies that will promote justice and empowerment?

Moreover, if one follows Welch's argument to its logical conclusion, it is ironic that the *one* condition of the sure ethical knowledge available to us (i.e., that our truths are relative) is the exposure to many perspectives (so that you at least know that your own perspective is limited). But those who have the most exposure to other perspectives are not always from the struggling, marginalized communities to which Welch points. Those with the greatest exposure to multiple perspectives are often the well educated, the most widely traveled, and the best read. She does not seem too far off from Richard Rorty, who, for similar reasons, dubbed the literary critic to be the new "moral advisor" or saint of our age.[140]

In spite of Welch's denial of universal claims or common human experience, her arguments are undergirded by strikingly broad implicit claims. Humans are relational. There are no independent moral actors. Human experience is contextual. Humans have the capacity to choose. Human flourishing is promoted in an atmosphere of mutual empowerment and suffers under conditions of domination. The integrity of particularity is affirmed. The importance of mutual criticism and of the recognition of the limited nature of our claims is assumed. These broad affirmations and assumptions about human nature and human community as such are difficult for Welch to account for, given her original philosophical assumptions.

Thus, we see in this discussion of the self, communities, and discourse, that Welch's argument is internally inconsistent. Her radical relativism, her broad claims about liberation and beloved communities, and her implicit "liberal" assumptions simply do not cohere.

A CHANGE OF CONTEXT

Welch's *context* is also relevant to this discussion of discourse. One of the primary issues to which Welch has responded is the nuclear crisis of the mid to late 1980s. She saw the ethics of control in the mentalities of the superpowers "obsessed" with security and order. She rejects this ethic because of its potential effects in encouraging a nuclear war. With the end of the cold war and the collapse of the Soviet Union, the global threats are much different. Our focus is no longer on two superpowers "obsessed" with order, security, and control. Instead, we face multiple conflicts in which there is very little security or order. In many of the places of conflict today, the underlying problem is not too much unified control but too little. We face the threat of anarchy and chaos. Within this very different political context, it is hard to imagine the possibility of Welch's model of noncoercive power and her completely open communities with no guidelines or shared assumptions. International law and even some threat of force, for example, may be necessary to blunt the worst of the very real attempts at genocide and forced relocation.

IMPLICATIONS FOR A FEMINIST CHRISTIAN REALISM: FREEDOM, TRANSCENDENCE, AND DOMINATION

As we have seen, Welch begins with a commitment to alleviate domination and promote empowerment. In the service of this cause, she allies herself with Foucault and insists that truth claims are radically relative. A given model is made true by winning in the "battle for truth." Yet, Welch rejects the ethic of control and a belief in a powerful, transcendent God as the support for a whole system of domination. Our hope is to turn away from this ethic of control and theology of transcendence toward an ethic of risk and a theology of immanence. To that end, we are called to participate in open communities of solidarity, where finite, particular voices are heard and mutually criticized. We enter the "battle for truth," the struggle against the powers and principalities of the world, in solidarity with open communities of mutual criticism and undergirded by a model of noncoercive power.

Thus, in the interest of curbing domination, Welch leaves herself and her communities open and vulnerable to the excesses and the domination of the very tyrants she wishes to transform. Her outright rejection of the models of power expressed in the traditional ethics and theology of the West (including coercion and restraint of the wicked) leaves her ethic of risk and theology of radical immanence unable to meet the stark realities of domination and human brutality that she describes so clearly. She is left with the victory of the powerful and the justification of the status quo. A realistic feminist ethic of risk would need to reconsider some of the components of an ethic of control and theology of power.

These issues bring us back to freedom and transcendence. Welch denies the possibility of individual self-transcendence. Transcendence of one's perspective is possible only in mutually critical community discourse. From a feminist perspective, this is a crucial problem within Welch's system. Without some moment of radical freedom from or over social context and experience, how can we make sense of the feminist criticism of patriarchy and the experience of liberation? Feminist judgments and experiences presuppose that humans not only are bound to social context but also have the capacity to transcend or stand outside the patriarchal mentality. If one denies the possibility for limited self-transcendence or freedom over culture, it is difficult to make sense of feminist experience. Indeed, as I have argued, freedom or self-transcendence is the condition of liberating moral experience.

Welch's rejection of moral realism is also troubling for feminists. Without a basic human experience of freedom or some other grounding for broad claims and judgments, the status quo is enshrined. The truth is what wins. And over the course of history, the winners were rarely women. For feminists who see the brutalization and domination of women and others throughout history, this lack of real critical leverage and normative grounding is profoundly troubling.

Welch's understanding of God provides no critical leverage or grounding. The divine is the projection of our values. But within Welch's system, our values are the truths that have won. God is the power of our relationships. But given the "battle" character of moral discourse and the way that truth is created by power, what *sort* of relational power is divine? Welch rejects models of divine sovereignty or controlling power because of their effects in promoting coercive human power. But if one accepts a system in which powers fight for truth on "battle" grounds and if the divine is the projection of our values, then a controlling God is oddly fitting. Within this understanding, God does not judge our systems of power and domination or call us to higher forms of life; both God and moral truths are intimately tied to whatever perspective has sufficient power to define itself as true and to connect its own values with the divine. These are the effects of truth in Welch's system.

For many Christians, Welch's equation of truth with that which wins and her likening of God to the values and relationships that are made true not only turns the biblical witness on its head but also destroys hope for the enactment of justice. Finally, what is needed to respond to Welch is a feminist realism—in this case, a feminist Christian realism—that redefines both divine transcendence and human freedom in a way that values the finite and undermines hierarchical domination without leaving us ultimately bound to the contingencies of a given patriarchal culture and history.

This bleak picture is not what Welch wants. She clearly wants to support struggles for justice and liberation. But her radically relativist theory conflicts with her pretheoretical commitment to liberation and her models of discursive communities. Ironically, she claims that she turned to Foucault and relativism to support her liberation commitment. Given Welch's suspicion of theory, her radical relativism, and her focus on "effects of truth," why not turn to a theory that allows her to have the "effects" that she wants?

Appropriations

Though I have raised many criticisms of Welch's position, I also draw on her work as a resource for a feminist Christian realism. Welch provides a helpful resource for reflecting on the critical role of communities. Her insistence on the fully social formation of the self and her idea of horizontal transcendence is a helpful counter to Niebuhr's claim that communities have no organ for self-transcendence and so are ultimately uncritical. Her suspicious political realism extends much further than that of Ruether. She is critical not only of patriarchy but also of feminism. Welch's position would be more consistent, however, if she were equally suspicious of her own relativism and her reliance on Foucault.

Thus, Welch has a very strong, if not fully consistent, political realism. But unlike both Niebuhr and Ruether, she lacks a moral realism. Any claims about shared human experience or nature are questioned by her relativist political realism. She does focus on the normative implications of human boundedness to community, but those implications are finally critical. Her appeal to community boundedness is an aspect not of moral realism but of political realism. Moreover, because the divine is the quality and power of relationships or the projection of our finite values, Welch also lacks a theological realism. In the end, her understanding of the divine is an aspect of her political realism. Many of these difficulties in Welch's position stem from her dual allegiance to a relativist epistemology and liberation claims and practices, as well as her unacknowledged liberal assumptions. These allegiances and assumptions make it difficult for her to coherently maintain the tension between boundedness and freedom that has been so central for our other figures.

SIX

Dueling Realisms

Ruether, Welch, Niebuhr, and a Feminist Christian Realism

THROUGHOUT this study, I have maintained that appeals to human freedom and boundedness, as well as to divine transcendence and immanence, help to account for feminist moral experience. The differences evident in the theological ethics of Niebuhr, Ruether, and Welch reflect their contrasting definitions and assessments of these four categories. Out of the mutually critical interaction among the three figures emerges an alternate option—a feminist Christian realism.

The theological ethics of Ruether, Welch, and Niebuhr center around their models of human life as both bound to and somehow transcending context. The location and extent of human boundedness as well as the degree and limits of transcendence shape their realist ethics, including their models of the divine. Within Niebuhr's realism, freedom is primary. The critical and positive requirements of freedom are the basis of theological and moral reflection. Human boundedness is important but is so transformed by freedom that it is not as significant a source for the grounding of moral norms.

In contrast, Ruether emphasizes boundedness as the source of moral norms and knowledge of the divine. Human consciousness, which makes freedom and social transformation possible, is a part of human boundedness. It is continuous with the natural evolutionary process. Welch, on the other hand, locates human boundedness and the divine not in nature but in finite communities. Humans are bound to the relative truths of an age; the only transcendence possible is a recognition of the relativity of our truth through multicultural community interactions. Therefore, the communities to which humans are bound both form and question radically relative truths. Both the divine and any transcendence of those truths are bound to community.

The fourth option, a feminist Christian realism, would retain the substantive and critical role of freedom in moral and theological discourse that is so central to Niebuhr. At the same time, it would give boundedness to nature and community a more ethically substantive role than one finds in Niebuhr. A feminist Christian realism would retain Ruether's grounding of moral claims in nature, while both avoiding her uncritical certainty about the content of the natural law and also granting radical human freedom a much more critical role in questioning and transforming the natural. Moreover, while incorporating Welch's idea of transcendence in community, this position would avoid her radical relativism, which undermines the grounding of feminist moral claims. It would draw on Niebuhr's model of divine transcendence as it relativizes, unifies, and gives meaning to our finite moral lives. At the same time, it would broaden his focus on divine presence in the cross.

A feminist Christian realism begins with and modifies Niebuhr's model of the self and God by drawing from Ruether's and Welch's alternative views and by accounting for feminist criticisms. Though disagreeing with Niebuhr on some points, this position relies heavily on and even furthers his model of human experience, particularly his understanding of freedom. This modified realist position is, in some ways, more Niebuhrian than Niebuhr. How does a feminist Christian realism emerge from the critical interaction among these figures?

Contrasting Realisms

Niebuhr

As we have seen, human freedom or self-transcendence is the crucial feature of Niebuhr's ethic. Though humans are both bound and free, freedom carries greater normative and critical weight. Freedom, though a part of the nature of the self, also sets itself in discontinuity with nature. The human capacity for self-transcendence allows for such a profound transformation of the givenness of natural and social lives that it limits what we can know about our natural state. In addition, the existence of a certain pattern in nature does not necessarily make that pattern preferable to its historical alteration through freedom. Freedom's transformations can improve nature. At the same time, the transforming aspects of freedom can also be distorted. Human self-transcendence can, for example, lead the self to claim that those structures serving its own interests are "natural."

Though Niebuhr briefly suggests that there are also minimal ethical norms that can be drawn from nature, he does not develop or reflect on them as extensively as he does on freedom. His primary emphasis is on the potential of human freedom to transform the natural. This critical analysis of freedom, particularly its self-interested and destructive aspects, undergirds Niebuhr's political realism and gives his moral realism a self-critical, dynamic aspect. Freedom not only plays the primary critical role in Niebuhr but also leads to positive normative requirements. From the "fact" of human freedom, Niebuhr moves to faith, hope, love, minimal political demands, and the human need for God.

Niebuhr's model of God also relates to his emphasis on freedom. It is through freedom that humans are drawn toward faith. The self-transcendent human, seeing the limits of its own claims, norms, and systems, longs for a norm beyond its finite norms. Only through faith in a transcendent God who unifies and gives meaning to our finite claims is the moral life of this bound and free self made possible. Moreover, Niebuhr uses the metaphor of freedom to speak of divine transcendence. God's "freedom" beyond the structures of the world and finite human claims both relativizes and unifies them. Even God's presence in Christ is an expression of God's "freedom." Throughout his work, then, Niebuhr's theological realism is formed in relation to his understanding of freedom.

Ruether

Ruether's theological ethic reverses this emphasis. Human boundedness to the natural evolutionary process is the crucial feature of her moral realism. The responsible moral life is made possible by observing and obeying both the laws of Gaia (cooperative interdependence) and the laws of human consciousness and altruism. Even these human laws are a conscious extension of the laws of Gaia. Thus, though human consciousness allows the self to reflect on its broader natural context, it is finally an expression of and continuous with that natural evolutionary process. In the human, the natural organic process is made conscious of itself.

Ruether's model emphasizes, then, the profound continuity between nature and human consciousness. Even so, human consciousness makes possible the reflection on and transformation of the natural. Through this social transformation, humans further the evolutionary process. But transformation is moral only if it follows the laws of nature. Boundedness to nature provides the moral limits and direction of the transformation. Those ethical systems that go against these laws of cooperative interdependence (such as "patriarchy") are rejected as unethical. Thus, even though Ruether includes both boundedness and freedom within her ethic, it is human boundedness to nature that is crucial. Nature, broadly conceived, provides the moral norms for responsible human actions and social structures. Because humans have the capacity to both know and follow these laws faithfully, Ruether is less suspicious than are many political realists about the resulting social and political changes.

Ruether's model of the divine also emphasizes this boundedness or continuity. God/ess, the source or "encompassing matrix" of this process, unifies human moral experience and all of life (thus providing a kind of theological realism). But because it is so continuous with nature, the divine does not have the same relativizing role that we saw in Niebuhr.

Welch

Welch's model of human boundedness and freedom stands in sharp contrast to the moral realism found in both Niebuhr and Ruether. For all their differences, Niebuhr and Ruether draw on common human experiences of boundedness and freedom. Welch, however, denies such common experiences or natures, claiming instead that humans are radically bound to the context and truths of their particular community and historical age. Moral truths are created by the powers of each age and do not refer to any universal or common human experiences (either of freedom or of boundedness). The truth is simply that which is made true or effective. Thus, for Welch, the moral norms of the self are radically relative to its age and community.

Within this community-centered ethic, moral responsibility is not, however, the consistent living out of these contingent community norms. Because of Welch's critical bent from her liberation and feminist commitments, she criticizes communitarian ethics as supporting the status quo. Thus, moral responsibility is not living faithfully within the norms of one's community; it is, instead, engagement in open, diverse, multicultural communities in which one's own cultural perspective is shown to be limited. The transcendence of the truth of one's context is made possible through interactions with those who define truth differently. Our boundedness to community shapes our truth; our interactions with the truths of other communities remind us of the limits of our own. Out of these critical interactions, one may "choose" another perspective. There are, however, no independent standards or truths to which one could appeal to explain a choice. There is no moral grounding beyond the relative truths of an age; ultimately, one is left only with the freedom to recognize that one's truths are relative and to opt for another relative truth.

Moreover, for Welch, the divine *is* the power or quality of these community interactions. The divine is, therefore, the quality of whatever structures and relationships win or survive in these battles for truth. The divine is transcendent only in the sense that the community (of which the divine is a quality or power) offers a sort of critical transcendence of one's particular truth through the expression of diverse truths. Consequently, the divine is so bound to these diverse, conflicting relationships in community that it offers neither unity nor meaning within the conflict. Indeed, the divine *is* the quality of these diverse, conflicting relationships. Thus, in her understanding of human boundedness to community, her affirmation of community-centered "transcendence," and her equation of God with the qualities of existing communities, Welch denies any substantive moral and theological realism while affirming a stark political realism.

A Feminist Christian Realism

A feminist Christian realism both draws on and differs from these three options. It shares components of the moral realism of both Ruether and Niebuhr, the political realism of Welch and Niebuhr, and the theological realism of Ruether and Niebuhr. Feminist moral experience presupposes radical human freedom, at least some minimal moral grounding, and a critical mechanism by which the limits of all claims are acknowledged. Without these features, it cannot account for its judgment of patriarchy, its support of an alternate ethic and theology, the reality of radical transformation for the good, and a continuing critical capacity allowing for assessment of all new systems and structures. A feminist Christian realism begins with these feminist presuppositions. In a review of feminist appropriations and realist definitions of divine transcendence in chapter 1, it was suggested that God's transcendence could unify and relativize diverse human claims. Given these concerns, I turned to the theological ethics of Niebuhr, Welch, and Ruether as resources for a feminist Christian realism.

This position draws its moral realism from both Niebuhr's emphasis on human freedom and Ruether's focus on human boundedness to nature. With Niebuhr, it claims that freedom carries thick positive and critical moral implications. The human capacity to transcend self and context offers a critical perspective on all human claims. At the same time, the "fact" of human freedom offers minimal grounding for moral, religious, and political reflection. Thus, with Niebuhr and in contrast to Ruether, this position grounds moral claims and finds a perspective for moral judgment from the human experience of freedom over nature, self, and community. This position moves beyond Niebuhr, however, in its greater attentiveness to the moral implications of human boundedness that one finds in Ruether and Welch.

Drawing on Ruether's ethic, boundedness to nature carries thick positive moral implications within a feminist moral realism. With Ruether, a feminist Christian realism would attend to creation, including patterns within the natural environment and common human nature and experience, as a source for moral norms. Where Ruether focuses on an ecological reading of the environment, this alternative position would also consider a broader range of human experiences. As diverse as human cultures are, the fact of our common boundedness to bodies and social groups offers a source for ethical reflection on shared natural moral norms. Humans have basic needs for food, shelter, health care, community, and protection from the perils of the natural environment (including other humans). Humans ask similar moral and religious questions and share many common bodily and social activities.[1] Though social construction forms human understanding of pain and pleasure, the bodily experiences themselves are shared. The tremendous care required by long human childhood demands stable social groups across cultures. These are a few examples of shared human experiences.

My focus on a broader range of experiences to ground moral claims extends Ruether's natural moral realism but is consistent with it. Likewise, this moral realism would draw much more heavily from nature than does Niebuhr's ethic. Yet, given his occasional references to the moral demands of our creaturely life, this position, though moving beyond Niebuhr's claims, is consistent with his argument. Moreover, because Niebuhr's emphasis on freedom is retained, these moral claims based in our boundedness are always subject to critical judgment and revision. This is a helpful check on a tendency in Ruether's more confident naturalist moral realism to uncritically underwrite some appeals to nature.

The moral realism found in Ruether, Niebuhr, and my alternative model contrasts sharply with Welch's relativist ethic. In Welch's case, human boundedness to community does not provide grounding for moral claims; on the contrary, it shows the finitude of those claims. When all claims to moral truth are radically relative to context and are created by structures of power, how does one ground or justify feminist claims? If moral claims are made true by forces of power in community struggles, it is difficult to imagine that women and other less powerful groups could win and, thus, have their truth be made true. The ethical difficulties that arise from Welch's relativism point to the need for at least minimal grounding for moral claims. The feminist moral realism described here is one option for this grounding.

Yet, the turn to experience and nature for grounding is not without difficulties. Ruether's confident and somewhat uncritical turn to the environment and to human experience to ground certain moral norms raises many questions for feminists. Some feminists claim that broad appeals to common human experience impose Western values, deny the radical particularity of human claims, and are ultimately oppressive.[2] Moreover, feminist critics of natural law arguments point to the dangers of justifying gender roles from nature or common human experience.[3] To account for these concerns, any feminist argument from nature or experience needs a built-in critical mechanism that acknowledges the contingency and limitations of human claims.

In a feminist Christian realism, a crucial aspect of this critical mechanism is freedom. Because freedom always stands over nature, judging and transforming it, a feminist Christian realism would insist that "natural law" claims are subject both to error and to change. With Niebuhr, this ethic emphasizes more than the human capacity for positive creative transformation of nature and social boundedness; it also notes the destructive possibilities of that transformation. The human tendency, noted in Niebuhr and Welch, to seek its own interests while hiding those interests casts suspicion on all moral claims. With Welch and Niebuhr, this position insists both that humans are limited by the contingent truth claims of a community and that these claims often have a self-interested nature. This "political realist" argument does not, however, necessarily undercut the possibility of reflection on and the grounding of moral claims in nature and human experience; it simply notes the contingent nature of that reflection.

Out of the need for an internal critical mechanism, a feminist Christian realism combines Niebuhr's focus on self-transcendence with Welch's horizontal transcendence in community. As noted previously, Niebuhr's insistence on the transformative capacity of human self-transcendence gives his system an internal dynamism and critical mechanism by which moral claims, natural patterns, social structures, and ideologies are criticized and transformed. At the same time, Welch is a helpful counter to one aspect of Niebuhr's argument. Niebuhr limits the critical capacity for self-transcendence to individuals. Because communities lack an organ for self-transcendence, they are both more selfish than individuals and less aware of that selfishness. In contrast, Welch insists that transcendence is possible not for a single individual but only in community. The limitations of one's truth become evident in the confrontation with other perspectives. Welch's emphasis on horizontal transcendence is a helpful counter to Niebuhr's pessimism about the moral capacity of human communities. A feminist Christian realism incorporates both of these factors.

A feminist Christian realism also draws on these three figures for its model of God. Its understanding of divine transcendence emerges from Niebuhr and in contrast to Welch and Ruether. Within a Niebuhrian model, divine transcendence helps to unify, relativize, and give meaning to diverse human values and claims. Because of the high vision made possible by human freedom and its finite, contingent reality, only faith in a transcendent God can unify and give meaning to our diverse, finite moral lives. Divine transcendence also plays a politically realist role, standing in judgment on all contingent human claims. Thus, a feminist Christian realism draws on this model of theological realism that includes both a positive aspect and a critical aspect.

In contrast to this position, Welch understands God as the power and quality of existing communities. In the end, such a model of God does not unify or relativize diverse, conflicting human relationships; it simply reflects them. Thus, Welch's God, contrary to her stated intention, does not encourage radical social transformation but reflects the relationships that exist, whether liberating or oppressive. At one level, then, her model of God can be seen as a confirmation of what exists—of the status quo. This is ironic because Welch turns to this radically "immanent," "finite" model of God precisely because she believes that classical models of divine transcendence and power support the conservation of human structures of domination.

Ruether's model of God/ess stands in sharp contrast to the models of Welch, Niebuhr, and a feminist Christian realism. God/ess, the matrix of all life, gives unity to diverse claims and experiences. Because Ruether's understanding of God is so profoundly continuous with creation, however, it lacks a critical relativizing aspect over natural claims. This position is difficult for feminism because it tends to sacralize the natural. Thus, because Ruether and Welch focus on the boundedness of God to nature (Ruether) and to existing relationships (Welch), they unintentionally support the status quo and undermine radical transformation.

At the same time, Ruether's emphasis on the immanence of the divine in creation and Welch's focus on the divine in community are helpful counterperspectives to Niebuhr. As we saw before, feminists have criticized Niebuhr for his central focus on God's presence in the cross. Even this immanence is understood finally as the highest expression of God's transcendence or "freedom." Moreover, his focus on the cross is the source of his moral norm of sacrificial love. Many feminists claim that this norm is dangerous for women and others who have little power.

A feminist Christian realism, then, retains Niebuhr's model of divine transcendence while giving greater emphasis to the divine presence in creation, liberation, judgment, incarnation, community, and the power of the Holy Spirit. While the atonement is included, it is balanced by a more comprehensive model of God's presence. This broader focus is in keeping with Niebuhr's overall argument and with his references to common human experiences of dependence, moral obligation, and a desire for mercy (which correspond to God as creator, judge, and redeemer). A feminist Christian realism merely develops these aspects more fully.

This more comprehensive model of divine presence has significant ethical implications. Whereas Niebuhr's focus on the cross led him to elevate the norm of self-sacrificial love, the turn to a broader understanding of divine presence offers other norms as well. In the biblical witness, we read of divine activity not only in the self-sacrificial love of the atonement but also in the love expressed in creation, in the liberation of the oppressed, in the judgment of injustice and idolatry, and in the sustaining comfort of the Holy Spirit. The biblical witness to these divine activities offers additional transcendent norms, such as justice, liberation, and creative and sustaining love. This shift not only responds to feminist criticisms but also reflects more fully both the biblical witness and a broader range of human experiences.

Within the analysis of this section and throughout the larger project, I have placed Niebuhr, Welch, and Ruether in mutually critical interaction. The synthetic position that emerges from this interaction incorporates and rejects some aspects of each position. Even so, it does not draw equally from the three figures. Because of his model of human experience as self-transcendent, Niebuhr has an internal critical mechanism by which to respond to criticisms and to be modified by them. This is the reason that I focus on the centrality of freedom in feminist ethics from the beginning of this argument; it works. It helps to make sense of feminist moral experience, to account for the problems of other positions, and to incorporate their criticisms.

A feminist reader more closely aligned with Ruether or Welch might charge that I have constructed a circular argument. She might suggest that having begun with a Niebuhrian analysis of the demands of feminist moral experience and a Niebuhrian emphasis on self-transcendence, it is hardly surprising that I find the theological ethics of Ruether and Welch to be insufficient. In addition, she might observe that my criticisms or modifications of Niebuhr's ethic do not challenge his broader model but, in fact, claim to be consistent with it. In the end, she could argue, this is a Niebuhrian position that asks Niebuhrian questions and then finds some feminists wanting when they do not give Niebuhrian answers.

At one level, I would have to agree with this critic. Though my argument is a *feminist* Niebuhrian argument, it is still in many ways Niebuhrian. Certainly, because of my feminist commitments and concerns, I have appropriated some aspects of Ruether's and Welch's ethics, and I have substantially modified Niebuhr's ethic. But these modifications are consistent with his broader model. Indeed, in some instances, my feminist Christian realism is more consistently Niebuhrian than Niebuhr himself.

This admission does not, however, discredit the argument. A modified Christian realism is able to fulfill certain tasks successfully. It can make sense of our moral experience, coherently incorporate the criticisms of others, and account for internal problems in its own model and other models. That is what a good argument does.[4] The fact that the argument is, in many ways, Niebuhrian does not take away from its efficacy. Niebuhr's understanding of self-transcendence as transformative builds in an internal critical principle that allows for the modification of his own ethic. The ability of a feminist realist model of human freedom to account for the gaps or problems within other feminist positions and to coherently incorporate their criticisms exemplifies the efficacy of this realist model.

Of course, for this alternate model, a feminist Christian realism, human self-transcendence does more than offer an internal critical mechanism. At the heart of this model is a redefinition both of Niebuhr's model of the self as free and of feminist models of the self as profoundly bound to social context and nature.[5] My alternate model not only responds to feminist criticisms of Niebuhr but also is more adequate than Niebuhr or many feminist models in accounting for a wide range of human experiences—particularly those experiences where human freedom and boundedness meet.

In this alternate model, radical freedom is a transforming quality that infuses the fully bound person. This quality is not a separate element distinct from boundedness but a creative quality of boundedness. It not only transforms the bound but is formed (positively and negatively) within it. This transforming quality is formed, for example, by biology; it is a physiological component of our nature. Moreover, it finds its source in the bonds of human community. Within the bonds of family and friendship, humans are made free; they learn to act freely and to discern freedom's proper ends. Within the bonds of political community, humans practice freedom and protect and nurture the freedom of others. In these relationships, boundedness is not only a limit and a negation to freedom but also its source, end, and joy.

As we saw before, my alternate model also modifies feminist and Niebuhrian understandings of God. Within this model, God's freedom is a transforming quality in the world. It is the source of our boundedness, including our transforming capacities. God works and is known in the world not only in sacrifice and judgment but also in more positive expressions of creation, incarnation, and sanctification. God enacts God's freedom not only in the suffering of the cross but also in the abundance of creation. And God not only creates but also gives laws to guide. God liberates us from the bonds of slavery and oppression. In Christ, God enters into human form and takes on the full joy and sorrow of the bound human life. God, through the power of the Holy Spirit, can draw forth our human creative, transformative capacities. Because God sustains and guides, we listen carefully and dare to follow. God also judges us and all of our transformations. But because God also redeems and forgives, we can risk mistakes. By emphasizing a broad spectrum of the biblical witness of God's activity, a feminist Christian realism can also include a broader understanding of human loves. The highest norms for human life include but are not limited to sacrificial love.

This transforming quality not only is formed by our boundedness but also transforms boundedness. It is the source of creative transformation and critical reflection because it allows us to imagine that some of the given elements of our lives might be different, to devise and enact strategies for subsequent transformation, to critically reflect on those transformations by recognizing that they may be flawed and distorted, and to imagine, again, how our lives might be made different. This creative cycle is driven not only by the transforming quality of an individual person but also by the transforming qualities of communities of conversation and action (and, at times, we hope and pray, even by the transforming power of God). Within this model, both persons and communities are unceasingly dynamic.

This cycle of creative transformation is always critical. Because of this transforming quality, we constantly judge both the given reality and the proposed transformations; because of its critical elements, we are often not sure which transformations are best (much less which ones are prompted by the Holy Spirit!). Even so, this model is not left without norms. As we have seen, the biological and social realities of our bound existence (including its freedom) provide a source for minimal norms. Norms can be derived, for example, from the human need for food and community. In addition, norms can be derived from the fact that freedom needs protection and nurture in families and political structures.

The transforming quality is more than a positive source of norms, however; it is also a kind of antinorm. The capacity offers a critical mechanism by which we recognize the tentative nature of our norms and models (including the model of the transforming person). Though this essential, fully bound quality is a part of our bound nature, it is a critical, dynamic part. The person is always transforming and critically evaluating claims about the essential. This model offers, then, a kind of dynamic, critical naturalism—an antiessentialist essentialism.[6] Bonds form freedom, and freedom transforms bonds; bonds free, and freedom binds.

Afterword

As I FINISH the final manuscript revisions for publication, the subject of this project—the intersection between human boundedness and freedom—assumes a real and embodied presence in our household. The final revisions coincide with the last days of preparation before the birth of our second child. In the vocation of parenting and the relationship between parent and child, freedom and boundedness meet head on. The baby, still in my womb, is already beginning the long process of self-differentiation so central to life as a free, agential self. And yet the schoolyard for this education in freedom is, at the moment, the utter bonds of the womb and will soon be the close attachment of the household—replete with near-endless holding, touching, gazing, and nursing. She has already learned to kick and move in response to our touch and to our voices. I expect that our infant, like her sister who is now a year and half old, will learn to be a free self who can make things happen as an agent in the world in the context and in the daily practices of the deep bonds of love and care provided, in our case and most cases, by the family. In the best of circumstances, all of us, not just the children in my house, learn to be free and to responsibly enact our freedom in the bonds of dependence and love. And as our children are formed for freedom, they are able to enact and practice that freedom in the larger society. Moreover, as they reach an age of responsibility, they will be able, we hope, to establish bonds that nurture and protect the freedom of others. Freedom is formed, trained, enacted, and protected within the bonds of human community.

Of course, as my husband and I reflect on freedom and parenting, we think not only about our daughters but also about ourselves. As much as we love the work of parenting and the deep bonds of attachment and care in the family, we cannot help but notice that our freedom has been curtailed in a thousand ways. Every decision about how we divide our time, how we make and spend money, where we go and when, how much we sleep and where, and how we fulfill our vocations in the larger world are constrained by the seemingly unending needs of our children. Our lives are no longer our own.

But the truth is, of course, that they never were. As people of faith, we know that we live in utter dependence on God and that a life of faithfulness is a life given in love to the world. Though we may never meet this ideal, it is the ultimate reality and present lure of the life of faith. In the end, the loss of freedom in care for our children or for any of God's children is the highest expression of our freedom. And the truth, of course, is that the losses entailed in care for others are not simply loss, either of freedom or of other aspects of our bound life; they are also our highest purpose and our greatest joy. We are formed in freedom and bound in love as we care for others and are cared for by them. This is our nature and our delight. Might the same be true for God? Perhaps God enacts God's freedom on our behalf not only in negation and loss on the cross but also in joy and love as God creates, redeems, and sanctifies us.

Perhaps the medieval Christian mystic Meister Eckhart reveals something of both divine and human life at the intersection between boundedness and freedom when he writes of the joy God finds on entering human life and finding God's image there: "It is just as enjoyable for [God] as when someone lets a horse run loose on a meadow that is completely level and smooth. Such is the horse's nature that it pours itself out with all its might in jumping about the meadow. This it would find delightful; such is its nature."[1]

God pours Godself into the world, delighting in incarnation. This is the highest expression of God's freedom. This is God's nature. So, too, we humans, created in God's image, find our greatest delight as we give ourselves to the world, as we bind ourselves to others. This is our created nature. This is the highest expression of our freedom.

Notes

Acknowledgments

1. Thomas Aquinas, *Summa Theologica* (III,96,7), vol. 20, *The Great Books of the Western World*, Robert Maynard Hutchins, ed. (Chicago: Encyclopaedia Britannica, 1952), 1061.
2. Ibid. (I,II,27,4), vol. 19, 738.
3. Michael Ventura, *The Zoo Where You're Fed to God* (New York: Simon and Schuster, 1994), 43–59.
4. Charles Dickens, *David Copperfield* (Oxford: Oxford University Press, 1989), 203.

Chapter 1

1. "Christian realism" and other terms central to this argument, such as moral realism and political realism, are defined in the section on Definitions. The phrase "feminist moral experience" is defined in the section on Feminist Reality and Feminist Assumptions.
2. See Beverly Wildung Harrison, *Making the Connections: Essays in Feminist Social Ethics*, Carol Robb, ed. (Boston: Beacon Press, 1985); Sheila Collins, *A Different Heaven and Earth* (Valley Forge, PA: Judson Press, 1974); and Rosemary Radford Ruether, *Sexism and God-Talk: Toward a Feminist Theology* (Boston: Beacon Press, 1983).
3. This is not an exhaustive study of Ruether and Welch. They are useful here because they illustrate clearly and forcefully the benefits and dangers of the broader feminist move toward immanence and boundedness. They also serve as representatives of two general options within feminism.
4. Where Niebuhr refers to finitude or the finite, I use the words *boundedness* or *bound*. The word *finitude* tends to be viewed suspiciously by some feminists, who see it as a negative reflection on human contingency and ultimate relation to nature and society. The words *boundedness* and *bound* are consistent with Niebuhr's meaning but more compatible with feminist affirmations of human boundedness in body and community.
5. I will return to this point in the concluding chapter.
6. The discussion of Niebuhr in chapters 2 and 3 is not exhaustive. I have focused on those issues that are most relevant to feminist concerns. My feminist reappropriation of Niebuhr centers on the ethical implications of his understanding of human selves as bound and free. Niebuhr's definition of human self-transcendence as freedom and his use of the metaphor of freedom to speak of divine transcendence provide a helpful alterna-

tive to the spatial and antimaterial definitions of transcendence that many feminists criticize.

7. Ruether is a process Catholic natural law thinker with an ecofeminist and liberation emphasis.

8. Welch represents a postmodern linguistic constructivist position informed by its "choice" for liberation.

9. For a review of the history of Christian realism, see Robin W. Lovin, "Theology, Ethics and Culture," *The Modern Theologians: An Introduction to Christian Theology in the Twentieth Century,* David F. Ford, ed. (Oxford: Basil Blackwell, 1989), 75–88; William R. Hutchison, *The Modernist Impulse in American Protestantism* (Cambridge, MA: Harvard University Press, 1976), especially 288–311; Martin Marty, *Modern American Religion: The Noise of Conflict, 1919–1941* (Chicago: University of Chicago Press, 1991), 303–40; Donald Meyer, *The Protestant Search for Political Realism: 1919–1941* (Middletown, CT: Wesleyan University Press, 1988), especially chapter 14; Robert T. Cornelison, *The Christian Realism of Reinhold Niebuhr and the Political Theology of Jürgen Moltmann in Dialogue: The Realism of Hope* (San Francisco: Mellen Research University Press, 1992), especially chapter 1; and Robin W. Lovin, *Reinhold Niebuhr and Christian Realism* (Cambridge: Cambridge University Press, 1995), especially 1–32.

10. The phrase "the faith of modernism" is taken from a book of that title that outlines the standard themes of modernism: Shailer Mathews, *The Faith of Modernism* (New York: Macmillan, 1924).

11. These emphases are evident in early realist texts. See, for example, Walter M. Horton, *Realistic Theology* (New York: Harper and Brothers, 1934); John C. Bennett, *Christian Realism* (New York: Charles Scribner's Sons, 1941); Douglas C. MacIntosh, ed., *Religious Realism* (New York: Macmillan, 1931); and Reinhold Niebuhr, "Will Christians Stop Fooling Themselves?" *Christian Century* 51 (May 16, 1934): 659. Reinhold Niebuhr reflects on the Augustinian roots of his political realism in an often quoted essay, "Augustine's Political Realism," *Christian Realism and Political Problems* (New York: Charles Scribner's Sons, 1953). Walter Horton also credited his change in theology during the 1930s to his reading of Augustine. See Hutchison, *The Modernist Impulse,* 305.

12. Walter Rauschenbusch, *Christianity and the Social Crisis* (Louisville, KY: Westminster/John Knox Press, 1991), 420. Rauschenbusch's faith in human possibility is also evident in *A Theology for the Social Gospel* (New York: Macmillan, 1917; Reprint. Nashville: Abingdon Press, 1960).

13. Bennett, *Christian Realism,* 4.

14. Horton, *Realistic Theology,* 12.

15. Niebuhr, *Christian Realism and Political Problems,* 119.

16. For an analysis of early criticisms of Christian realism from Shirley Jackson Case, Edward Scribner Ames, Ernest F. Tittle, Robert Calhoun, and others, see Hutchison, *The Modernist Impulse,* 298ff.

17. Rubem Alves, "Christian Realism: The Ideology of the Establishment," *Christianity and Crisis* 33 (September 17, 1973), 173–76. Alves's article was a part of a heated debate about liberation theology and Christian realism in the issues of *Christianity and Crisis* from the fall of 1973.

18. It is ironic that Alves's criticism of realist arguments has such a strong "realist" cast to it.

19. Collins, *A Different Heaven and Earth,* 157. Beverly Harrison, Rosemary Ruether, Judith Vaughan, and other feminists have also criticized Christian realism. See chapter 2.

20. Rosemary Radford Ruether, *The Radical Kingdom: The Western Experience of Messianic Hope* (New York: Harper and Row, 1970), 287.

21. Harrison, *Making the Connections*, 65–67.
22. Conservative thinker Michael Novak, a realist disciple of Niebuhr, confirms the suspicions of Ruether and other feminists. The criticisms of liberation theology by Thomas Sanders are another example: Thomas Sanders, "The Theology of Liberation: Christian Utopianism," *Christianity and Crisis* 33 (September 17, 1973): 167–73.
23. Others have made this argument. See, for example, John Coleman Bennett, "Liberation Theology and Christian Realism," *Christianity and Crisis* 33 (October 15, 1973): 197–98; and Robert McAffee Brown, "Liberation Theology and Christian Realism," *Christianity and Crisis* 33 (October 15, 1973): 199–200.
24. Niebuhr, *Christian Realism and Political Problems*, 119.
25. Bennett, *Christian Realism*, 4.
26. Ibid., 65.
27. Horton, *Realistic Theology*, 38.
28. These factors will be examined more closely in chapter 3.
29. Lovin, *Reinhold Niebuhr and Christian Realism*. My account of realism relies heavily on Lovin's definitions.
30. See Horton, Niebuhr, and Bennett in the previous historical sketch.
31. For Robin Lovin's definition of political realism, see *Reinhold Niebuhr and Christian Realism*, 3ff.
32. I refer to idealism here not as a fully developed philosophical perspective but simply in contrast to political realism's suspicions not only about human nature generally but also about human social and political visions.
33. Lovin, *Reinhold Niebuhr and Christian Realism*, 11ff.
34. Ibid., 18ff.
35. By using the terms *self-transcendence, freedom,* or even *radical freedom,* the fact of human boundedness is not rejected or disparaged. For a Niebuhrian realism and for a feminist Christian realism, human boundedness and self-transcendence are always held in tension; neither is denied. Freedom does not negate boundedness. It is the capacity of the self to reflect on, judge, and partially transform its bound situation. This capacity is "radical" because of its transformative character, *not* because of any denial of our bound condition.
36. Christian realism will be described more fully later.
37. See David Tracy, *Blessed Rage for Order* (Minneapolis: Winston-Seabury Press, 1975); and *The Analogical Imagination* (New York: Crossroad, 1981).
38. See, for example, Rosemary Ruether, *Sexism and God-Talk*, 18–19; and Beverly Harrison, *Making the Connections*, 122.
39. Although I focus primarily on European American feminist theologies in this project, some of the same themes are found in the theologies of women from other groups. See, for example, Chung Hyun Kyung, *Struggle to Be the Sun Again: Introducing Asian Women's Theology* (Maryknoll, NY: Orbis Press, 1990).
40. Sara Ruddick, *Maternal Thinking: Toward a Politics of Peace* (Boston: Beacon Press, 1989); and Bonnie Miller-McLemore, *Also a Mother: Work and Family as Theological Dilemma* (Nashville: Abingdon Press, 1994).
41. Kathryn Rabuzzi, *The Sacred and the Feminine: Toward a Theology of Housework* (New York: Seabury, 1982).
42. Grace D. Cumming Long, *Passion and Reason: Womenviews of Christian Life* (Louisville, KY: Westminster/John Knox Press, 1993). The metaphors of weaving and quilting are found in scores of feminist theologies.
43. Rita Nakashima Brock, *Journeys by Heart: A Christology of Erotic Power* (New York: Crossroad, 1988).

44. Mary Hunt, *Fierce Tenderness: A Feminist Theology of Friendship* (New York: Crossroad Press, 1991); and Carter Heyward, *Our Passion for Justice: Images of Power, Sexuality and Liberation* (New York: Pilgrim Press, 1984).

45. Sheila Davaney, "The Limits of the Appeal to Women's Experience," in *Shaping New Visions: Gender and Values in American Culture*, Clarissa W. Atkinson, Constance H. Buchanan, and Margaret R. Miles, eds. (Ann Arbor, MI: UMI Research Press, 1987), 31–49; Susan Thistlethwaite, *Sex, Race, and God* (New York: Crossroad, 1989); and Jacquelyn Grant, *White Women's Christ and Black Women's Jesus: White Feminist Christology and Womanist Response* (Atlanta: Scholars Press, 1989).

46. See, for example, Katie Geneva Cannon, *Black Womanist Ethics* (Atlanta: Scholars Press, 1988); Delores Williams, "The Color of Feminism," *Christianity and Crisis* 45 (April 29, 1985): 164–65; Ada María Isasi-Díaz, *Hispanic Women, Prophetic Voice in the Church: Toward a Hispanic Women's Liberation Theology* (San Francisco: Harper & Row, 1988); Elsa Tamez, ed. *Through Her Eyes: Women's Theology from Latin America* (Maryknoll, NY: Orbis Press, 1989); Chung, *Struggle to Be the Sun Again*; and Cheryl Sanders et al., "Roundtable Discussion: Christian Ethics and Theology in Womanist Perspective," *Journal of Feminist Studies in Religion* 5 (Fall 1989): 83–112.

47. Sanders, "Roundtable Discussion," 83ff.

48. Ada María Isasi-Díaz, et al., "Mujeristas: Who We Are and What We Are About," *Journal of Feminist Studies in Religion* 8 (Spring 1992): 105–25.

49. C. W. Maggie Kim, Susan M. St. Ville, and Susan M. Simonaitis, eds., *Transfigurations: Theology and the French Feminists* (Minneapolis: Fortress Press, 1993).

50. See Starhawk, *Truth or Dare: Encounters with Power, Authority, and Mystery* (San Francisco: Harper & Row, 1987), for example.

51. These charges are widespread in feminist theology. For example, see works by Rosemary Ruether, Mary Daly, Sharon Welch, Sallie McFague, Rita Brock, and Susan Thistlethwaite.

52. These reflections form the heart of many works in feminist theology. For good summaries of the arguments and reconstructions in systematic form, see Ruether, *Sexism and God-Talk*; Daphne Hampson, *Theology and Feminism* (Oxford: Basil Blackwell, 1990); Catherine LaCugna, ed., *Freeing Theology: The Essentials of Theology in Feminist Perspective* (San Francisco: HarperCollins, 1993); and Anne Carr, *Transforming Grace: Christian Tradition and Women's Experience* (New York: Harper and Row, 1988).

53. See, for example, Harrison, *Making the Connections*, 122; and Ruether, *Sexism and God-Talk*, 18–19.

54. Sallie McFague, *The Body of God: An Ecological Theology* (Minneapolis: Augsburg Fortress Press, 1993); Rosemary Ruether, *Gaia and God: An Ecofeminist Theology of Earth-Healing* (San Francisco: HarperCollins, 1992); Starhawk, *Dreaming the Dark* (Boston: Beacon Press, 1982); Sallie McFague, *Metaphorical Theology: Models of God in Religious Language* (Philadelphia: Fortress Press, 1982); and Eleanor Rae, *Women, the Earth, the Divine* (Maryknoll, NY: Orbis, 1994).

55. For a discussion of feminist redefinitions of power, see Nancy Harstock, *Money, Sex, and Power: Toward a Feminist Historical Materialism* (Boston: Northeastern University Press, 1985); Starhawk, *Dreaming the Dark*; Sharon Welch, *A Feminist Ethic of Risk* (Minneapolis: Fortress Press, 1990); Christine Hinze, *Comprehending Power in Christian Social Ethics* (Atlanta: Scholars Press, 1995); Brock, *Journeys by Heart*; Joanna Rogers Macy, *Despair and Personal Power in the Nuclear Age* (Philadelphia: New Society Publishers, 1983); and Martha Ellen Stortz, *PastorPower* (Nashville: Abingdon Press, 1993). Welch (*A Feminist Ethic of Risk,* 182) claims that the words "power over and "power-with" were coined by Mary Parker Follett in the 1920s.

56. Several of these redefinitions rely on models of power and the human self drawn from process theology. Rita Brock, for example, relies on Bernard Loomer's understanding of power.

57. There are a few exceptions. Martha Ellen Stortz, for example, suggests that "power over" may be appropriate in some circumstances.

58. Ruether, *Sexism and God-Talk;* and *Gaia and God;* Sallie McFague, *Models of God: Theology for an Ecological, Nuclear Age* (Philadelphia: Fortress Press, 1987); I. Carter Heyward, *The Redemption of God: A Theology of Mutual Liberation* (Washington, DC: University Press of America, 1982); I. Carter Heyward, *Our Passion for Justice: Images of Power, Sexuality and Liberation* (New York: Pilgrim Press, 1984); Long, *Passion and Reason;* Welch, *A Feminist Ethic of Risk;* Brock, *Journeys by Heart;* and Hampson, *Theology and Feminism.*

59. Hampson, *Theology and Feminism,* 152–53.

60. Mary Farrell Bednarowski, "The Significance of Immanence in Women's Theologies" (paper presented at the Comparative Studies in Religion Section, American Academy of Religion Annual Meeting, Washington, DC, November 1993).

61. Ruddick, *Maternal Thinking;* Welch, *A Feminist Ethic of Risk;* Thistlethwaite, *Sex, Race, and God;* Brock, *Journeys by Heart;* and Ruether, *Gaia and God.*

62. This claim is found throughout many feminist arguments. See, for example, Welch, *A Feminist Ethic of Risk;* Ruether, *Sexism and God-Talk;* and Long, *Passion and Reason.*

63. Welch, *A Feminist Ethic of Risk.*

64. Carol Gilligan, *In a Different Voice* (Cambridge, MA: Harvard University Press, 1982); and Nancy Chodorow, *The Reproduction of Mothering: Psychoanalysis and the Sociology of Gender* (Berkeley: University of California Press, 1978).

65. Catherine Keller, *From a Broken Web: Separation, Sexism, and Self* (Boston: Beacon Press, 1986); and Ann Wilson Shaef, *Women's Reality: An Emerging Female System in White Male Society* (Minneapolis: Winston Press, 1981).

66. Keller, *From a Broken Web,* 36.

67. Hampson, *Theology and Feminism,* 151.

68. Ruether, *New Woman/New Earth: Sexist Ideologies and Human Liberation* (New York: Seabury Press, 1975); Collins, *A Different Heaven and Earth;* and Simone de Beauvoir, *The Second Sex,* trans. H. M. Parshley (New York: Vintage Books, 1974).

69. Ruether, *New Woman/New Earth.*

70. It is ironic that many feminists have first criticized the traditional Christian focus on transcendence as an expression of male needs for separation and independent power and then gone on to suggest more immanent understandings of God. If, as the argument goes, the traditional focus on transcendence is an expression of "male sin," then perhaps this tendency toward increasing immanence, relationality, and boundedness could reflect what many have called "female sin." If a focus on transcendence is an expression of male issues about separation and autonomy, is a focus on immanence and boundedness an expression of female issues about overconnectedness and relationality? If, as Keller, Ruether, Collins, and others have argued, a transcendent God was created in the image of sinful man, has a new immanent God/ess been created in the image of sinful woman? Of course, many women deny these fundamental differences between women and men.

71. See, for example, Ruether, *Sexism and God-Talk;* Collins, *A Different Heaven and Earth;* Welch, *A Feminist Ethic of Risk;* and Long, *Passion and Reason.*

72. Heyward, *The Redemption of God,* 156.

73. Judith Plaskow, *Standing Again at Sinai: Judaism from a Feminist Perspective* (New York: Harper and Row, 1990), 132. Many other feminist theologians have written of this pattern of hierarchical dualisms of which God is the highest point and legitimator. See, for example, Anne Carr, *Transforming Grace,* 136–38; Hampson, *Theology and Feminism,*

152–53; Shaef, *Women's Reality*, 164; Ruether, *New Woman/New Earth*, 74; Collins, *Different Heaven and Earth*, 51–52; and McFague, *Metaphorical Theology*, 148.

74. Hunt, *Fierce Tenderness*; McFague, *Models of God*; Ruether, *Sexism and God-Talk*; Brock, *Journeys by Heart*; Grace M. Jantzen, *God's World, God's Body* (Philadelphia: Westminster Press, 1984); and Heyward, *The Redemption of God*.

75. McFague, *The Body of God*, xi, 132–33, and 140.

76. Welch, *A Feminist Ethic of Risk*; Starhawk, *Dreaming the Dark*; and Carol P. Christ, *Laughter of Aphrodite* (San Francisco: Harper and Row, 1987).

77. McFague, *The Body of God*, 126ff.

78. Ibid., 157ff.

79. Mary Hunt, "Friends in Deed," in *Sex and God*, Linda Hurcombe, ed. (New York: Routledge and Kegan Paul, 1987), 52–53. See also Hunt, *Fierce Tenderness*, 166–67.

80. I. Carter Heyward, *Touching Our Strength: The Erotic as Power and the Love of God* (San Francisco: Harper and Row, 1989), 188. See also Heyward, *Our Passion for Justice and The Redemption of God*.

81. Welch, *A Feminist Ethic of Risk*, 173.

82. Ibid., 176.

83. Carol Christ, "Why Women Need the Goddess: Phenomenological, Psychological and Political Reflections," in *Womanspirit Rising: A Feminist Reader in Religion*, Carol Christ and Judith Plaskow, eds. (New York: Harper and Row, 1979), 278.

84. Emily Culpepper, "Contemporary Goddess Theology," in *Shaping New Vision*, Clarissa Atkinson, Constance Hall Buchanan, and Margaret Miles, eds. (Ann Arbor, MI: UMI Research Press, 1987), 60.

85. Mary Daly, *Gyn/Ecology: The Metaethics of Radical Feminism* (Boston: Beacon Press, 1978), 111.

86. Brock, *Journeys by Heart*; Kim, St. Ville, and Simonaitis, *Transfigurations*; Rebecca Chopp, *The Power to Speak: Feminism, Language, God* (New York: Crossroad, 1989); Davaney, "The Limits of the Appeal to Women's Experience," in *Shaping New Vision: Gender and Values in American Culture*, Clarissa W. Atkinson, Constance H. Buchanan and Margaret R. Miles, eds. (Ann Arbor, MI: UMI Research Press, 1987); and "Problems with Feminist Theory: Historicity and the Search for Sure Foundations," in *Embodied Love: Sensuality and Relationship as Feminist Values*, Paula M. Cooey, Sharon Farmer, and Mary Ellen Ross, eds. (San Francisco: Harper and Row, 1987), 79–95; Thistlethwaite, *Sex, Race, and God*; Sharon Welch, *Communities of Resistance and Solidarity: A Feminist Theology of Liberation* (Maryknoll, NY: Orbis Press, 1985); and *A Feminist Ethic of Risk*.

87. Typologies of women's theologies center on several different issues. Pamela Dickey Young, for example, types feminists according to the ways women's experience and Christian tradition are appropriated: Pamela Dickey Young, *Christian Theology/Feminist Theology: In Search of Method* (Minneapolis: Fortress Press, 1990), chapter 1. In the beginning of this section, I outlined the differences that arise depending on the kind of experience to which the feminist appeals (e.g., motherhood, sexuality, ethnicity). The division between the two groups mentioned here centers on their contrasting conceptions of the status and grounding of moral and theological claims.

88. Ruether, *Gaia and God*.

89. Ruether's represents an ecofeminist process version of a classic Catholic, natural law position.

90. This position will be explained more fully in chapter 5.

91. See Welch, *A Feminist Ethic of Risk*, especially part 3.

92. For an account of these limitations, see *The World's Women: Trends and Statistics* (New York: United Nations Press, 1991).

93. See, for example, Susan Faludi, *Backlash: The Undeclared War against American Women* (New York: Crown Press, 1991); and Naomi Wolf, *The Beauty Myth* (New York: Doubleday, 1992).

94. See, for example, Judith Plaskow, *Sex, Sin, and Grace: Women's Experience and the Theologies of Reinhold Niebuhr and Paul Tillich* (Washington, DC: University Press of America, 1980); Susan Dunfee, *Christianity and the Liberation of Women* (Ph.D. dissertation, Claremont Graduate School, 1985); Judith Vaughan, *Sociality, Ethics and Social Change: A Critical Appraisal of Reinhold Niebuhr's Ethics in the Light of Rosemary Ruether's Works* (Lanham, MD: University Press of America, 1983); Hampson, *Theology and Feminism*; and Valerie Saiving, "The Human Situation: A Feminine View," *Journal of Religion* 40 (April 1960): 108–10. These discussions of sin will be examined later.

95. See, for example, Ruether, *New Woman/New Earth*, as well as her *Gaia and God*; and Brock, *Journeys by Heart*.

96. See, for example, the "Seneca Falls Declaration" and Mary Wollstonecraft, "A Vindication of the Rights of Woman," in *The Feminist Papers: From Adams to de Beauvoir*, Alice Rossi, ed. (New York: Bantam Books, 1973).

97. The liberal or Enlightenment roots of feminism are noted in many recent accounts. See, for example, Josephine Donovan, *Feminist Theory: The Intellectual Traditions of American Feminism* (New York: Continuum, 1994); Susan Okin, *Women in Western Political Thought* (Princeton, NJ: Princeton University Press, 1979); and Zillah Eisenstein, *The Radical Future of Liberal Feminism* (New York: Longman, 1981). Feminist theologian Sheila Davaney ("The Limits of the Appeal to Women's Experience") suggests that some feminist theologies still carry Enlightenment assumptions.

98. De Beauvoir, *The Second Sex*, xxxiii and xxxiv.

99. Ibid., xxxiv.

100. Ibid., 813.

101. Ibid., 56.

102. Ibid., 755.

103. See, for example, Iris Young, *Justice and the Politics of Difference* (Princeton, NJ: Princeton University Press, 1990); Jane Flax, "Postmodernism and Gender Relations in Feminist Theory," *Signs* 12 (Summer 1987), 621–43; and Carole Pateman, *The Sexual Contract* (Stanford: Stanford, CA: Stanford University Press, 1988). Postmodern feminist theologians such as Sharon Welch and Sheila Davaney address similar issues.

104. Keller, *From a Broken Web*, 18.

105. See, for example, Susan Bordo, "Feminism, Postmodernism, and Gender Skepticism," in *Feminism/Postmodernism*, Linda J. Nicholson, ed. (New York: Routledge, 1990), 133–56; Sandra Harding, *The Science Question in Feminism* (Ithaca, NY: Cornell University Press, 1986); and Mary E. Hawkesworth, *Beyond Oppression: Feminist Theory and Political Strategy* (New York: Continuum, 1990). My own argument expresses similar concerns.

106. See, for example, Anne Carr, *Transforming Grace*; Elizabeth Johnson, *She Who Is: The Mystery of God in Feminist Theological Discourse* (New York: Crossroad, 1992); and Mercy Amba Oduyoye, *Hearing and Knowing: Theological Reflections on Christianity in Africa* (Maryknoll, NY: Orbis Press, 1986).

107. Carr, *Transforming Grace*, 138.

108. Ibid., 134.

109. Ibid.

110. Johnson, *She Who Is*, 104.

111. Ibid., 111.

112. Oduyoye, *Hearing and Knowing*, chapters 6 and 7.

113. Jantzen, *God's World, God's Body*.

114. Ibid., 129.

115. This analogy from the human experience of self-transcendence is certainly not new to theology. Jantzen notes similar analogies in the work of Karl Rahner and J. R. Illingsworth. And, of course, Reinhold Niebuhr also draws his model of divine transcendence from the human experience of self-transcendence or freedom.

116. Jantzen, *God's World, God's Body*, 125.

117. Ibid.

118. Ibid., 128.

119. Ibid.

120. Ibid., 128–29.

121. Ibid., 156.

122. Ibid., 150.

123. Ibid.

124. Ibid., 149–50.

125. Plaskow, *Standing Again at Sinai*. See particularly chapters 3 and 4.

126. Ibid., 128ff.

127. Ibid., 130–34.

128. Ibid., 132.

129. Ibid., 167.

130. Ibid.

131. Ibid.

132. Ibid., 144.

133. Ibid., 151.

134. Ibid.

135. Ibid., 134–35.

136. For a review of this debate, see Edward Farley, *The Transcendence of God* (Philadelphia: Westminster Press, 1960); Stanley Grenz and Roger Olson, *Twentieth Century Theology: God and the World in a Transitional Age* (Downers Grove, IL: InterVarsity Press, 1992); and A. C. McGiffert, "Immanence," *Encyclopedia of Religion and Ethics*, vol. 8 (New York: Charles Scribner's Sons, n. d.).

137. Ruether notes this dependency on Teilhard de Chardin. See, for example, *Gaia and God*, 240–45.

138. See, for example, Davaney, *Feminism and Process Thought: The Harvard Divinity School/Claremont Center for Process Studies Symposium Papers* (New York: Edwin Mellen Press, 1981); Marjorie Suchocki, "Weaving the World: Feminism and Process Thought," *Process Studies* 14 (Summer 1985): 76–86; and Brock, *Journeys by Heart*.

139. See Mark C. Taylor, *Erring: A Postmodern A/Theology* (Chicago: University of Chicago Press, 1984).

140. Keller, *From a Broken Web*, 42. See also Vaughan, *Sociality, Ethics and Social Change*.

Chapter 2

1. In an informal survey of feminist works, I found that he is more frequently criticized than any other twentieth century scholar of religion. Criticisms of Niebuhr can be found in many feminist works, including the following: Judith Plaskow, *Sex, Sin, and Grace*; Judith Vaughan, *Sociality, Ethics and Social Change*; Daphne Hampson, *Theology and Feminism*; Susan Dunfee, *Christianity and the Liberation of Women*; Valerie Saiving, "The Human Situation: A Feminine View," 108–10; Ruth L. Smith, *The Individual and Society in Reinhold Niebuhr and Karl Marx* (Ph.D. Dissertation, Boston University, 1982) and "Feminism and

the Moral Subject," *Women's Consciousness, Women's Conscience,* Barbara Hilkert Andolsen, Christine E. Gudorf, and Mary D. Pellauer, eds. (Minneapolis: Winston Press, 1985), 235–50; Daphne Hampson, "Reinhold Niebuhr on Sin: A Critique," *Reinhold Niebuhr and the Issues of Our Time,* Richard Harries, ed. (Grand Rapids, MI: Eerdmans, 1986), 46–60; Beverly Wildung Harrison, *Making the Connections,* 27–28 and 56–67; Sheila Collins, *A Different Heaven and Earth,* 154–60; Rosemary Radford Ruether, *New Woman/New Earth,* 199–200; Grace D. Cumming Long, *Passion and Reason,* 15–17; Mary Stewart Van Leeuwen et al., *After Eden: Facing the Challenge of Gender Reconciliation* (Grand Rapids, MI: Eerdman's, 1993), 409–14; and Barbara Hilkert Andolsen, "Agape in Feminist Ethics," *Journal of Religious Ethics* 9 (Spring 1981): 69–83. Not all feminist readings of Niebuhr are simply dismissive. Both Beverly Harrison and Rosemary Ruether find positive features in his arguments. See Rosemary Ruether, *The Radical Kingdom,* 119–30; and Beverly Harrison, *Making the Connections,* 27–28 and 58–67.

2. Keller, *From a Broken Web,* 40.
3. Vaughan, *Sociality, Ethics and Social Change,* 194.
4. Collins, *A Different Heaven and Earth,* 157.
5. Ibid.
6. Ibid.
7. Keller, *From A Broken Web,* 40.
8. Harrison, *Making the Connections,* 28, emphasis mine.
9. Ibid.

10. To my knowledge, this is the first full examination of and response to some of the feminist charges of overt sexism in Niebuhr's account of gender roles and family life. Though I do agree with some of the charges, they represent, in part, a misreading or caricature of Niebuhr.

11. See Vaughan, *Sociality, Ethics and Social Change;* Smith, *The Individual and Society;* Keller, *From A Broken Web;* Hampson, "Reinhold Niebuhr on Sin: A Critique;" and *Theology and Feminism.*

12. As we saw in chapter 1, this argument is common among feminists. See, for example, Keller, *From A Broken Web;* Ruether, *Sexism and God-Talk;* and Collins, *Different Heaven and Earth.*

13. See, for example, Hampson, *Theology and Feminism;* and Vaughan, *Sociality, Ethics and Social Change.* Even Welch, a self-professed antiessentialist, seems to suggest that humans are essentially relational.

14. Smith, *The Individual and Society in Reinhold Niebuhr and Karl Marx,* v.
15. Ibid., vi.
16. Ibid., 248. Actually, Niebuhr insists on the unity of the self.
17. Vaughan, *Sociality, Ethics and Social Change,* 38. See also 21–27, 38–40, and 187–89.
18. Ibid., 190.
19. Ibid., 160ff.
20. Ibid., 187–98.
21. Ibid., 194.
22. Hampson, *Theology and Feminism,* 123–24.
23. Ibid., 122.
24. Ibid., 124.
25. Keller, *From A Broken Web,* 42.
26. Ibid.
27. Ibid.
28. Ibid., 42–43.
29. Ibid., 43–44.

30. Ibid., 44.
31. Ibid. Rosemary Ruether, Sheila Collins, and Grace Long offer similar arguments.
32. See, for example, Reinhold Niebuhr, *Man's Nature and His Communities: Essays on the Dynamics and Enigmas of Man's Personal and Social Existence* (New York: Charles Scribner's Sons, 1965); and *The Self and the Dramas of History* (New York: Charles Scribner's Sons, 1955).
33. Smith, *The Individual and Society in Reinhold Niebuhr and Karl Marx*, v.
34. These insights will be developed more fully in chapter 5.
35. Gilligan, *In a Different Voice*.
36. See Hampson, *Theology and Feminism*; Saiving, "The Human Situation"; Judith Plaskow, *Sex, Sin, and Grace*; Vaughan, *Sociality, Ethics and Social Change*; and Susan Dunfee, *Christianity and the Liberation of Women*.
37. Keller, *From A Broken Web*, 40.
38. Niebuhr's understanding of sin will be examined more fully in the next chapter.
39. Hampson, *Theology and Feminism*, 121.
40. Plaskow, *Sex, Sin, and Grace*, 3.
41. Dunfee, *Christianity and the Liberation of Women*.
42. Plaskow, *Sex, Sin, and Grace*, 62–63 and 69. See Reinhold Niebuhr, *The Nature and Destiny of Man: A Christian Interpretation*, vol. 1, *Human Nature* (New York: Charles Scribner's Sons, 1941).
43. We will examine Niebuhr's understanding of sensuality and other aspects of sin more fully in chapter 3.
44. As we will see in chapter 3, Niebuhr expresses ambivalence about this traditional formulation.
45. Plaskow, *Sex, Sin, and Grace*, 63 and 67–68.
46. Ibid., 69.
47. Ibid.
48. Carr, *Transforming Grace*, 211. Carr is examining feminist arguments about salvation.
49. Lovin, *Reinhold Niebuhr and Christian Realism*, 147–49.
50. This argument will be examined more fully later.
51. This point will be made more fully in chapter 3.
52. See Harrison, *Making the Connections*; Collins, *A Different Heaven and Earth*; and Ruether, *Radical Kingdom*.
53. Ibid.
54. Collins, *A Different Heaven and Earth*, 157–58.
55. Harrison, *Making the Connections*, 63.
56. Ibid., 59 and 63.
57. Ibid., 59.
58. Collins, *A Different Heaven and Earth*.
59. See Collins and Ruether.
60. Harrison, *Making the Connections*, 27.
61. Ibid.
62. Ibid., 28.
63. Ibid., 27–28.
64. Rosemary Ruether, *New Woman/New Earth*, 199–200.
65. Ibid., 199.
66. Ibid.
67. Ibid.
68. Ibid.

69. Ibid.
70. Ibid., 199–200; and Collins, *A Different Heaven and Earth*.
71. Ruether, *New Woman/New Earth*, 200.
72. Collins, *A Different Heaven and Earth*, 157–60.
73. Ibid., 158.
74. Ibid., 158–59.
75. Ibid., 159.
76. Ibid.
77. Ibid.
78. Ibid., 159–60.
79. Hampson, *Theology and Feminism*, 126.
80. Ibid.
81. Ibid.
82. Ibid.
83. For example, this is a reoccurring theme in Fyodor Dostoevsky, *The Brothers Karamazov* (Chicago: Encyclopaedia Britannica, 1952).
84. Niebuhr's understanding of morality in the public realm will be examined more fully later.
85. Niebuhr often speaks of the injustices and distortions of the family and the demand for justice within it. See, for example, *Moral Man and Immoral Society: A Study in Ethics and Politics* (New York: Charles Scribner's Sons, 1932), 46; *The Self and the Dramas of History*, 191-92 and 234; *Love and Justice*, D. B. Robertson, ed. (Cleveland, OH: Meridian Books, 1967), 26 and 90; *Christianity and Power Politics* (New York: Charles Scribner's Sons, 1940), 27; *The Nature and Destiny of Man*, vol. 1, 282ff.; and *Man's Nature and His Communities*, 32ff.
86. Niebuhr, *The Self and the Dramas of History*, 191.
87. Niebuhr, *Moral Man and Immoral Society*, 46–47.
88. Ibid.
89. See, for example, Niebuhr, *Love and Justice*, 26; and *The Self and the Dramas of History*, 234.
90. Niebuhr, *Christianity and Power Politics*, 27, emphasis mine.
91. Niebuhr, *The Self and the Dramas of History*, 234.
92. Ibid., 191.
93. Niebuhr, *The Nature and Destiny of Man: A Christian Interpretation*, vol. 2, *Human Destiny* (New York: Charles Scribner's Sons, 1943), 124.
94. Niebuhr, *Moral Man and Immoral Society*, 46.
95. Niebuhr, *The Self and the Dramas of History*, 192. See also *Moral Man and Immoral Society*, 46; and *Love and Justice*, 26.
96. Niebuhr, *Christianity and Power Politics*, 27.
97. Niebuhr, *Moral Man and Immoral Society*, 46–47.
98. Niebuhr, *The Nature and Destiny of Man*, vol. 1, 282ff.
99. Niebuhr, *Essays in Applied Christianity*, ed. D. B. Robertson (New York: Meridian Books, 1959), 179ff.
100. Niebuhr, *The Structure of Nations and Empires: A Study of the Recurring Patterns and Problems of the Political Order in Relation to the Unique Problems of the Nuclear Age* (New York: Charles Scribner's Sons, 1959), 40ff.; and *Man's Nature and His Communities*, 34ff.
101. Niebuhr, *The Nature and Destiny of Man*, vol. 1, 282.
102. Niebuhr, *Moral Man and Immoral Society*, 266.
103. This argument was first published in an article pulled from this chapter. See my

"Freeing Bonds and Binding Freedom: Reinhold Niebuhr and Feminist Critics on Paternal Authority and Maternal Constraint," *The Annual of the Society of Christian Ethics* (1996): 121–43.

104. Vaughan, *Sociality, Ethics and Social Change*, 115.

105. Niebuhr's reflections on gender roles in the family are found throughout his work. See, for example, Reinhold Niebuhr, *Christianity and Power Politics*, 62-63 and 27; *Essays in Applied Christianity*, 93–94 and 179–82; *Faith and History: A Comparison of Christian and Modern Views of History* (New York: Charles Scribner's Sons, 1949), 80–85; *An Interpretation of Christian Ethics* (New York: Meridian Books, 1956), 132–39; *Man's Nature and His Communities*, 30–35 and 46–47; *The Nature and Destiny of Man*, vol. 1, 280–83; vol. 2, 197–98; *Reflections on the End of an Era* (New York: Charles Scribner's Sons, 1934), 89–90; *The Structure of Nations and Empires*, 33–41; "Sex Standards in America," *Christianity and Crisis* 8 (May 24, 1948): 65–66; "Sex and Religion in the Kinsey Report," *Christianity and Crisis* 13 (November 2, 1953): 138–41; "More on Kinsey," *Christianity and Crisis* 13 (January 11, 1953): 182–83; "Christian Attitudes toward Sex and Family," *Christianity and Crisis* 24 (April 27, 1964): 73–80; and "The Problem of Justice and the Power of Love," *United Church Herald* 2 (January 1, 1959): 13. For a personal look at family and gender roles in Niebuhr's own life, see Ursula M. Niebuhr, *Remembering Reinhold Niebuhr: Letters of Reinhold and Ursula Niebuhr* (New York: HarperCollins Publishers, 1991); and Richard Fox, *Reinhold Niebuhr: A Biography* (New York: Pantheon Books, 1985).

106. Vaughan, *Sociality, Ethics and Social Change*, 115. See also Keller, *From a Broken Web*, 41; and Hampson, *Theology and Feminism*, 126.

107. Vaughan, *Sociality, Ethics and Social Change*, 115.

108. Vaughan draws from Niebuhr's *Structure of Nations and Empires*, 40 and 33. Vaughan, *Sociality, Ethics and Social Change*, 116.

109. For Niebuhr's arguments about paternal authority see *The Nature and Destiny of Man*, vol. 1, 280–83; *The Structure of Nations and Empires*, 33–41; *Man's Nature and His Communities*, 30–35 and 46–47; and "More on Kinsey,"182–83. For related arguments about male authority, see *Christianity and Power Politics*, 27; and *Essays in Applied Christianity*, 179–82.

110. See especially Niebuhr's *Structure of Nations and Empires*, 33–41; and *Man's Nature and His Communities*, 30–35 and 46–47.

111. Niebuhr, *Structure of Nations and Empires*, 40.

112. Ibid.

113. Ibid. (emphasis mine).

114. Niebuhr, *Man's Nature and His Communities*, 34.

115. Niebuhr, *The Nature and Destiny of Man*, vol. 1, 282.

116. Niebuhr emphasizes the injustices of the family throughout his work. See, for example, Niebuhr, *Moral Man and Immoral Society*, 46–47; *The Self and the Dramas of History*, 191–92 and 234; *Christianity and Power Politics*, 27; *The Nature and Destiny of Man*, vol. 1, 109 and 282, and vol. 2, 124; *Man's Nature and His Communities*, 32–35; and *An Interpretation of Christian Ethics*, 132–39 and 194; *Love and Justice*, 26 and 90; and *Justice and Mercy* (New York: Harper and Row, 1974), 59.

117. Niebuhr, *Moral Man and Immoral Society*, 46–47. It is surprising that Niebuhr's *Moral Man and Immoral Society* contains such strong allegations of male injustice in the family. This book supposedly depicts Niebuhr at his most romantic about intimate relationships and the family. Indeed, his wife, Ursula, commenting on *Moral Man*, teased him over his "sentimentality about the family." See Ursula M. Niebuhr, *Remembering Reinhold Niebuhr*, 415. Of course, it is not so unusual that he *would* be at his most romantic and sen-

timental about intimate relationships in a book conceived during their engagement and written in their first year of marriage. Yet even here, at his most romantic, he is slamming the "tyranny" and "autocracy" of males in the family.

118. See *The Self and the Dramas of History*, 192; *Love and Justice*, 26; *Moral Man and Immoral Society*, 46–47; and *Christianity and Power Politics*, 27.

119. Niebuhr, *The Self and the Dramas of History*, 190–91 and 234; and *Love and Justice*, 26.

120. Niebuhr, *Christianity and Power Politics*, 27, emphasis mine.

121. Niebuhr, *The Self and the Dramas of History*, 234.

122. For years Niebuhr and his wife called for churches to grant women full rights and participation, including ordination. Letters between Ursula and Reinhold Niebuhr provide an interesting commentary on the international struggle for ordination. In 1944, the bishop of Hong Kong, R. O. Hall, wrote to the Niebuhrs after he had ordained a deaconess to the priesthood. Acknowledging their influence, he noted, "I want you to know that you had a share in this, perhaps also a share in your prayers." Ursula M. Niebuhr, *Remembering Reinhold Niebuhr*, 192.

123. Niebuhr, *Essays in Applied Christianity*, 93–94.

124. Ibid., 93.

125. Niebuhr, *The Nature and Destiny of Man*, vol. 2, 85.

126. Niebuhr, *Essays in Applied Christianity*, 179–82.

127. Ibid., 179.

128. See Niebuhr, *The Nature and Destiny of Man*, vol. 1, 280–83; *Man's Nature and His Communities*, 33; "Sex and Religion in the Kinsey Report," 138–41; "More on Kinsey," 183; and "Christian Attitudes toward Sex and Family," 73–80.

129. Niebuhr, *Man's Nature and His Communities*, 33. Though Niebuhr doubts that monogamy is "natural" for men, he insists that it is a universal, "permanent norm" known and "maintained" by the "cumulative experience" of the human race. See Niebuhr, *The Nature and Destiny of Man*, vol. 1, 282–83. Here, then, we have a universal norm that is contrary to nature; it is freedom's improvement on nature.

130. Niebuhr, "More on Kinsey," 183. For Niebuhr's personal reflections on marriage as mutual partnership, see his letters to his fiancée soon before their marriage. Ursula M. Niebuhr, *Remembering Reinhold Niebuhr*. For a less sympathetic interpretation of their marriage as a mutual partnership, see Richard Fox, *Reinhold Niebuhr*, 206.

131. For Niebuhr's reflections on motherhood and the limitations it places on women, see *The Nature and Destiny of Man*, vol. 1, 280–83; *Christianity and Power Politics*, 62–63; *Faith and History*, 85; *An Interpretation of Christian Ethics*, 139; "Sex and Religion in the Kinsey Report," 138–41; and "Christian Attitudes toward Sex and Family," 73–80.

132. I focus here on the arguments of Vaughan, Hampson, and Keller.

133. Vaughan, *Sociality, Ethics and Social Change*, 115, emphasis mine. These are Vaughan's words, not Niebuhr's.

134. Hampson, *Theology and Feminism*, 126.

135. Keller, *From A Broken Web*, 41, emphasis mine. These are Keller's words, not Niebuhr's.

136. Ibid.

137. Niebuhr, *The Nature and Destiny of Man*, vol.1, 282.

138. Niebuhr criticizes, for example, those feminists who do not recognize the "facts" of sex differentiation: "A rationalistic feminism is undoubtedly inclined to transgress inexorable bounds set by nature." Niebuhr, *The Nature and Destiny of Man*, vol. 1, 282. For similar comments on "utopian" or "rationalistic" feminism, see Niebuhr, *Reflections*, 90; *Christianity and Power Politics*, 62–63; and *Faith and History*, 85.

139. Niebuhr, *An Interpretation of Christian Ethics*, 132-39; *Christianity and Power Politics*, 62-63; *Reflections*, 89-90; and *Faith and History*, 85.

140. Niebuhr, *An Interpretation of Christian Ethics*, 135, emphasis mine.

141. Vaughan, *Sociality, Ethics and Social Change*, 115.

142. Niebuhr, *Faith and History*, 85. See also Niebuhr, "More on Kinsey," 183.

143. Niebuhr, *Faith and History*, 85. These issues are reflected in Niebuhr's own life. He and his wife, Ursula, were facing decisions about having children and pursuing careers. In a letter from May 1936, Reinhold Niebuhr wrote enthusiastically about a possible job offer she was considering at Sarah Lawrence College. The letter shows that they were weighing the timing of the job with their plans for a second child. See Fox, *Reinhold Niebuhr*, 105. Ursula Niebuhr did not take a teaching position until 1940, when she joined the faculty at Barnard College. They continued to struggle with the tension between her vocations as teacher and mother. It is not unlikely that their experiences informed his comments about motherhood and vocational decisions.

144. Indeed, some feminists have also reflected on the difference that pregnancy and lactation make for women's lives and theologies. See, for example, Sara Ruddick, *Maternal Thinking*; and Bonnie Miller-McLemore, *Also a Mother*.

145. His specific statements about motherhood may be connected to these events in his own life. The early references to the limitations placed on women by pregnancy were written around the time of his wife's first miscarriage (and subsequent surgery and hospitalization) and then during her pregnancy with their first child, Christopher. See Niebuhr, *An Interpretation of Christian Ethics*, 132–39; and *Reflections*, 89–90. The references noted by Vaughan, Hampson, and Keller are from the first set of Gifford Lectures, which were begun in the summer of 1938, while Ursula Niebuhr was pregnant with their daughter, Elizabeth. See Niebuhr, *The Nature and Destiny of Man*, vol. 1, 280–83. Because she had experienced a second miscarriage and was having trouble with the pregnancy, she was confined to bed. So, while writing the early chapters of the first volume of *The Nature and Destiny of Man*, Reinhold Niebuhr was caring for their son, Christopher, and worrying about his wife. The lectures were completed and delivered during the first months of his daughter's life. It is not unlikely that his wife's experiences were on his mind when he wrote about the physical limitations placed on mothers. Certainly, Niebuhr's letters to his wife and friends express his concern about the difficulties she suffered with the pregnancies and miscarriages. He wrote to a friend that her nausea lasted twenty-four hours a day, adding that "nature is a little too unkind to her." See Fox, *Reinhold Niebuhr*, 186. See also Ursula Niebuhr, *Remembering Reinhold Niebuhr*, 132–42 and 80; and Fox, *Reinhold Niebuhr*, 150–51.

146. Niebuhr, *Faith and History*, 85. See also Niebuhr, "More on Kinsey," 183; and "Christian Attitudes toward Sex and Family," 73-80.

147. Niebuhr, *Faith and History*, 85, emphasis mine. See also Niebuhr, *An Interpretation of Christian Ethics*, 135–39. Ursula Niebuhr makes a similar point, writing that motherhood is "more central, physiologically and vocationally than fatherhood." She also emphasizes the natural givenness of sex differentiation. These comments were "asides" in an article supporting women's ordination. She and her husband took the Christian church to task for its conservatism about women's roles in church and family. See Ursula M. Niebuhr, "Women and the Church and the Fact of Sex," *Christianity and Crisis* 11(August 6, 1951): 106–10.

148. Niebuhr, "Sex and Religion in the Kinsey Report," 138–41. See also "Christian Attitudes toward Sex and Family," 73–80. We see here the romanticizing of the family and the maternal role for which Harrison, Ruether, and others criticize him.

149. Implicit in Niebuhr's comments, some feminist criticisms, and my analysis are

modern, North American notions of family life. The discussion centers around roles of mothers and fathers in nuclear families. The larger role of kinship groups or community in child raising is not addressed. The main point of the paragraph still stands; in most cultures, women bear the primary responsibilities for the care of children.

150. Niebuhr, *The Nature and Destiny of Man*, vol. 1, 282.

151. I intentionally let Niebuhr speak the "self-critical" word here. I hesitate to push the personal criticism of Niebuhr too far because internal psychological motivations are barely known to the actors themselves, much less to observers several generations removed. On the other hand, the criticism is too Niebuhrian to leave out.

152. Implicit in the discussion of maternal vocation are professional, middle-class assumptions. He refers to vocational choices in a way that seems most relevant to professional, white-collar jobs. The discussion also assumes that humans can and do "choose" vocation. He does not address here the fact that these "choices" may be limited by other social realities. For a further exploration of this criticism, see Katie Geneva Cannon, *Black Womanist Ethics*.

153. The rejection or neglect of divine transcendence within feminism undercuts another mechanism to criticize human distortion and domination.

154. Feminism needs a sharpened capacity for criticizing not only patriarchal ideas but also feminist ideas. Though feminists, myself included, have been quick to see male sin and pretense, we have at times been blind to our own sin and pretense. Some womanists and feminists have charged that many middle-class white feminist theologians have been oppressive in their assumption that their own perspective was women's perspective. See, for example, Sheila Davaney, "The Limits of the Appeal to Women's Experience"; Susan Thistlethwaite, *Sex, Race and God*; Jacquelyn Grant, *White Women's Christ and Black Women's Jesus*; and Delores Williams, "The Color of Feminism." Similarly, British feminist Mary Grey is suspicious of the claims of middle-class feminists that women's sin is the loss of self. Given their role in structures that dominate others, Grey suggests that this idea is a pretentious cover for their own complicity in oppression. She asks, "Was it the sin of passivity which was responsible for racism within the feminist movement?" See Mary Grey, *Feminism, Redemption and the Christian Tradition* (Mystic, CT: Twenty-Third Publications, 1990), 23.

155. Though this emphasis is neglected, it is not absent. Niebuhr is more sympathetic to *minimal* claims about the moral implications of our bound natures than some of his interpreters (and even his own rhetoric about natural law) suggest. G. A. Lindbeck claims that "Niebuhr is a natural law thinker despite himself." See Niebuhr, *Love and Justice*, 17. Niebuhr notes, however, that even these minimal natural law claims are "tentative." Ibid., 54.

156. Given feminist criticisms of Niebuhr's model of the self, it is crucial to clarify several points. Niebuhr does *not* propose two selves or a fully divided self. The self is unified but has two essential, distinct elements: boundedness and freedom. He is also not devaluing the bound but insists on its goodness. See, for example, Niebuhr, *The Nature and Destiny of Man*, vol. 1, 12, 13, and 169. In addition, he recognizes and affirms the social nature of human selves. See Niebuhr, *The Self and the Dramas of History*, 34–35; *Man's Nature and His Communities*, 106–9; and *The Children of Light and the Children of Darkness: A Vindication of Democracy and a Critique of Its Traditional Defence* (New York: Charles Scribner's Sons, 1944), 52–56.

157. Niebuhr insists, of course, that agape love is not fully realized, even in intimate relationships. For Niebuhr's account of sacrificial love, see *The Nature and Destiny of Man*, vol. 2, 68–76. For his correlation of sacrificial love and motherhood, see *Love and Justice*, 11; and "Some Things I Have Learned," *Saturday Review* (November 6, 1965): 22.

158. Niebuhr, *The Nature and Destiny of Man*, vol. 2, 67 and 70–76. This point will be explored more fully later.

159. The tension caused by this two-part model of the self is evident in other aspects of Niebuhr's work. He has a hard time accounting for freedom's positive expression and ground, not only in ordinary physical boundedness but also in the self's boundedness to community. Niebuhr's insistence, particularly in his early work, that radical freedom is a capacity of the individual self and his subsequent ambivalence about community is also an example of this tension. The self is free as it transcends the boundedness of community. Niebuhr has a hard time accounting for the possibility of freedom finding its source and end in the bonds of community. Niebuhr's hesitation about ontology can be traced to this same tension in his model of the self. Niebuhr rejects ontologies because freedom always radically transforms nature and any philosophies of nature. Yet what he fails to acknowledge is that his model of the person as radically free is itself an ontology. Niebuhr's most interesting reflections on ontology emerge from discussions with Paul Tillich. See, for example, Charles W. Kegley, ed., *The Theology of Paul Tillich*, (New York: Macmillan, 1956), 338–39 and 217–27; Charles W. Kegley and Robert W. Bretall, eds., *Reinhold Niebuhr: His Religious, Social and Political Thought* (New York: Macmillan, 1956), 36–43 and 432–33; and Harold Landon, *Reinhold Niebuhr: A Prophetic Voice in Our Time* (Greenwich, CT: Seabury Press, 1962), 29–54 and 120.

Chapter 3

1. Harrison, *Making the Connections*, 29; Collins, *A Different Heaven and Earth*, 157; and Vaughan, *Sociality, Ethics, and Social Change*, 194.

2. The critical tension between boundedness and freedom is reiterated again and again. See, for example, Niebuhr, *The Nature and Destiny of Man*, vol. 1, 12–13, 150, and 270, and vol. 2, vii and 1; *Structure of Nations and Empires*, 287; *Christian Realism and Political Problems*, 6; *The Children of Light and the Children of Darkness*, 13 and 14; and *Man's Nature and His Communities*, 30–31 and 83.

3. In spite of Niebuhr's criticism of ontological claims about human life, he refers to boundedness and freedom as a part of the human self's "essential nature." *The Nature and Destiny of Man*, vol. 1, 270.

4. Niebuhr, *The Children of Light and the Children of Darkness*, 3–4.

5. Neibuhr, *The Nature and Destiny of Man*, vol. 1, 146 and 163, and vol. 2, 40.

6. Niebuhr, *The Nature and Destiny of Man*, vol. 1, 271.

7. Ibid., 125.

8. See, for example, Niebuhr, *The Nature and Destiny of Man*, vol. 2, 66–67; and *The Self and the Dramas of History*, 64–72. As we will see later, Niebuhr is not using the language of divine personality or freedom literally. Myths speak to truths of human life in ways that do not deny the tensions and paradoxes of human life but point beyond them. References to divine personality and freedom will be examined more fully later.

9. Niebuhr, *Beyond Tragedy: Essays on the Christian Interpretation of Nature* (New York: Charles Scribner's Sons, 1937), 6.

10. Ibid., 4.

11. Niebuhr, *The Self and the Dramas of History*, 97.

12. Niebuhr, *An Interpretation of Christian Ethics*, 14 and 18.

13. Ibid., 19.

14. See Niebuhr, *Love and Justice*, 49ff.; *The Children of Light and the Children of Darkness*; and *An Interpretation of Christian Ethics*, 13ff.

15. See, for example, Niebuhr, *Love and Justice*, 49ff.
16. Niebuhr, *Faith and History*, 116.
17. Ibid., 30.
18. Kegley and Bretall, *Reinhold Niebuhr*, 36.
19. James Gustafson, "Theology in the Service of Ethics: An Interpretation of Reinhold Niebuhr's Theological Ethic," *Reinhold Niebuhr and the Issues of Our Time*, Richard Harries, ed. (Grand Rapids, MI: Eerdman's, 1986), 30.
20. See Kegley, *The Theology of Paul Tillich*. The point here is not whether Niebuhr is right or wrong about this claim or whether he does or does not have an ontology. The point is that his emphasis on freedom influences the structure of his ethical system.
21. Kegley and Bretall, *Reinhold Niebuhr*, 433.
22. Landon, *Reinhold Niebuhr*, 36. The discussion between Tillich and Niebuhr is found in several exchanges. See Kegley, *The Theology of Paul Tillich*, 338–39 and 217–27; Kegley and Bretall, *Reinhold Niebuhr*, 36–43 and 432–33; and Landon, *Reinhold Niebuhr*, 29–54 and 120.
23. Landon, *Reinhold Niebuhr*, 38–39; and Kegley and Bretall, *Reinhold Niebuhr*, 41.
24. Landon, *Reinhold Niebuhr*, 36. Tillich uses similar language when he claims that "in speaking of 'the self,' [Niebuhr] ontologizes against his will." Kegley and Bretall, *Reinhold Niebuhr*, 41.
25. See, for example, Gustafson, "Theology in the Service of Ethics," 39–40.
26. Ibid., 44.
27. Niebuhr, *The Nature and Destiny of Man*, vol. 1, 270.
28. See Kegley, *The Theology of Paul Tillich*, 216. Other descriptions of this two-part human nature are found throughout his work. See, for example, Niebuhr, *The Nature and Destiny of Man*, vol. 1, 1, 3, and 270.
29. Niebuhr, *The Nature and Destiny of Man*, vol. 1, 155. Niebuhr also relates self-transcendence to memory in *The Self and the Dramas of History*, 23.
30. Niebuhr, *The Self and the Dramas of History*, 12.
31. Ibid.
32. Ibid., 13.
33. Ibid., 16–17.
34. Ibid., 18.
35. Ibid., 23–25 and 12–19.
36. Niebuhr, *The Nature and Destiny of Man*, vol. 1, 2, 3, 13, and 125; and *Christian Realism and Political Problems*, 6. See also *The Self and the Dramas of History*, 23–25, where Niebuhr discusses the self's relation to space and time.
37. Niebuhr, *The Self and the Dramas of History*, 13 and 20.
38. The self's dialogues form the structure of Niebuhr's *Self and the Dramas of History*. The self's internal dialogues are the subject of the earlier chapters. See *The Self and the Dramas of History*, 4 and 6–22.
39. This argument runs throughout his work. See, for example, *The Nature and Destiny of Man*, vol. 1, 1 and 4; and *The Self and the Dramas of History*, 3, 4, and 61.
40. Niebuhr, *The Nature and Destiny of Man*, vol. 1, 1. Note the contrast between these statements and Ruth Smith's claims about Niebuhr discussed in chapter 2.
41. See Kegley, *The Theology of Paul Tillich*, 217.
42. In later descriptions of self-transcendence, Niebuhr includes reason as one aspect of the transcendent self.
43. Niebuhr, *The Nature and Destiny of Man*, vol. 1, 72.
44. Ibid., 2.

45. Niebuhr's unwillingness to associate self-transcendence with mind or reason stands in contrast to some feminist criticisms. As we saw in chapter 2, Ruth Smith claims that Niebuhr equates self-transcendence with reason.

46. Niebuhr, *The Nature and Destiny of Man*, vol. 2, 214.

47. Niebuhr, *Beyond Tragedy*, 28–29.

48. Ibid., 26–46.

49. We will examine the requirements of freedom later.

50. See Robert McAfee Brown, ed., *The Essential Reinhold Niebuhr: Selected Essays and Addresses* (New Haven: Yale University Press, 1986), 49ff.

51. Niebuhr, *Man's Nature and His Communities*, 30.

52. Niebuhr, *The Nature and Destiny of Man*, vol. 1, 68–69.

53. Niebuhr writes of freedom as the basis for history and transformation of context on many occasions. See, for example, *Man's Nature and His Communities*, 30ff.; *The Nature and Destiny of Man*, vol. 1, 40, 55 and 68-69; and *The Children of Light and the Children of Darkness*, 3.

54. Niebuhr, *Faith and History; The Self and the Dramas of History*, 23–41; *The Nature and Destiny of Man*, vol. 1, 4 and 5; and Kegley and Bretall, *Reinhold Neibuhr*, 10.

55. Niebuhr, *The Nature and Destiny of Man*, vol. 1, 270.

56. Niebuhr, *The Self and the Dramas of History*, 34–40.

57. These criticisms were explored in chapter 2.

58. Niebuhr, *Moral Man and Immoral Society*, 9.

59. This is especially evident in his later work. See *Man's Nature and His Communities* and *The Self and the Dramas of History*. Niebuhr (*Man's Nature and His Communities*, 22) notes that he should have entitled *Moral Man and Immoral Society* as "The Not So Moral Man in His Less Moral Communities."

60. Niebuhr, *The Children of Light and the Children of Darkness*, 52–56; *The Self and the Dramas of History*, 34–35; and *Man's Nature and His Communities*, 106–9.

61. Niebuhr, *Justice and Mercy*, 24–25 and 46–47.

62. Niebuhr, *The Children of Light and the Children of Darkness*, 52–56.

63. Niebuhr, *The Self and the Dramas of History*, 15.

64. Niebuhr, *The Children of Light and the Children of Darkness*, 53. See also *The Self and the Dramas of History*, 34.

65. Niebuhr emphasizes the social nature of human life throughout his work. See, for example, *The Self and the Dramas of History*, 34ff.

66. Niebuhr, *Moral Man and Immoral Society*, 2.

67. Niebuhr, *The Self and the Dramas of History*, 34.

68. Ibid.

69. Ibid., 4–5. See also *The Children of Light and the Children of Darkness*.

70. Niebuhr, *Man's Nature and His Communities*, 109.

71. Ibid., 107. Note that Niebuhr says "mothering one" instead of "mother." Niebuhr recognized that a child could have a primary caretaker who is not the biological mother.

72. Ibid., 108.

73. Ibid.

74. Ibid., 107–8.

75. Ibid., 108–9.

76. Hampson, *Theology and Feminism*, 124–25; Keller, *From a Broken Web*, 42; and Vaughan, *Sociality, Ethics and Social Change*.

77. See, for example, Ruether, *The Radical Kingdom*; and Collins, *A Different Heaven and Earth*.

78. Niebuhr continued to insist on the limitations of community: *The Self and the Dramas of History*, 37.
79. See Niebuhr, *The Self and the Dramas of History*; and *Man's Nature and His Communities*.
80. Niebuhr, *The Self and the Dramas of History*, 26.
81. Niebuhr, *The Nature and Destiny of Man*, vol. 1, 12, 4, and 5; and *The Self and the Dramas of History*, 26.
82. Niebuhr, *The Nature and Destiny of Man*, vol. 1, 7.
83. Ibid.
84. Ibid., 12, 13, and 169.
85. Niebuhr, *Faith and History*, 53.
86. Niebuhr, *The Nature and Destiny of Man*, vol. 1, 167.
87. Ibid., 19.
88. Plaskow, *Sex, Sin and Grace*, 69.
89. Niebuhr, *The Nature and Destiny of Man*, vol. 1, 150 and 167.
90. Ibid., 167.
91. Ibid., 3, emphasis mine.
92. Ibid., 14.
93. Ibid., 124–25.
94. See previously.
95. Robert McAfee Brown has also noticed this theme in Niebuhr's prayers. See Brown, *The Essential Reinhold Niebuhr*, xix.
96. Niebuhr, *Justice and Mercy*. See, for example, 10, 23, 24, 26, 47, 49, 75, and 119.
97. Ibid., 119.
98. Ibid., 23.
99. Ibid., 26.
100. Niebuhr, *The Nature and Destiny of Man*, vol. 1, 270 and 280.
101. Ibid., 271.
102. Ibid., 270–72.
103. Ibid., 281.
104. This is one of Niebuhr's favorite examples of the limits of the natural law. Consequently, it reappears throughout his work. See, for example, *The Nature and Destiny of Man*, vol. 1, 282–83; *Man's Nature and His Communities*, 34ff.; and *Structure of Nations and Empires*, 33–41. See chapter 2 for further citations.
105. Niebuhr, *The Nature and Destiny of Man*, vol. 1, 282.
106. Ibid., 270ff.
107. As Niebuhr himself notes, "We may call this natural law. But we had better realize how tentative it is" (*Love and Justice*, 54). In addition, G. A. Lindbeck claims that "Niebuhr is a natural law thinker despite himself" (quoted in *Love and Justice*, 17).
108. Niebuhr, *The Nature and Destiny of Man*, vol. 1, 280.
109. Niebuhr, *Love and Justice*, 46–54.
110. Ibid., 50.
111. Niebuhr, *The Nature and Destiny of Man*, vol. 1, 270.
112. Niebuhr, *Christianity and Power Politics*, 197.
113. Ibid.
114. Niebuhr, *The Nature and Destiny of Man*, vol. 1, 163.
115. Ibid., 122.
116. Ibid., 146 and 163; *The Nature and Destiny of Man*, vol. 2, 40.
117. Niebuhr, *The Nature and Destiny of Man*, vol. 1, 146.

118. Ibid., 13 and 15.
119. Ibid., 125.
120. Niebuhr's discussions of the human search for meaning beyond its finite world are found throughout his work. See *The Nature and Destiny of Man*, vol. 2, 63; *The Self and the Dramas of History*, 61ff.; *The Nature and Destiny of Man*, vol. 1, 164; and *Christianity and Power Politics*, chapter 2.
121. Niebuhr, *Christian Realism and Political Problems*, 178.
122. Niebuhr, *The Self and the Dramas of History*, 61.
123. See previously. Also, *The Self and the Dramas of History*, 5; and *The Nature and Destiny of Man*, vol. 2, 63.
124. Niebuhr, *The Nature and Destiny of Man*, vol. 1, 271.
125. Ibid., 289.
126. Ibid., 271.
127. Ibid., 289.
128. Ibid., 271.
129. Ibid., 272.
130. Ibid.
131. Ibid., 293–94.
132. The difficulty of the language of Fall and "original righteousness" is that it suggests the classical chronological understanding of Creation and Fall that Niebuhr does not accept. The Creation and Fall myth speaks of the human condition over time and in each moment.
133. Niebuhr, *The Nature and Destiny of Man*, vol. 1, 127.
134. Ibid., 136. Note that Niebuhr does not suggest that special revelation actually reveals true knowledge of God's nature that humans can then know with certainty. Instead, it is the historical record of discernment.
135. Niebuhr, *The Nature and Destiny of Man*, vol. 1, 127 and 131.
136. Ibid., 131.
137. Ibid.
138. Ibid., 133.
139. Ibid., 132.
140. Ibid., 133–34.
141. Ibid., 136.
142. Ibid., 137.
143. Ibid., 142.
144. Ibid.
145. Niebuhr, *The Self and the Dramas of History*, 66. See also *The Nature and Destiny of Man*, vol. 1, 136.
146. Niebuhr, *The Nature and Destiny of Man*, vol. 2, 64–65.
147. Ibid., 65–66.
148. Niebuhr's focus on "personality" as a way to talk about divine freedom and transcendence is evident in works as early as *Does Civilization Need Religion? A Study in the Social Resources and Limitations of Religion in Modern Life* (New York: Macmillan Company, 1941) and even his Yale B.D. thesis. Richard Fox suggests that this emphasis came from Niebuhr's teacher, D. C. MacIntosh. See Richard Fox, *Reinhold Niebuhr: A Biography*, 29–33. Though Niebuhr rejected many assumptions of personalism, the similarity between Niebuhr's use of these themes and that of the personalists is striking.
149. References to the metaphor of divine personality are found throughout Niebuhr's later work as well. See, for example, *The Self and the Dramas of History*, 64–72; *The Nature and Destiny of Man*, vol. 2, 64–67; Charles Brown, ed., *A Reinhold Niebuhr Reader: Selected*

Essays, Articles, and Book Reviews (Philadelphia: Trinity Press International, 1992), 16–17; Kegley and Bretall, *Reinhold Niebuhr* 10, 19, 442–43, and 448; and Kegley, *The Theology of Paul Tillich*, 216–17.

150. Niebuhr, *The Self and the Dramas of History*, 64.

151. In addition to the previous citations, Niebuhr often writes of transcendence through the metaphor of human freedom without using the words *person* or *personality*. See, for example, *Reflections on the End of an Era*, 200–201; and *The Nature and Destiny of Man*, vol. 1, 133.

152. Others have noted Niebuhr's use of personhood to talk about God, particularly about divine immanence and transcendence or freedom. See, for example, Farley, *The Transcendence of God*, 43ff.; and Hans Hofmann, *The Theology of Reinhold Niebuhr* (New York: Charles Scribner's and Sons, 1956), 18–20 and 22. The exchange between Tillich and Niebuhr in the Kegley and Bretall volumes also relates to these issues of freedom, personhood, and God. See Paul Tillich "Reinhold Niebuhr's Doctrine of Knowledge," in *Reinhold Niebuhr*, ed. Kegley and Bretall, particularly 39–42. See also Niebuhr's "Reply to Interpretation and Criticism," in *Reinhold Niebuhr*, ed. Kegley and Bretall, especially 432–33.

153. Niebuhr, *The Self and the Dramas of History*, 71.

154. See, for example, Kegley and Bretall, *Reinhold Niebuhr*, 19; Brown, *A Reinhold Niebuhr Reader* 16–17; and Niebuhr, *The Self and the Dramas of History*, 64ff.

155. Brown, *A Reinhold Niebuhr Reader*, 17.

156. Niebuhr, *Beyond Tragedy*, 3ff.

157. Niebuhr, *The Nature and Destiny of Man*, vol. 2, 66.

158. Ibid., 67.

159. Niebuhr, *The Self and the Dramas of History*, 66 and 71.

160. See the discussion of Ruether, Collins, Long, and Hampson in chapters 1 and 2.

161. Hampson, *Theology and Feminism*, 151.

162. Niebuhr, *The Self and the Dramas of History*.

163. Ibid., 4.

164. Ibid.

165. See Harlan Beckley, *Passion for Justice: Retrieving the Legacies of Walter Rauschenbusch, John A. Ryan, and Reinhold Niebuhr* (Louisville: Westminster/John Knox Press, 1992), 189ff.; and James Gustafson, "Theology in the Service of Ethics," 38.

166. Paul Lehmann, "The Christology of Reinhold Niebuhr," *Reinhold Niebuhr: His Religious, Social and Political Thought*, ed. Kegley and Bretall, 253.

167. Niebuhr, *The Nature and Destiny of Man*, vol. 2, 67.

168. Ibid., 66–67.

169. Ibid., 68.

170. Ibid., 69.

171. Ibid., 247.

172. Ibid., 78.

173. Ibid., 247.

174. Ibid., 69.

175. Ibid.

176. See the discussion of the importance of justice in family life in the last chapter. See also Niebuhr, *Moral Man and Immoral Society*, 46–47; *The Self and the Dramas of History*, 191 and 234; and *Love and Justice*, 26.

177. Niebuhr, *Love and Justice*, 43.

178. Ibid., 25–26.

179. Niebuhr, *Christian Realism and Political Problems*, 119.

180. Niebuhr, *The Nature and Destiny of Man*, vol. 2, 78.

181. Niebuhr, *Love and Justice*, 49.
182. Ibid.
183. Niebuhr, *The Nature and Destiny of Man*, vol. 2, 246.
184. Ibid., 254.
185. Niebuhr, *The Children of Light and the Children of Darkness*, 3–5.
186. Niebuhr, *The Nature and Destiny of Man*, vol. 2, 254.
187. See, for example, Brock, *Journeys by Heart*; and Hampson, *Theology and Feminism*.
188. Brock, *Journeys by Heart*. Most of these types of feminist analyses of the atonement focus on Jesus as an innocent human. Because they have low Christologies, the atonement is not God suffering for humans but God arbitrarily sacrificing an innocent human. They tend to work out of low Christologies without reflecting on the difference that makes for a concept like the atonement.
189. Niebuhr, *The Nature and Destiny of Man*, vol. 1, 180.
190. Ibid., 180–81.
191. Ibid., 182.
192. Ibid., 185.
193. Ibid., 186.
194. Ibid., 206.
195. Ibid., 208.
196. Ibid., 179.
197. Ibid.
198. Ibid., 188.
199. Ibid., 194.
200. Ibid., 190.
201. Ibid., 192.
202. Ibid., 200.
203. Ibid.
204. Ibid., 203.
205. Ibid., 185.
206. Ibid., 186.
207. Ibid., 186–87 and 228.
208. Ibid., 228.
209. Ibid.
210. Ibid., 232.
211. Ibid., 233.
212. Ibid.
213. Ibid., 233–34.
214. Ibid., 236.
215. Ibid.
216. Ibid., 237.
217. Ibid.
218. Ibid., 240, emphasis mine.
219. For example, both Katie Geneva Cannon and Susan Brooks Thistlethwaite trace the cruelty of white women toward black slave women in the American South. Thistlethwaite, *Sex, Race and God*, 27ff.; and Cannon, *Black Womanist Ethics*, 38ff.
220. See Thistlethwaite, *Sex, Race and God*; Davaney, "The Limits of the Appeal to Women's Experience"; Williams, "The Color of Feminism"; and Grant, *White Woman's Christ and Black Woman's Jesus*.
221. Mary Grey, *Feminism, Redemption and the Christian Tradition*, 22ff.
222. See the feminist analysis of sin in chapter 2.

223. Niebuhr, *Christian Realism and Political Problems*, 119.

224. See Thistlethwaite, *Sex, Race and God*; Davaney, "The Limits of the Appeal to Women's Experience"; and Grey, *Feminism, Redemption and the Christian Tradition*.

Chapter 4

1. Because Ruether has not outlined her ethic as systematically as she has her theology, my own explication is itself an argument. I rely heavily on the naturalist ethic sketched in *Gaia and God*, where she explores the four themes of creation, Fall, evil, and healing, subsequently developing an "ecological ethic" and an "ecofeminist theology." The ethic presented is consistent with her earlier work and builds on her systematic feminist theology outlined in *Sexism and God-Talk*. Drawing from these two books, as well as from themes in her earlier works, I have formulated the composite position presented here.

2. Rosemary Ruether et al., "Gaia and God: Responses to R. R. Ruether's New Book" (Papers presented at the American Academy of Religion annual meeting, San Francisco, November 1992).

3. Ruether, *Gaia and God*, 12.

4. Ruether, *New Woman/New Earth*, 210–11.

5. For a more detailed account of this distinction, see chapter 1.

6. Ruether, *Gaia and God*, 256.

7. See, for example, *Sexism and God-Talk*, 75ff., and *New Woman/New Earth*, 31ff.

8. Ruether, *Sexism and God-Talk*, 45.

9. William Shannon, ed., *Thomas Merton: The Hidden Ground of Love, Letters on Religious Experience and Social Concerns* (New York: Farrer, Straus, Giroux, 1985), 497.

10. Ruether, *Sexism and God-Talk*, 12–13.

11. Ruether's turn to Teilhard de Chardin will be examined more fully later. Ruether is explicit about her appropriation of Teilhard in several places. See, for example, *Sexism and God-Talk*, 86ff.; *The Radical Kingdom*, 202; and *Gaia and God*, 242ff. The dependence is evident throughout her more recent work.

12. We will explore this dependency more fully later.

13. Ruether, *Sexism and God-Talk*, 68–69. See also Ruether, *Womanguides: Readings toward a Feminist Theology* (Boston, Beacon Press, 1985), 8.

14. Her understanding of God will be explored more fully later. See *Sexism and God-Talk*, 85ff., 114, and 265–66; and *Gaia and God*, 86 and 252–53.

15. Ruether, *New Woman/New Earth*, 204.

16. Ibid., 204–5.

17. Ibid., 31.

18. Ruether, *Gaia and God*, 111.

19. Ibid., 256.

20. Ibid., 256–57.

21. Ibid., 141.

22. Ruether, *Sexism and God-Talk*, 180ff.

23. Ruether, *Gaia and God*, 141.

24. See, for example, Saiving, "The Human Situation," 108–10; Plaskow, *Sex, Sin and Grace*; Carr, *Transforming Grace*; Hampson, *Theology and Feminism*; Vaughan, *Sociality, Ethics and Social Change*; and Keller, *From a Broken Web*.

25. See Nancy Chodorow, *The Reproduction of Mothering*; Dorothy Dinnerstein, *The Mermaid and the Minotaur: Sexual Arrangements and Human Malaise* (New York: Harper and Row, 1976); and Peggy R. Sanday, *Female Power and Male Dominance: On the Origins of Sexual Inequality* (Cambridge: Cambridge University Press, 1981), chapter 1.

26. Ruether, *Gaia and God*, 169.
27. Ibid., 171.
28. Ruether, *Sexism and God-Talk*, 220; and *Gaia and God*, 171–72.
29. Ruether, *Liberation Theology: Human Hope Confronts Christian History and American Power* (New York: Paulist Press, 1972), 95; *New Woman/New Earth*, 14, 18, and 204; and *Gaia and God*, 140.
30. Ruether, *New Woman/New Earth*, 14.
31. Ibid., 25.
32. Ibid., 74.
33. For example, Ruether, *Gaia and God*, 143ff. These theories are put forward in Marija Gimbutas, *Goddesses and Gods of Old Europe, 6500–3500 BC: Myths and Cult Images* (Berkeley: University of California Press, 1982); and Riane Eisler, *The Chalice and the Blade* (San Francisco: Harper and Row, 1987).
34. Ruether, *Gaia and God*, 200.
35. This analysis appears throughout Ruether's work. See, for example, Ruether, *Liberation Theology*, 119ff.; *New Woman/New Earth*, 5–17; *Sexism and God-Talk*, 47ff.; and *Gaia and God*, 201.
36. Ruether, *New Woman/New Earth*, 10–11.
37. Ruether, *Sexism and God-Talk*, 48.
38. Ruether, *New Woman/New Earth*, 7.
39. Ruether, *Sexism and God-Talk*, 54.
40. Ruether, *New Woman/New Earth*, 14.
41. Ruether, *Gaia and God*, 200.
42. Ruether, *New Woman/New Earth*, 13–14.
43. Ruether, *Liberation Theology*, 122.
44. Ruether, *New Woman/New Earth*, 4; and *Liberation Theology*, 102.
45. Ruether, *New Woman/New Earth*, 89–110, especially 105ff.
46. Ruether, *Sexism and God-Talk*, 89.
47. Ibid., 89–91.
48. Ruether's critical analysis of several categories of Christian theology and her alternate proposals will be considered later.
49. Ruether, *Disputed Questions: On Being a Christian* (Maryknoll, NY: Orbis Books, 1989), 51.
50. Ruether, *New Woman/New Earth*, 211.
51. Ruether, *Gaia and God*, 58.
52. Ibid., 47.
53. These concepts will be described more fully later.
54. Ruether, *Gaia and God*, 249.
55. Ibid., 31.
56. Ibid., 1.
57. J. E. Lovelock, *Gaia: A New Look at Life on Earth* (Oxford: Oxford University Press, 1987); and Lynn Margulis and J.E. Lovelock, "Gaia and Geognosy," *Global Ecology: Towards a Science of Biosphere*, Mitchell B. Rambler et al., eds. (San Diego, CA: Academic Press of America, 1989).
58. This is a continual theme in Ruether's work. From 1966 to 1968, Ruether and Thomas Merton exchanged letters. In their discussions of human creation and vocation, Merton suggested that while she wrote about "God's good creation, the goodness of the body, and all that," she was removed from the sensuality of close contact with the earth and was actually "a very academic, cerebral, abstract type." Ruether's next letter to Merton closed with the words: "P.S. I'm as fleshy as you, baby." See, Shannon, *Thomas Merton*, 506 and 509.

59. Ruether, *Gaia and God*, 47.
60. Ibid.
61. Ibid., 48.
62. Ibid., 49.
63. See Margulis and Lovelock, "Gaia and Geognosy."
64. Ruether, *Gaia and God*, 56.
65. Ibid.
66. Ibid., 31.
67. Ibid., 57.
68. Ibid., 31.
69. Ibid., 115.

70. At the most general level, Ruether's model of human concsiousness is similar in some ways to Niebuhr's model of human self-transcendence. The self stands out from its environment and is thereby able to transform it. For both thinkers, ethical responsibility is rooted in this capacity. The differences between the two models, however, are also striking. For Ruether, consciousness is more closely tied to human rationality. It develops as an extension of the natural evolutionary process and will ideally further that development. By contrast, Niebuhr links this unique human capacity not with rationality but with freedom. Moreover, while it is a part of human nature, it is much more deeply discontinuous with nature than in Ruether's model. These differences will be discussed more fully later.

71. Ruether, *Gaia and God*, 47.
72. Ibid., 249, emphasis mine.
73. Ruether turns to Teilhard throughout her work. See, for example, *Sexism and God-Talk*, 86; *Gaia and God*, 242ff.; and *Womanguides*, 198.
74. Ruether, *Sexism and God-Talk*, 86.
75. Ruether, *Gaia and God*, 250.
76. Ibid., 31.
77. Ibid., 5.
78. Ibid.
79. Ruether, *Sexism and God-Talk*, 87–88.
80. Ibid., 89.
81. Ibid., 91–92.
82. Ibid., 88.
83. Ibid., 18–19.

84. This pattern will become more evident later as we examine her systematic categories.

85. Ruether, *Gaia and God*, 258.
86. Ruether, *Sexism and God-Talk*, 24.
87. Ibid.
88. Ruether, *Womanguides*, ix.
89. Ibid., ixff.
90. Ibid.

91. Ibid. The authors included in this new canon range from Plato, Philo, and Aquinas to Mary Baker Eddy, Friedrich Engels, and Pierre Teilhard de Chardin.

92. Ruether, *Sexism and God-Talk*, 45.

93. Kathryn Rabuzzi, "The Socialist Feminist Vision of Rosemary Radford Ruether: A Challenge to Liberal Feminism," *Religious Studies Review* 15 (January 1989): 6.

94. For a further explication of Ruether's criticism of transcendence, see previous discussion.

95. Ruether, *Sexism and God-Talk*, 54.

96. Ruether, *Liberation Theology*, 115–16.
97. Ruether, *New Woman/New Earth*, 74.
98. See, for example, Sheila Collins, Carol Christ, and Mary Daly.
99. Ruether, *New Woman/New Earth*, 63ff.; *Sexism and God-Talk*, 193ff.; and *Women-Church: Theology and Practice of Feminist Liturgical Communities* (San Francisco: Harper and Row, 1985), 75–95.
100. Ruether, *Women-Church*, 85–86.
101. Ruether, *New Woman/New Earth*, 74–76, emphasis mine.
102. It is ironic, of course, that Ruether, while rejecting simple dualisms of good and evil, seems to fall into the very thing she criticizes when she sets up such strong normative distinctions between oppressors and oppressed.
103. Ruether, *Sexism and God-Talk*, 163–64.
104. Ruether, *To Change the World: Christology and Cultural Criticism* (New York: Crossroad, 1981); *Sexism and God-Talk*, 116ff.; and *Disputed Questions*, 56ff.
105. Ruether, *Sexism and God-Talk*, 125.
106. Ibid., 138.
107. Ruether, *New Woman/New Earth*, 36ff.; and *Sexism and God-Talk*, 139ff.
108. Ruether, *New Woman/New Earth*, 56.
109. Ruether, *Sexism and God-Talk*, 154.
110. Ruether, *New Woman/New Earth*, 58.
111. Ruether, *Sexism and God-Talk*, 69.
112. Ibid., 46.
113. Ruether, *Gaia and God*, 247.
114. Ibid., 248–49.
115. Ruether, *Sexism and God-Talk*, 45ff., 85ff., and 266; and *Gaia and God*, 253.
116. Ruether, *Gaia and God*, 31.
117. Ibid., 249–50, emphasis mine.
118. Ibid., 253.
119. Ibid., 5.
120. Ibid., 31.
121. Ruether emphasizes the distortion of patriarchal theology and the authentic nature of biophilic theology in several places. See, for example, *Sexism and God-Talk*, 48ff. and 71.
122. Ibid., 71.
123. Ruether, *Gaia and God*, 258.
124. Ruether, *Sexism and God Talk*, 233; and *Gaia and God*, 266.
125. Ruether, *Gaia and God*, 266.
126. Ruether, *Sexism and God-Talk*, 201ff. and 231ff.
127. Ruether, *Gaia and God*, 272.
128. Ruether, *Women-Church*.
129. Ruether, *Gaia and God*, 268–69.
130. Ibid., 266.
131. Ibid., 268.
132. Ibid.
133. Ruether, *New Woman/New Earth*, 204ff.; *Sexism and God-Talk*, 232ff.; and *Gaia and God*, 258ff.
134. Ruether, *Gaia and God*, 261.
135. Ruether, "Gaia and God: Responses to R. R. Ruether's New Book." See my section on Ruether's Task: A Summary.
136. Ruether, *New Woman/New Earth*, 178–79, emphasis mine.

137. Indeed, in the early years, he was also a socialist, even running for Congress on a Socialist ticket. He became, of course, increasingly critical of socialism over the course of his life. See Fox, Reinhold Niebuhr, 135–36.

138. It would be easy to overdraw the distinction here. Though I have appropriately conditioned this contrast, I believe it still stands.

139. This point will be discussed more fully in the final chapter. In addition, I will explore how self-transcendence might be understood so that radical human freedom is maintained while taking into account some of Ruether's criticisms.

140. A more complete account of the function of divine transcendence in theology and ethics (especially my own) will be included in the final chapter.

141. This exploration of Ruether responds to criticisms of Niebuhr. As I noted in chapters 2 and 3, Niebuhr's relative ambivalence about human creatureliness and his neglect of boundedness as a source for moral claims is a problem for some feminist critics.

Chapter 5

1. I use the term "theological ethic" loosely. Welch, like Ruether, is primarily a theologian. Even so, she addresses ethical concerns and proposes the outlines of an ethic.
2. Sharon Welch, *Communities of Resistance and Solidarity*, 5.
3. Ibid., ix.
4. Ibid.
5. Ibid., 13–14.
6. Welch, *A Feminist Ethic of Risk*. Welch describes herself as Christian in *Communities of Resistance and Solidarity* and post-Christian in *A Feminist Ethic of Risk*.
7. This ethic will be examined later.
8. Welch, *Communities of Resistance and Solidarity*, 9–15 and 23–31.
9. Welch, *A Feminist Ethic of Risk*, 173.
10. Ibid., 178.
11. Welch, *Communities of Resistance and Solidarity*, 1–3.
12. Ibid, 7.
13. Ibid.
14. Ibid.
15. Welch, *A Feminist Ethic of Risk*, 177.
16. Welch, *Communities of Resistance and Solidarity*, 3. This strikes me as an unusual way to state the problem. Is the task of liberal Christian theologians (or any Christian theologians) to discover "evidence" to "establish" the "reality of God" with "certainty"?
17. Ibid., 4.
18. Welch, "The Nuclear Arms Race as a Test of Faith," *Union Seminary Quarterly Review* 40 (1985): 38.
19. Welch, *Communities of Resistance and Solidarity*, 4. This makes sense when we remember that, for Welch, God is the projection of our moral values and our values are what are made true in practice.
20. Welch, *A Feminist Ethic of Risk*, 104.
21. Welch, *Communities of Resistance and Solidarity*, 2.
22. Welch, *A Feminist Ethic of Risk*, 104 and 111.
23. Ibid., 111.
24. Welch, *Communities of Resistance and Solidarity*, 6.
25. Welch, "A Genealogy of the Logic of Deterrence: Habermas, Foucault, and a Feminist Ethic of Risk," *Union Seminary Quarterly Review* 41 (1987): 23–25; and *A Feminist Ethic of Risk*, 23ff.

26. Welch, *Communities of Resistance and Solidarity*, 4.
27. Ibid., 24.
28. Ibid., 35, emphasis mine.
29. This chapter is neither an analysis of Foucault nor an examination of the validity of Welch's interpretation of Foucault. It is an analysis of Welch. Consequently, whether or not her reading is correct, it is the reading that tells us the most about Welch. Foucault's understanding of freedom seems somewhat at odds with Welch's ethic. I suspect that Welch is closer philosophically to Richard Rorty. They are both "liberal ironists." Richard Rorty, *Contingency, Irony and Solidarity* (Cambridge: Cambridge University Press), 1989.
30. Welch, *Communities of Resistance and Solidarity*, 9ff.
31. Ibid., 20ff.
32. Welch, "A Genealogy of the Logic of Deterrence," 13ff.; and *Communities of Resistance and Solidarity*, 12 and 28.
33. Welch, *Communities of Resistance and Solidarity*, 26–27.
34. Welch, "A Genealogy of the Logic of Deterrence," 14; "The Nuclear Arms Race as a Test of Faith," 42–43; and *Communities of Resistance and Solidarity*, 26–27.
35. Welch, *Communities of Resistance and Solidarity*, 27. See also 13–14.
36. "The Nuclear Arms Race as a Test of Faith," 38 and 40–41.
37. Welch, *Communities of Resistance and Solidarity*, 36–38.
38. Ibid., 41, emphasis mine.
39. Welch, "A Genealogy of the Logic of Deterrence," 13; and *Communities of Resistance and Solidarity*, 28.
40. Welch, *Communities of Resistance and Solidarity*, 26–27.
41. Ibid., 26.
42. As we will see later, Cornel West criticizes Welch's "choice" for liberation as "ideological fideism" or an "intuitionist/confessional political commitment." See Cornel West, "Faith, Struggle and Reality: Communities of Resistance and Solidarity," *Christianity and Crisis* (October 14, 1985): 402.
43. Welch, *Communities of Resistance and Solidarity*, 23–31.
44. Ibid., 23 and 84–85.
45. Ibid., 29 and 86–87.
46. Ibid., 25. See also "Beloved Community" in *A Feminist Ethic of Risk*, 160–61.
47. Welch, *Communities of Resistance and Solidarity*, 25.
48. Ibid.
49. Ibid., 31.
50. Ibid.
51. Ibid., 52–53.
52. Ibid., 31.
53. Ibid., 91; and "The Nuclear Arms Race as a Test of Faith," 41.
54. For example, we saw this in our examination of Reinhold Niebuhr in chapter 3. In Welch's criticisms of H. R. Niebuhr, she recognizes his insistence on the finitude of all human claims (*A Feminist Ethic of Risk*, 120–21).
55. Welch, *Communities of Resistance and Solidarity*, 87, emphasis mine.
56. Ibid., 83.
57. Ibid., 82.
58. Ibid.
59. Ibid., 80.
60. Welch, "Ideology and Social Change," *Weaving the Visions: New Patterns in Feminist Spirituality*, Judith Plaskow and Carol Christ, eds. (New York: Harper and Row, 1989), 341; and "Sporting Power: American Feminisms, French Feminisms and an Ethic of Conflict,"

Transfigurations: Theology and the French Feminists, C. W. Kim, Susan Simonaitis, and Susan St. Ville, eds. (Minneapolis: Fortress, 1993), 184.

61. Welch, "Ideology and Social Change," 341; and "Sporting Power," 184.
62. Ibid.
63. Welch, "Ideology and Social Change," 342.
64. From an earlier, unpublished version of "Sporting Power," Conference on Feminist Theologies and French Feminism, University of Chicago (Spring 1991), 12.
65. Welch, *A Feminist Ethic of Risk*, part 1.
66. Ibid., 187–88.
67. Ibid., 127.
68. Rubem Alves is one notable exception. See Rubem A. Alves, *A Theology of Human Hope* (New York: Corpus Books, 1971). Even Cornel West has much thicker assumptions than Welch.
69. Welch, *A Feminist Ethic of Risk*, 1ff.; and "The Nuclear Arms Race," 37ff.
70. One reviewer commented on the theme of despair in this work. "If you sometimes feel, as the Hebrew prophets Elijah and Jonah did, like going into a barren place, lying down under a tree and saying, 'I have had enough Lord . . . I want to die,' Welch's *A Feminist Ethic of Risk* is for you." Brenda Carr, "With Integrity and Risk," review of *A Feminist Ethic of Risk*, *Sojourners* 21 (May 1992): 39.
71. Welch, "A Genealogy of the Logic of Deterrence," 24.
72. Ibid., 14; and *A Feminist Ethic of Risk*, 6 and 182.
73. See, for example, Starhawk, *Dreaming the Dark*; Hampson, "On Power and Gender," *Modern Theology* 4 (1988): 234–50; Welch, "A Genealogy of the Logic of Deterrence"; and Hampson, *Theology and Feminism*.
74. Welch, *Communities of Resistance and Solidarity*, 80–81, emphasis mine.
75. Ibid., 72.
76. Welch, *A Feminist Ethic of Risk*, 38. See also 117 and 125.
77. Welch, *Communities of Resistance and Solidarity*, 68.
78. Ibid., 63–64.
79. Welch, *A Feminist Ethic of Risk*, 111–16.
80. Ibid., 111.
81. Ibid., 111–14.
82. Ibid., 112.
83. Ibid., 118.
84. Welch, *Communities of Resistance and Solidarity*, 72. Her reading of H. R. Niebuhr is unusual.
85. Welch, *A Feminist Ethic of Risk*, 111; and *Communities of Resistance and Solidarity*, 41–42.
86. Welch, *Communities of Resistance and Solidarity*, 2.
87. Welch, *A Feminist Ethic of Risk*, 104.
88. Welch "The Nuclear Arms Race as a Test of Faith," 41–42.
89. Welch, *A Feminist Ethic of Risk*, 106–11.
90. Note the similarity between this argument and the feminist criticisms in chapter 2 that Reinhold Niebuhr's focus on the limits of human claims and the relativizing function of divine transcendence was basically conservative.
91. Welch, *Communities of Resistance and Solidarity*, 45.
92. Welch, *A Feminist Ethic of Risk*, 122.
93. Ibid., 173.
94. Ibid., 1–2. See also "A Genealogy of the Logic of Deterrence," 26–27.
95. Welch, *A Feminist Ethic of Risk*, 129.

96. An African American womanist pastor, Irene Moore, notes that Welch draws on African American resources but calls her ethic "a feminist ethic of risk" without noting in the title her dependence on womanist work. See Welch, "Sporting Power," 181. Also Emilie Townes et al., "Critical Book Discussion: Sharon Welch's *A Feminist Ethic of Risk,*" audio recording of papers presented at the annual meeting of the Society of Christian Ethics, Philadelphia (January 1992).

97. Welch, "A Genealogy of the Logic of Deterrence," 26–30. See also *A Feminist Ethic of Risk*, 19–22.

98. Ibid., 27–28.

99. Ibid., 29.

100. Welch, *A Feminist Ethic of Risk*, 38. See also 117 and 125.

101. Ibid., 6 and 182; and "A Genealogy of the Logic of Deterrence," 15–16. For further discussion of these terms, see chapters 1 and 4.

102. Welch, "A Genealogy of the Logic of Deterrence," 15–16.

103. Welch, "The Nuclear Arms Race as a Test of Faith," 41.

104. Gary Burrill, "This Mortar, These Dreams: Sharon Welch and the Ethic of Risk," *The World* (November-December, 1989): 15.

105. Welch joined the Unitarian Universalists because of their theological openness and political commitments. She was raised in a large, tight-knit Latter-day Saints family in a small town on the Texas panhandle. While in graduate school at Vanderbilt, she left the Latter-day Saints church because of its hierarchical and exclusivist structure. She continues to value, however, its strong focus on community. Burrill, "This Mortar, These Dreams."

106. Welch, *A Feminist Ethic of Risk*, 178.

107. Ibid., 173.

108. Ibid., 176.

109. Ibid., 179.

110. Ibid., 179–80.

111. Ibid., 179.

112. Ibid.

113. Ibid., 196–97. Welch notes that her use of the "beloved community" is closer to King's understanding than to Josiah Royce's focus on Christian community from which King drew. I will claim later that her model is quite different from King's as well.

114. Ibid., 160–61.

115. Ibid., 169–71.

116. Ibid., 172.

117. Ibid., 167.

118. Ibid., 123–24.

119. Ibid., 125. Despite Welch's charge, MacIntyre does move beyond a concern for "shared moral criteria" to reflect on the importance of "critique." Indeed, the most "mature" systems of rationality, according to MacIntyre, are the ones that have internal critical mechanisms and can respond to and account for alternate traditions. See Alasdair MacIntyre, *Whose Justice? Which Rationality?* (Notre Dame, IN: University of Notre Dame Press, 1988), 354ff.

120. Welch, *A Feminist Ethic of Risk*, 125. Welch writes earlier that because of the partiality of all of our claims, we must work in community, where mutual critique and strategy are more possible. She writes, then, that "a single actor cannot be moral" (*A Feminist Ethic of Risk*, 38).

121. Ibid., 126.

122. Ibid., 105–6.

123. Ibid., 126.

124. Cannon, *Black Womanist Ethics*, 169–73. This claim is evident throughout King's work, especially when he talks about the limits of white "good will" and the necessity of civil rights legislation to enforce justice.

125. Welch, *A Feminist Ethic of Risk*, 197.

126. James M. Washington, ed., "An Experiment in Love," *A Testament of Hope: The Essential Writings and Speeches of Martin Luther King, Jr.* (New York: HarperCollins Publishers, 1986), 16–20.

127. Welch, *A Feminist Ethic of Risk*, 129, emphasis mine. Given this extraordinary admission, it is puzzling that Welch does not question her reliance on Foucault's epistemology.

128. Ibid., 129ff. See also "A Genealogy of the Logic of Deterrence," 13–14.

129. Welch, *A Feminist Ethic of Risk*, 131–32.

130. Ibid., 132–33. Welch does not ask how a community has solidarity without consensus.

131. Again, Welch may be closer to Richard Rorty than she is to either Habermas or Foucault. Rorty describes himself as a "liberal ironist." He is liberal because of his hatred of suffering and cruelty and his preference for human solidarity; he is an ironist because of his insistence on the contingency of all moral claims, including those that judge suffering and cruelty. According to Rorty, Foucault is an ironist but not a liberal, and Habermas is a liberal but not an ironist. Given this typology, Welch finds herself encamped with neither Habermas nor Foucault, but with Rorty, the postmodern heir of Christian liberalism and grandson of Walter Rauschenbusch.

132. Welch, *A Feminist Ethic of Risk*, 150–51. See also "A Genealogy of the Logic of Deterrence," 13.

133. Welch, "A Genealogy of the Logic of Deterrence," 15.

134. Welch, *A Feminist Ethic of Risk*, 151.

135. Some feminists appropriate Welch after adding an aside about disagreeing with her Foucauldian relativist framework. The difficulty with this move is that the framework is so central to her argument. This is similar, of course, to the sorts of appropriations that Welch often makes. For example, she appropriates King's beloved community without King's understanding of God, human nature, or moral norms. See Mary McClintock Fulkerson, *Changing the Subject: Women's Discourses and Feminist Theology* (Minneapolis: Fortress Press, 1994), 361–62.

136. Welch, *Communities of Resistance and Solidarity*, 13.

137. Welch, "Ideology and Social Change," 341.

138. West, "Faith, Struggle and Reality," 402; and Carol Wayne White, *Postmodern Religion and the Problem of Historicity* (Ph.D. dissertation, Iliff School of Theology and University of Denver, 1993) make similar arguments.

139. West, "Faith, Struggle, and Reality," 402.

140. Rorty, *Contingency, Irony and Solidarity*, 80–81.

Chapter 6

1. See Martha Nussbaum, "Non-Relative Virtues: An Aristotelian Approach," *Midwest Studies in Philosophy* 13 (1988): 32–53.

2. In addition to Welch, see Sheila Davaney, Mary McClintock Fulkerson, and Susan Thistlethwaite.

3. We saw this concern in chapter 2 when we examined feminist criticisms of gender roles in Niebuhr.

4. Alasdair MacIntyre writes of the capacity of "mature rationalities" to incorporate and be modified by the arguments of other systems. See MacIntyre, *Whose Justice? Which*

Rationality? See also Kathryn Tanner, *The Politics of God: Christian Theologies and Social Justice* (Minneapolis: Fortress Press, 1992).

5. This argument and parts of the text were first published in an article taken largely from chapter 2 of this study. See my "Freeing Bonds and Binding Freedom."

6. Throughout this project, Niebuhr, Ruether, and Welch have not been the only thinkers in my line of vision. Always present (though rarely mentioned) were other figures central in contemporary theological and philosophical debates—particularly those associated with both the communitarian and deconstructionist wings of postmodernism. The background task of this project has become the central, foreground task of my current research. How might a Christian realist model of God and the transforming person offer an alternative to deconstructionist and communitarian models, taking seriously the contextual nature of all human claims and allowing for the dynamic nature of human existence and human models of the truth (including truth claims about God and the self) without undermining the grounding or possibility of moral truth? Moreover, how can this alternate model be formed and articulated within the structures and language of classical Christian theology?

Afterword

1. Meister Eckhart, "Sermon 12: Qui audit me, non confundetur," in *Meister Eckhart: Teacher and Preacher*, Bernard McGinn, ed. (New York: Paulist Press, 1986), 269.

Bibliography

Alves, Rubem A. "Christian Realism: The Ideology of the Establishment." *Christianity and Crisis* 33 (September 17, 1973): 173–76
———. *A Theology of Human Hope.* New York: Corpus Books, 1971.
Andolsen, Barbara H. "Agape in Feminist Ethics." *Journal of Religious Ethics* 9 (Spring 1981): 69–83.
Andolsen, Barbara H., Christine Gudorf, and Mary Pellauer, eds. *Women's Consciousness, Women's Conscience: A Reader in Feminist Ethics.* Minneapolis: Winston Press, 1985.
Beauvoir, Simone de. *The Second Sex.* Translated by H. M. Parshley. New York: Vintage Books, 1974.
Beckley, Harlan. *Passion for Justice: Retrieving the Legacies of Walter Rauschenbusch, John A. Ryan, and Reinhold Niebuhr.* Louisville, KY: Westminster/John Knox Press, 1992.
Bednarowski, Mary Farrell. "The Significance of Immanence in Women's Theologies." Paper presented at the Comparative Studies in Religion Section, American Academy of Religion annual meeting, Washington, DC, November 1993.
Benhabib, Seyla. "The Generalized and the Concrete Other: The Kohlberg-Gilligan Controversy and Moral Theory." In *Women and Moral Theory,* edited by Eva Feder Kittay and Diana T. Myers, 154–77. Totowa, NJ: Rowan & Littlefield, 1987.
Benhabib, Seyla, and Drucilla Cornell, eds. *Feminism as Critique.* Minneapolis: University of Minnesota Press, 1987.
Bennett, John Coleman. *Christian Realism.* New York: Charles Scribner's Sons, 1941.
———. "Liberation Theology and Christian Realism." *Christianity and Crisis* 33 (October 15, 1973): 197–98.
Bordo, Susan. "Feminism, Postmodernism, and Gender Skepticism." In *Feminism/Postmodernism,* edited by Linda J. Nicholson, 133–56. New York: Routledge, 1990.
———. *The Flight to Objectivity: Essays on Cartesianism and Culture.* Albany: State University of New York Press, 1987.
Brock, Rita Nakashima. *Journeys by Heart: A Christology of Erotic Power.* New York: Crossroad, 1988.
Brown, Charles C. *A Reinhold Niebuhr Reader: Selected Essays, Articles, and Book Reviews* Philadelphia: Trinity Press International, 1992.
Brown, Robert McAfee, ed. *The Essential Reinhold Niebuhr: Selected Essays and Addresses.* New Haven: Yale University Press, 1986.
———. "Liberation Theology and Christian Realism." *Christianity and Crisis* 33 (October 15, 1973): 199–200.

Burrill, Gary. "This Mortar, These Dreams: Sharon Welch and the Ethic of Risk." *The World* (November-December, 1989): 15.
Cahill, Lisa. *Between the Sexes: Foundations for a Christian Ethics of Sexuality*. Philadelphia: Fortress Press, 1985.
———. "Feminist Ethics." *Theological Studies* 51 (March 1990): 49–64.
Cairns, David. *God Up There?* Edinburgh: T. and A. Constable, 1967.
Cannon, Katie Geneva. *Black Womanist Ethics*. Atlanta: Scholars Press, 1988.
———. "The Emergence of Black Feminist Consciousness." In *Feminist Interpretation of the Bible*, edited by Letty Russell, 30–40. Philadelphia: Westminster Press, 1985.
———. "Hitting a Straight Lick with a Crooked Stick: The Womanist Dilemma in the Development of a Black Liberation Ethic." *The Annual of the Society of Christian Ethics*, 165–77. Knoxville, TN: Society of Christian Ethics, 1987.
———. "Moral Wisdom in the Black Women's Literary Tradition." *The Annual of the Society of Christian Ethics*, 171–92. Vancouver, BC: Society of Christian Ethics, 1984.
Carr, Anne E. *Transforming Grace: Christian Tradition and Women's Experience*. New York: Harper and Row, 1988.
Carr, Brenda. "With Integrity and Risk." A Review of *A Feminist Ethic of Risk*. *Sojourners* 21 (May 1992): 39.
Case-Winters, Anna. *God's Power: Traditional Understandings and Contemporary Challenges*. Louisville, KY: Westminster/John Knox Press, 1990.
Chodorow, Nancy. *The Reproduction of Mothering: Psychoanalysis and the Sociology of Gender*. Berkeley: University of California Press, 1978.
Chopp, Rebecca. "Feminism's Theological Pragmatics: A Social Naturalism of Women's Experience." *Journal of Religion* 67 (April 1987): 239–56.
———. *The Power to Speak: Feminism, Language, God*. New York: Crossroad, 1989.
———. *The Praxis of Suffering: An Interpretation of Liberation and Political Theologies*. Maryknoll, NY: Orbis Books, 1986.
———. "Seeing and Naming the World Anew: The Works of Rosemary Radford Ruether." *Religious Studies Review* 15 (January 1989): 8–11.
Christ, Carol P. *Laughter of Aphrodite*. San Francisco: Harper and Row, 1987.
Christ, Carol, and Judith Plaskow, eds. *Womanspirit Rising. A Feminist Reader in Religion*. New York: Harper and Row, 1979.
Chung, Hyun Kyung. *Struggle to Be the Sun Again: Introducing Asian Women's Theology*. Maryknoll, NY: Orbis Press, 1990.
Collins, Sheila D. *A Different Heaven and Earth*. Valley Forge, PA: Judson Press, 1974.
Cooey, Paula. "The Power of Transformation and the Transformation of Power." *Journal of Feminist Studies in Religion* 1 (1985): 22–36.
Cornelison, Robert Thomas. *The Christian Realism of Reinhold Niebuhr and the Political Theology of Jürgen Moltmann in Dialogue: The Realism of Hope*. San Francisco: Mellen Research University Press, 1992.
Daly, Mary. *Beyond God the Father: Toward a Philosophy of Women's Liberation*. Boston: Beacon Press, 1973.
———. *Gyn/Ecology: The Metaethics of Radical Feminism*. Boston: Beacon Press, 1978.
———. *Pure Lust: Elemental Feminist Philosophy*. Boston: Beacon Press, 1984.
Davaney, Sheila Greeve. *Divine Power: A Study of Karl Barth and Charles Hartshorne*. Harvard Dissertations Series in Religion. Philadelphia: Fortress Press, 1986.
———, ed. *Feminism and Process Thought*. Harvard Divinity School/Claremont Center for Process Studies Symposium Papers: New York: E. Mellen Press, 1981.
———. "The Limits of the Appeal to Women's Experience." In *Shaping New Vision: Gender and Values in American Culture*, edited by Clarissa W. Atkinson, Constance

H. Buchanan, and Margaret R. Miles, 31–49. Ann Arbor, MI: UMI Research Press, 1987.

———. "Problems with Feminist Theory: Historicity and the Search for Sure Foundations." In *Embodied Love: Sensuality and Relationship as Feminist Values*, edited by Paula M. Cooey, Sharon Farmer, and Mary Ellen Ross, 79–95. San Francisco: Harper and Row, 1987.

Diamond, Irene, and Lee Quinby, eds. *Feminism & Foucault: Reflections on Resistance*. Boston: Northeastern University Press, 1988.

Dinnerstein, Dorothy. *The Mermaid and the Minotaur: Sexual Arrangements and Human Malaise*. New York: Harper and Row, 1976.

Donovan, Josephine. *Feminist Theory: The Intellectual Traditions of American Feminism*. New York: Continuum, 1994.

Dunfee, Susan. *Christianity and the Liberation of Women*. Ph.D. dissertation, Claremont Graduate School, 1985.

Eckhart, Meister. "Sermon 12: Qui audit me, non confundetur." In *Meister Eckhart: Teacher and Preacher*, edited by Bernard McGinn, 267–71. New York: Paulist Press, 1986.

Eisenstein, Zillah, ed. *The Radical Future of Liberal Feminism*. New York: Longman, 1981.

Eisler, Riane. *The Chalice and the Blade*. San Francisco: Harper and Row, 1987.

Fabella, Virginia, and Mercy Amba Oduyoye, eds. *With Passion and Compassion: Third World Women Doing Theology*. Maryknoll, NY: Orbis Books, 1988.

Fabella, Virginia, and Sun Ai Lee Park, eds. *We Dare to Dream: Doing Theology as Asian Women*. Kowloon, Hong Kong: Asian Women's Resource Centre for Culture and Theology, 1989.

Faludi, Susan. *Backlash: The Undeclared War against American Women*. New York: Crown Press, 1991.

Farley, Edward. *The Transcendence of God*. Philadelphia: Westminster Press, 1960.

Fiorenza, Elizabeth Schüssler. *In Memory of Her: A Feminist Theological Reconstruction of Christian Origins*. New York: Crossroad, 1983.

Flax, Jane. "Postmodernism and Gender Relations in Feminist Theory." *Signs* 12 (Summer 1987): 621–43.

Foucault, Michel. *The Order of Things: An Archaeology of the Human Sciences*. New York: Vintage Books, 1973.

———. *Power/Knowledge: Selected Interviews and Other Writings 1972–1977*. New York: Pantheon, 1980.

Fox, Richard W. *Reinhold Niebuhr: A Biography*. New York: Pantheon, 1985.

French, Marilyn. *Beyond Power: Of Women, Men, and Morals*. New York: Summit Books, 1985.

Fulkerson, Mary McClintock. *Changing the Subject: Women's Discourses and Feminist Theology*. Minneapolis: Fortress Press, 1994.

Fuss, Diana. *Essentially Speaking: Feminism, Nature and Difference*. New York: Routledge, 1989.

Gill, Jerry H. *Mediated Transcendence: A Postmodern Reflection*. Macon, GA: Mercer University Press, 1989.

Gilligan, Carol. *In a Different Voice*. Cambridge, MA: Harvard University Press, 1982.

Gimbutas, Marija. *Goddesses and Gods of Old Europe, 6500–3500 BC: Myths and Cult Images*. Berkeley: University of California Press, 1982.

Goldenberg, Naomi R. *Changing of the Gods: Feminism and the End of Traditional Religions*. Boston: Beacon Press, 1979.

Grant, Jacquelyn. *White Women's Christ and Black Women's Jesus: White Feminist Christology and Womanist Response*. Atlanta: Scholars Press, 1989.

Grenz, Stanley J., and Roger E. Olson. *Twentieth Century Theology: God and the World in a Transitional Age*. Downers Grove, IL: InterVarsity Press, 1992.

Grey, Mary. *Feminism, Redemption and the Christian Tradition*. Mystic, CT: Twenty-Third Publications, 1990.

Gudorf, Christine. "Women's Choice for Motherhood: Beginning a Cross-Cultural Approach." In *Motherhood: Experience, Institution, Theology*, edited by Anne Carr and Elisabeth Schüssler Fiorenza, 55–63. Edinburgh: T & T Clark, 1989.

Gustafson, James. "Theology in the Service of Ethics: An Interpretation of Reinhold Niebuhr's Theological Ethic." In *Reinhold Niebuhr and the Issues of Our Time*, edited by Richard Harries. Grand Rapids, MI: Eerdmans, 1986.

Hampson, Daphne. "On Power and Gender." Modern Theology 4 (1988): 234–50.

———. "Reinhold Niebuhr on Sin: A Critique." In *Reinhold Niebuhr and the Issues of Our Time*, edited by Richard Harries, 46–60. Grand Rapids, MI: Eerdmans, 1986.

———. *Theology and Feminism*. Oxford: Basil Blackwell, 1990.

Harding, Sandra. *The Science Question in Feminism*. Ithaca, NY: Cornell University Press, 1986.

Harland, Gordon. *The Thought of Reinhold Niebuhr*. New York: Oxford University Press, 1960.

Harries, Richard, ed. *Reinhold Niebuhr and the Issues of Our Time*. Grand Rapids, MI: Eerdmans, 1986.

Harrison, Beverly Wildung. *Making the Connections: Essays in Feminist Social Ethics*, Carol Robb, ed. Boston: Beacon Press, 1985.

Harstock, Nancy. *Money, Sex, and Power: Toward a Feminist Historical Materialism*. Boston: Northeastern University Press, 1985.

Hawkesworth, M. E. *Beyond Oppression: Feminist Theory and Political Strategy*. New York: Continuum, 1990.

Heine, Susanne. *Matriarchs, Goddesses, and Images of God*. Minneapolis: Augsburg Press, 1989.

Heschel, Susannah. "Anti-Judaism in Christian Feminist Theology." *Tikkun* 5 (May–June 1990): 25–28, 95–97.

———, ed. *On Being a Jewish Feminist: A Reader*. New York: Schocken Books, 1983.

Heyward, I. Carter. *Our Passion for Justice: Images of Power, Sexuality, and Liberation*. New York: Pilgrim Press, 1984.

———. *The Redemption of God: A Theology of Mutual Liberation*. Washington, DC: University Press of America, 1982.

———. *Touching Our Strength: The Erotic as Power and the Love of God*. San Francisco: Harper and Row, 1989.

Hinze, Christine Firer. *Comprehending Power in Christian Social Ethics*. Atlanta: Scholars Press, 1995.

———. "Power in Christian Ethics: Resources and Frontiers for Scholarly Exploration." *The Annual of the Society of Christian Ethics*, 277–90. Washington, DC: Georgetown University Press, 1992.

Hofmann, Hans. *The Theology of Reinhold Niebuhr*. Translated by Louise Pettibone Smith. New York: Charles Scribner's Sons, 1956.

Horton, Walter Marshall. *Realistic Theology*. New York: Harper and Brothers 1934.

Hunt, Mary E. *Fierce Tenderness: A Feminist Theology of Friendship*. New York: Crossroad, 1991.

———. "Friends in Deed." In *Sex and God*, edited by Linda Hurcombe, 46–54. New York: Routledge and Kegan Paul, 1987.

Hurcombe, Linda, ed. *Sex and God: Some Varieties of Women's Religious Experience.* New York: Routledge and Kegan Paul, 1987.
Hutchison, William. *The Modernist Impulse in American Protestantism.* Cambridge: Harvard University Press, 1976.
Illingworth, J. R. *Divine Transcendence.* New York: Macmillan, 1911.
Isasi-Díaz, Ada María. *En la Lucha/In the Struggle: A Hispanic Women's Liberation Theology.* Minneapolis: Fortress Press, 1993.
———. *Hispanic Women, Prophetic Voice in the Church: toward a Hispanic Women's Liberation Theology.* San Francisco: Harper and Row, 1988.
Isasi-Díaz, Ada María, et al. "Mujeristas: Who We Are and What We Are About." *Journal of Feminist Studies in Religion* 8 (Spring 1992): 105–25.
Jakobsen, Janet R. "Postmodern Multiplicity and Feminist Responsibility." Paper presented at the American Academy of Religion annual meeting, Kansas City, MO, 1991.
Jantzen, Grace M. *God's World, God's Body.* Philadelphia: Westminster Press, 1984.
Jenkins, David. *Guide to the Debate about God.* London: Lutterworth Press, 1966.
Johnson, Elizabeth A. *She Who Is: The Mystery of God in Feminist Theological Discourse.* New York: Crossroad, 1992.
Kegley, Charles W., and Robert W. Bretall, eds. *Reinhold Niebuhr: His Religious, Social and Political Thought.* New York: Macmillan, 1956.
Keley, Charles W. *The Theology of Paul Tillich.* New York: Macmillan, 1952.
Keller, Catherine. *From a Broken Web: Separation, Sexism, and Self.* Boston: Beacon, 1986.
Kim, C. W. Maggie, Susan M. St. Ville, and Susan M. Simonaitis, eds. *Transfigurations: Theology and the French Feminists.* Minneapolis: Fortress Press, 1993.
King, Ursula, ed. *Feminist Theology from the Third World.* Maryknoll, NY: Orbis Books, 1994.
LaCugna, Catherine. *God for Us: The Trinity and Christian Life.* San Francisco: HarperCollins, 1991.
———. ed. *Freeing Theology: The Essentials of Theology in Feminist Perspective.* San Francisco: HarperCollins, 1993.
Landon, Harold, ed. *Reinhold Niebuhr: A Prophetic Voice in Our Time.* Greenwich, CT: Seabury Press, 1962.
Lebacqz, Karen. "Love Your Enemy: Sex, Power, and Christian Ethics." *The Annual of the Society of Christian Ethics,* 3–23. Washington, DC: Georgetown University Press, 1990.
———. *Six Theories of Justice: Perspectives from Philosophical and Theological Ethics.* Minneapolis: Augsburg, 1986.
Lehman, Paul. "The Christology of Reinhold Niebuhr." In *Reinhold Niebuhr: His Religious, Social and Political Thought,* edited by Charles Kegley and Robert Bretall. New York: Macmillan, 1956.
Livezey, Lois Gehr. "Women, Power, and Politics: Feminist Theology in Process Perspective." *Process Studies* 17 (Summer 1988): 67–77.
Long, Grace D. Cumming. *Passion and Reason: Womenviews of Christian Life.* Louisville, KY: Westminster/John Knox Press, 1993.
Lorde, Audre. *Sister Outsider.* Trumansberg, NY: Crossing Press, 1984.
———. "Uses of the Erotic: The Erotic as Power." In *Weaving the Visions: New Patterns in Feminist Spirituality,* edited by Judith Plaskow and Carol Christ, 208–13. San Francisco: Harper and Row Publishers, 1989.
Lovelock, J. E. *Gaia: A New Look at Life on Earth.* Oxford: Oxford University Press, 1987.
Lovin, Robin W. *Reinhold Niebuhr and Christian Realism.* Cambridge: Cambridge University Press, 1995.

———. "Theology, Ethics, and Culture." In Vol. 2, *The Modern Theologians: An Introduction to Christian Theology in the Twentieth Century*, edited by David F. Ford, 75–88. Oxford: Basil Blackwell, 1989.

MacIntosh, Douglas C., ed. *Religious Realism*. New York: Macmillan, 1931.

MacIntyre, Alasdair. *Whose Justice? Which Rationality?* Notre Dame, IN: University of Notre Dame Press, 1988.

Macy, Joanna Rogers. *Despair and Personal Power in the Nuclear Age*. Philadelphia: New Society Publishers, 1983.

Margulis, Lynn, and J. E. Lovelock. "Gaia and Geognosy." In *Global Ecology: Towards a Science of Biosphere*, edited by Mitchell B. Rambler, et al. San Diego, CA: Academic Press of America, 1989.

Marty, Martin. *Modern American Religion: The Noise of Conflict, 1919–1941*. Chicago: University of Chicago Press, 1991.

Mathews, Shailer. *The Faith of Modernism*. New York: Macmillan, 1924.

McCann, Dennis P. *Christian Realism and Liberation Theology: Practical Theologies in Creative Conflict*. Maryknoll, NY: Orbis Press, 1981.

McFague, Sallie. *The Body of God: An Ecological Theology*. Minneapolis: Augsburg Fortress Press, 1993.

———. *Metaphorical Theology: Models of God in Religious Language*. Philadelphia: Fortress Press, 1982.

———. *Models of God: Theology for an Ecological, Nuclear Age*. Philadelphia: Fortress Press, 1987.

———. "Mother God." In *Motherhood: Experience, Institution, Theology*, edited by Anne Carr and Elisabeth Schüssler Fiorenza, 138–43. Edinburgh: T & T Clark, 1989.

McGiffert, A. C. "Immanence." In *Encyclopedia of Religion and Ethics*. Vol. 8. New York: Charles Scribner's Sons, n. d..

Meyer, Donald. *The Protestant Search for Political Realism: 1919–1941*. 2d ed. Middletown, CT: Wesleyan University Press, 1988.

Miles, Rebekah L. "Freeing Bonds and Binding Freedom: Reinhold Niebuhr and Feminist Critics on Paternal Authority and Maternal Constraint." *The Annual of the Society of Christian Ethics*, 121–43. Chicago: Society of Christian Ethics, 1996.

Miller-McLemore, Bonnie. *Also a Mother: Work and Family as Theological Dilemma*. Nashville, TN: Abingdon Press, 1994.

Minnema, Theodore. *The Social Ethics of Reinhold Niebuhr*. Grand Rapids, MI: Eerdmans, 1958.

Mollenkott, Virginia Ramey. *Godding: Human Responsibility and the Bible*. New York: Crossroad, 1987.

Nicholson, Linda J., ed. *Feminism/Postmodernism*. New York: Routledge, 1990.

Niebuhr, Reinhold. *Beyond Tragedy: Essays on the Christian Interpretation of History*. New York: Charles Scribner's Sons, 1937.

———. *The Children of Light and the Children of Darkness: A Vindication of Democracy and a Critique of Its Traditional Defence*. New York: Charles Scribner's Sons, 1944.

———. "Christian Attitudes toward Sex and Family." *Christianity and Crisis* 24 (April 27, 1964): 73–80.

———. *Christian Realism and Political Problems*. New York: Charles Scribner's Sons, 1953.

———. *Christianity and Power Politics*. New York: Charles Scribner's Sons, 1940.

———. *Does Civilization Need Religion? A Study in the Social Resources and Limitations of Religion in Modern Life*. New York: Macmillan, 1941.

———. *Essays in Applied Christianity*. D. B. Robertson, ed. New York: Meridian Books, 1959.

———. *Faith and History: A Comparison of Christian and Modern Views of History.* New York: Charles Scribner's Sons, 1949.
———. *An Interpretation of Christian Ethics.* New York: Meridian Books, 1956.
———. *The Irony of American History.* New York: Charles Scribner's Sons, 1952.
———. *Justice and Mercy.* Ursula M. Niebuhr, ed. New York: Harper & Row, 1974.
———. *Love and Justice.* D. B. Robertson, ed. Cleveland, OH: Meridian Books, 1967.
———. *Man's Nature and His Communities: Essays on the Dynamics and Enigmas of Man's Personal and Social Existence.* New York: Charles Scribner's Sons, 1965.
———. *Moral Man and Immoral Society: A Study in Ethics and Politics.* New York: Charles Scribner's Sons, 1932.
———. "More on Kinsey." *Christianity and Crisis* 13 (January 11, 1953): 182–83.
———. *The Nature and Destiny of Man: A Christian Interpretation.* Vol. 1. *Human Nature.* New York: Charles Scribner's Sons, 1941.
———. *The Nature and Destiny of Man: A Christian Interpretation.* Vol. 2. *Human Destiny.* New York: Charles Scribner's Sons, 1943.
———. "The Problem of Justice and the Power of Love." *United Church Herald* 2 (January 1, 1959): 13.
———. *Reflections on the End of an Era.* New York: Charles Scribner's Sons, 1934.
———. *The Self and the Dramas of History.* New York: Charles Scribner's Sons, 1955.
———. "Sex and Religion in the Kinsey Report." *Christianity and Crisis* 13 (November 2, 1953): 138–41.
———. "Sex Standards in America." *Christianity and Crisis* 8 (May 24, 1948): 65ff.
———. "Some Things I Have Learned." *Saturday Review* (November 6, 1965): 22.
———. *The Structure of Nations and Empires: A Study of the Recurring Patterns and Problems of the Political Order in Relation to the Unique Problems of the Nuclear Age.* New York: Charles Scribner's Sons, 1959.
———. "Will Christians Stop Fooling Themselves?" *Christian Century* 51 (May 16, 1934): 659.
Niebuhr, Ursula M. *Remembering Reinhold Niebuhr: Letters of Reinhold and Ursula Niebuhr.* New York: HarperCollins, 1991.
———. "Women and the Church and the Fact of Sex." *Christianity and Crisis* 11 (August 6, 1951): 106–10.
Noddings, Nel. *Caring: A Feminine Approach to Ethics and Moral Education.* Berkeley: University of California Press, 1984.
———. *Women and Evil.* Berkeley: University of California Press, 1989.
Nussbaum, Martha. "Non-Relative Virtues: An Aristotelian Approach." *Midwest Studies in Philosophy* 13 (1988): 32–53.
Ochshorn, Judith. *The Female Experience and the Nature of the Divine.* Bloomington: Indiana University Press, 1981.
Oduyoye, Mercy Amba. *Hearing and Knowing: Theological Reflections on Christianity in Africa.* Maryknoll, NY: Orbis Press, 1986.
Okin, Susan. *Women in Western Political Thought.* Princeton: Princeton University Press, 1979.
Pateman, Carole. *The Sexual Contract.* Stanford, CA: Stanford University Press, 1988.
Plaskow, Judith. "Christian Feminism and Anti-Judaism." *Cross Currents* 28 (Fall 1978): 306–9.
———. *Sex, Sin, and Grace: Women's Experience and the Theologies of Reinhold Niebuhr and Paul Tillich.* Washington, DC: University Press of America, 1980.
———. *Standing Again at Sinai: Judaism from a Feminist Perspective.* New York: Harper and Row, 1990.

Plaskow, Judith, and Carol P. Christ, eds. *Weaving the Visions: New Patterns in Feminist Spirituality.* San Francisco: Harper and Row, 1989.

Rabuzzi, Kathryn Allen. *The Sacred and the Feminine: Toward a Theology of Housework.* New York: Seabury, 1982.

———. "The Socialist Feminist Vision of Rosemary Radford Ruether: A Challenge to Liberal Feminism." *Religious Studies Review* 15 (January 1989): 4–8.

Rae, Eleanor. *Women, the Earth, the Divine.* Maryknoll, NY: Orbis, 1994.

Rauschenbusch, Walter. *Christianity and the Social Crisis.* Louisville, KY: Westminster/John Knox Press, 1991.

———. *A Theology for the Social Gospel.* New York: Macmillan, 1917; Reprint. Nashville: Abingdon Press, 1960.

Rorty, Richard. *Contingency, Irony, and Solidarity.* Cambridge: Cambridge University Press, 1989.

Rossi, Alice S., ed. *The Feminist Papers: From Adams to de Beauvoir.* New York: Bantam Books, 1974.

Ruddick, Sara. *Maternal Thinking: Toward a Politics of Peace.* Boston: Beacon Press, 1989.

Ruether, Rosemary Radford. "The Development of My Theology." *Religious Studies Review* 15 (January 1989): 1–4.

———. *Disputed Questions: On Being a Christian.* Maryknoll, NY: Orbis Books, 1989.

———. *Gaia and God: An Ecofeminist Theology of Earth-Healing.* San Francisco: HarperCollins, 1992.

———. *Liberation Theology: Human Hope Confronts Christian History and American Power.* New York: Paulist Press, 1972.

———. *New Woman/New Earth: Sexist Ideologies and Human Liberation.* New York: Seabury Press, 1975.

———. *The Radical Kingdom: The Western Experience of Messianic Hope.* New York: Harper and Row, 1970.

———. *Sexism and God-Talk: Toward a Feminist Theology.* Boston: Beacon Press, 1983.

———. *To Change the World: Christology and Cultural Criticism.* New York: Crossroad, 1981.

———. *Womanguides: Readings toward a Feminist Theology.* Boston: Beacon Press, 1985.

———. *Women-Church: Theology and Practice of Feminist Liturgical Communities.* San Francisco: Harper and Row, 1985.

Ruether, Rosemary, et al. "Gaia and God: Responses to R. R. Ruether's New Book." Papers presented at the American Academy of Religion annual meeting, November 1992, San Francisco.

Russell, Letty M., ed. *Feminist Interpretation of the Bible.* Philadelphia: Westminster Press, 1985.

———. *Household of Freedom: Authority in Feminist Theology.* Philadelphia: Westminster Press, 1987.

———. *Human Liberation in a Feminist Perspective: A Theology.* Philadelphia: Westminster Press, 1974.

Saiving, Valerie. "The Human Situation: A Feminine View." *Journal of Religion* 40 (April 1960): 108–10.

Sanday, Peggy R. *Female Power and Male Dominance: On the Origins of Sexual Inequality.* Cambridge: Cambridge University Press, 1981.

Sanders, Cheryl J., et al. "Black Women: Moral Agents." *Christianity and Crisis* 49 (December 11, 1989): 391–92.

———. "Roundtable Discussion: Christian Ethics and Theology in Womanist Perspective." *Journal of Feminist Studies in Religion* 5 (Fall 1989): 83–112.

Sanders, Thomas. "The Theology of Liberation: Christian Utopianism." *Christianity and Crisis* 33 (September 17, 1973): 167–73.

Schaef, Anne Wilson. *Women's Reality: An Emerging Female System in White Male Society.* Minneapolis: Winston Press, 1981.

Schweiker, William. "One World, Many Moralities: A Diagnosis of Our Moral Situation." *Criterion* (Spring 1993):12–21.

Scott, Nathan A., Jr., ed. *The Legacy of Reinhold Niebuhr.* Chicago: University of Chicago Press, 1975.

Shannon, William, ed. *Thomas Merton: The Hidden Ground of Love, Letters on Religious Experience and Social Concerns.* New York: Farrer, Straus, Giroux, 1985.

Smith, Ruth L. "Feminism and the Moral Subject." In *Women's Consciousness, Women's Conscience*, edited by Barbara Hilkert Andolsen, Christine E. Gudorf, and Mary D. Pellauer, 235–50. Minneapolis: Winston Press, 1985.

———. *The Individual and Society in Reinhold Niebuhr and Karl Marx.* Ph.D. dissertation, Boston University, 1982.

Starhawk. *Dreaming the Dark*, Boston: Beacon Press, 1982.

———. *Truth or Dare: Encounters with Power, Authority, and Mystery.* San Francisco: Harper and Row, 1987.

Stone, Ronald H. *Reinhold Niebuhr: Prophet to Politicians.* Nashville, TN: Abingdon Press, 1972.

Stortz, Martha Ellen. *PastorPower.* Nashville, TN: Abingdon Press, 1993.

Suchocki, Marjorie. "Weaving the World." *Process Studies* 14 (Summer 1985): 76–86.

Tamez, Elsa, ed. *Through Her Eyes: Women's Theology from Latin America.* Maryknoll, NY: Orbis Books, 1989.

Tanner, Kathryn. *The Politics of God: Christian Theologies and Social Justice.* Minneapolis: Fortress Press, 1992.

Taylor, Mark C. *Erring: A Postmodern A/Theology.* Chicago: University of Chicago Press, 1984.

Thistlethwaite, Susan Brooks. "God and Her Survival in a Nuclear Age." *Journal of Feminist Studies in Religion* 4 (Spring 1988): 73–88.

———. *Sex, Race, and God: Christian Feminism in Black and White.* New York: Crossroad, 1989.

Townes, Emilie, et al. "Critical Book Discussion: Sharon Welch's *A Feminist Ethic of Risk.*" Audio recording of papers presented at the Society of Christian Ethics annual meeting, Philadelphia, January 1992.

Tracy, David. *The Analogical Imagination.* New York: Crossroad, 1981.

———. *Blessed Rage for Order.* Minneapolis: Winston-Seabury Press, 1975.

Van Leeuwen, Mary Stewart. *After Eden: Facing the Challenge of Gender Reconciliation.* Grand Rapids, MI: Eerdmans, 1993.

Vaughan, Judith. *Sociality, Ethics and Social Change: A Critical Appraisal of Reinhold Niebuhr's Ethics in the Light of Rosemary Ruether's Works.* Lanham, MD: University Press of America, 1983.

Washington, James M., ed. *A Testament of Hope: The Essential Writings and Speeches of Martin Luther King, Jr.* New York: HarperCollins, 1986.

Welch, Sharon D. *Communities of Resistance and Solidarity: A Feminist Theology of Liberation.* Maryknoll, NY: Orbis Press, 1985.

———. "An Ethic of Solidarity and Difference." In *Postmodernism, Feminism, and Cultural Politics: Redrawing Educational Boundaries*, edited by Henry A. Giroux. Albany, NY: State University of New York Press, 1991.

———. *A Feminist Ethic of Risk.* Minneapolis: Fortress Press, 1990.

———. "A Genealogy of the Logic of Deterrence: Habermas, Foucault, and a Feminist Ethic of Risk." *Union Seminary Quarterly Review* 41 (1987): 13–32.

———. "Human Beings, White Supremacy, and Racial Justice." In *Reconstructing Christian Theology*, edited by Rebecca S. Chopp and Mark L. Taylor, 170–94. Minneapolis: Augsburg Fortress Press, 1994.

———. "Ideology and Social Change." In *Weaving the Visions: New Patterns in Feminist Spirituality*, edited by Judith Plaskow and Carol Christ, 336–43. San Francisco: Harper and Row, 1989.

———. "The Nuclear Arms Race as a Test of Faith." *Union Seminary Quarterly Review* 40 (1985): 37–46.

———. "Sporting Power: American Feminism, French Feminisms, and an Ethic of Conflict." In *Transfigurations: Theology and the French Feminists*, edited by C.W. Kim, Susan Simonaitis, and Susan St. Ville, 171–98. Minneapolis: Fortress Press, 1993.

West, Cornel. "Faith, Struggle and Reality." *Christianity and Crisis* (October 14, 1985): 402.

White, Carol Wayne. *Postmodern Religion and the Problem of Historicity*. Ph.D. dissertation, Iliff School of Theology and University of Denver, 1993.

Williams, Delores. "The Color of Feminism." *Christianity and Crisis* 45 (April 29, 1985): 164–65.

Wolf, Naomi. *The Beauty Myth*. New York: Doubleday, 1992.

Wollstonecraft, Mary. "A Vindication of the Rights of Woman." In *The Feminist Papers*, edited by Alice Rossi, 40–85. New York: Bantam Books, 1973.

Young, Iris Marion. *Justice and the Politics of Difference*. Princeton, NJ: Princeton University Press, 1990.

Young, Pamela Dickey. *Feminist Theology/Christian Theology: In Search of Method*. Minneapolis: Fortress Press, 1990.

Index

Alves, Rubem, 6
Aquinas, Thomas, 59
Augustine, 62

Bennett, John, 7
Bednarowski, Mary Farrell, 13, 163n.60
Brock, Rita, 11

Cannon, Katie, 138, 162n.46, 189n.124
Carr, Anne, 21
Chodorow, Nancy, 14
Christ, Carol, 15
Christian realism, 6–8, 10
    Divine immanence, 10
    Divine transcendence, 10
    Feminist criticisms of, 3–4, 6–7
    Historical background of, 6–7
    Human boundedness, 7, 10
    Human freedom, 10
    Human moral capacity, 7
    Human sin, 7
    Pessimism, 6–7, 37, 43, 59, 80
    Political, 7
    See also Feminist Christian realism; Niebuhr, Reinhold
Conversion, 18–19
Collins, Sheila, 37–39, 41
Culpepper, Emily, 15

Daly, Mary, 15, 132
Davaney, Sheila, 162n.39
De Beauvoir, Simone, 19–20
Divine immanence, 6, 8–9, 13–17. *See also* Feminist Christian realism; Feminist theologies; Niebuhr, Reinhold; Ruether, Rosemary; Welch, Sharon

Divine transcendence, 6, 8–9, 17, 20–23
    Feminist criticisms of, 3, 13–14, 17
    As separation, 14, 32, 77
    See also Feminist Christian realism; Feminist theologies; Niebuhr, Reinhold; Ruether, Rosemary; Welch, Sharon
Dunfee, Sue, 34

Eckhart, Meister, 158

Feminist Christian realism, 3–6, 9–11, 17–19, 26–27, 147–58
    Alternative to deconstructionism and communitarianism, 190n.6
    Assumptions and methodology, 10–11, 17–19, 26–27
    Christian realism, 3, 6–7
    Conversion, 18–19
    Creative transformation, 155
    Definitions, 7–10
    Divine immanence, 3, 9, 87–89, 153
    Divine transcendence, 3, 9, 19, 23, 87–89, 152–58
    Feminist moral experience, 3, 17–19, 150
    Feminist theology, criticism of, 3, 17–19, 23
    Historical transformation, 17–19, 88–89
    Human boundedness, 3, 9, 19, 20, 54, 87–89, 147–48, 157
    Human experience, 10, 17–19, 54–56, 87–89
    Human freedom, 3, 9, 17–19, 20, 26, 54–55, 87–89, 147–48, 152, 154–58
    Antinorm, 156
    Boundedness of, 54–55, 155, 157–58
    Transforming boundedness, 155

Index

Feminist Christian realism (*continued*)
  Internal critical mechanism, 4, 9, 10–11, 89, 152, 154, 156
  Judgment of social forms and theologies, 88–89
  Love, 81, 89
  Model of God, 152–55
  Model of the self, 54–55, 154–56
  Moral experience, 3, 17–19, 150
  Moral norms, 153–56
  Moral realism, 3–6, 8, 26, 88, 151
  Niebuhr, Reinhold, as resource, 3–6, 24–28, 87–89, 147–54
  Parenthood, 88, 157–58
  Political realism, 26, 67, 88
  Presuppositions of, 150–56
  Response to feminist criticisms of Niebuhr
    Family, 37–43, 55–56
    Gender roles, 43–45, 49–56
    Public and private dualism, 40–43, 55, 66–68
    Self, 33–34, 55, 66–68
    Sin, 35–36, 55, 86–87
    Summary, 55–56
    Transcendent norm, 40–43, 55
  Response to Reinhold Niebuhr, 4–5, 50–56, 88–89
  Response to Rosemary Reuther, 113–19
  Response to Sharon Welch, 140–44
  Ruether, Rosemary, as resource, 3–6, 26–27, 88–89, 90–120, 147–54
  Scripture as resource for norms, 153–154
  Self as transforming person, 54–55, 88–89, 154–56
  Sin, 18, 88
  Theological realism, 8–9, 88–89
  Transcendent norm or agape love, 81, 153–54
  Welch, Sharon, as resource, 3–6, 26–27, 88–89, 120, 145, 147–154
    Horizontal transcendence, 145, 152
    Political realism, 145
    Social self, 145
Feminist theologies
  Commonality and difference, 11–17
  Criticism of Christian theologies, 12
  Divine immanence, 3, 13–17, 21, 163n.70
  Divine transcendence, 20–23
  Human boundedness, 13–17, 163n.70
  Human freedom, 19–20
    as presupposition of feminist experience, 17–21
  Models of human flourishing, 12
  Models of self, 29–34, 52–53
  Moral experience, 3–4, 17–19, 26, 53, 87
    Presuppositions of, 17–19, 150
  Niebuhr, Reinhold
    Commonalities, 24, 28
    Criticisms of, 5, 28–56, 65, 66, 68–69, 77–78, 80–81, 84–87, 166–67n.1
  Norms, 12
Feuerbach, Ludwig, 122–23
Foucault, Michel, 124–25, 128, 130, 145
Freedom. *See* Human freedom

Gilligan, Carol, 14, 33
Gustafson, James, 60–62
Grey, Mary, 87

Habermas, Jürgen, 139
Hampson, Daphne, 13–14, 31, 34, 39, 48, 77
Harrison, Beverly, 6, 28, 37–38, 41, 47
Hauerwas, Stanley, 137–38, 141
Heyward, Carter, 11, 15, 135
Horton, Walter, 7
Human boundedness (finitude), 6, 8, 13–17, 44, 119, 159n.4. *See also* Feminist Christian realism; Feminist theologies; Niebuhr, Reinhold; Ruether, Rosemary; Welch, Sharon
Human freedom (self-transcendence), 6, 8, 44, 161n.35
  Feminist criticisms of, 3, 13–14, 17
  See also Feminist Christian realism; Feminist theologies; Niebuhr, Reinhold; Ruether, Rosemary; Welch, Sharon
Human wholeness, 18
Hunt, Mary, 11, 15

Irigaray, Luce, 136
Isasi-Díaz, Ada María, 162n.46

Jantzen, Grace, 21–23
Johnson, Elizabeth, 21

Keller, Catherine, 14, 28, 31–32, 48–49
King, Martin Luther, Jr., 136, 138, 189n.135

Lehman, Paul, 78
Liberal feminism, 19–20
Liberation theology, 6, 67, 124–127
Lindbeck, George, 138
Long, Grace Cumming, 11
Lorde, Audre, 136
Lovin, Robin, 7, 88
Luther, Martin, 59

MacIntyre, Alasdair, 137–38, 189n.4
Marshall, Paule, 129
Marx, Karl, 30
McFague, Sallie, 15–16
Merton, Thomas, 92
Miller-McLemore, Bonnie, 11
Moral realism, 4, 7–8, 26, 119. *See also* Feminist Christian realism; Niebuhr, Reinhold; Ruether, Rosemary; Welch, Sharon
Mujerista theology, 11–12

Naturalist feminism, 12
Niebuhr, H. R., 132, 186n.54
Niebuhr, Reinhold, 3–6, 10, 23, 24–28, 28–56, 57–89, 119–20, 132, 145, 148–49
  Christ, 25, 36, 74, 78–81
  Christian realism, 4, 6, 26
  Creation, goodness of, 68–69
  Dialogical understanding of God, 78
  Divine immanence, 25, 57–58, 62, 74–77, 153
  Divine (agape) love, 26, 28, 36, 40, 43, 78–81
  Divine personhood, 58, 74–78
  Divine transcendence, 4, 9, 25–26, 32–33, 40, 54–55, 58, 62, 65, 74–81, 84, 153
    Atonement as expression of, 78–79, 153
  Family, 29, 38–39, 40–55, 66–67, 170n.105, 170n.116
    Autobiographical link to his writings on, 50, 51, 170n.105, 170n.117, 171n.122, 171n.130, 172n.143, 172n.145, 172n.147
    Injustice in, 37–39, 40–42, 46, 67, 169n.85, 170n.116, 170n.117
    Injustice of fatherhood, 40–44, 46–47, 51
    Marriage as mutual partnership, 47, 171n.129, 171n.130
    Motherhood, 43–44, 48–56, 171n.131, 172n.143, 172n.145, 172n.147, 173n.157, 176n.71
    Questioning authority of fatherhood, 42–48, 51, 55, 170n.109
  Feminism, 171n.138
  Feminist criticisms of, 5, 28–56, 166–67n.1
  Feminist theology, commonalities, 24, 28
  Freedom's transformation of nature, 47
  Gender roles, 29, 38–39, 41–56, 170n.105. *See also* Niebuhr, family
  Grace, 66–67
  Hermeneutic of suspicion, 5, 67
  Human boundedness, 4–5, 7, 9, 25–26, 29–30, 35–36, 48–55, 57–58, 60, 62, 65–74, 76, 79, 81–87, 147–49, 159n.4, 174n.159
    Body, 68–69
    Society, 65–68
  Human freedom (self-transcendence), 4–5, 7, 9, 25–26, 29–30, 43–55, 57–65, 69–74, 76, 80–87, 147–49, 174n.159, 183n.70
    Conscience, 63, 66
    Consciousness, 63
    Faith, 72
    God, 64, 72, 74–78
    History, 64
    Hope, 73
    Love, 73, 78–79
    Reason, 63
    Sin, 81–87
    Transformation, 64
    Truth, 64, 82
    Using analogy to describe, 63
    Will, 63, 67
  Ideal and actual, 78–81
  Image of God, 9, 60, 62
  Internal critical mechanism, 4, 9–11, 26
  Justice, 36, 40–43, 46, 66, 79–81
    Equality and liberty, principles of, 80
  Justitia originalis, 71, 73

Niebuhr, Reinhold, (*continued*)
   Knowledge of God, 73–78
   Male leadership, criticizing, 40–48, 51, 55, 170n.109, 172n.147. *See also* Niebuhr, family
   Methodology and structure of argument, 59–62
   Monogamy, 47, 171n.129
   Moral realism, 4, 7–8
   Mutual love, 36, 40, 40–43, 46, 66, 75–76, 78–81
   Myth and religious language, 59
   Natural law, 43, 45, 49, 51, 59, 70–71
   Ontology, hesitation about, 60–61
   Political realism, 4, 7–8, 24, 28, 79–80
   Realism, 148–149
   Religious language, nature of, 58–59, 76–77
   Revelation, 73–74
   Self, 29–34, 40, 53–55, 58–59, 62–69, 71–73, 77–87
     Rejecting isolated self, 66–68
     Social aspects of, 65–68
     Unity of, 68
   Sin, 24–25, 28, 32, 34–36, 42, 47, 62, 69, 71, 73, 77, 81–87
     Pride, 34–36, 82–84, 86–87
     Relative to freedom and boundedness, 81–82
     Religious and moral aspects of, 83
     Sensuality, 34–36, 84–87
   Theological realism, 4, 7–8, 149
   Theological virtues, 59, 71–73, 148
   Women's equality, 40, 42, 46–47, 49, 51, 171n.122, 172n.147. *See also* Niebuhr, family
   See also Feminist Christian realism
Nussbaum, Martha, 189n.1

Oduyoye, Mercy Amba, 21

Pantheism, 22
Plaskow, Judith, 14–15, 22–23, 34–36, 68–69, 86
Political realism, 4, 7–8, 24, 26, 67, 119. *See also* Feminist Christian realism
Post-modern feminists, 12, 16, 18–20, 23
Power, Feminist analysis of, 12–13, 16–17, 131, 162n.55
Process Theology, 23, 92

Rabuzzi, Kathryn, 11, 105
Rahner, Karl, 21
Rorty, Richard, 143, 189n.131
Ruddick, Sara, 11
Ruether, Rosemary, 3–6, 10, 13, 16–17, 26–27, 38, 41, 47, 90–119, 120, 145, 149
   Biophilic mutuality, 91–93, 98–99, 103, 105, 107, 184n.121
   Clericalism, 106–07
   Criticisms of, 113–118
   Divine immanence, 90, 92, 96, 98, 100, 109–10, 153
   Divine transcendence, 14, 90–91, 95–98, 104–06, 107, 153, 183n.70
   Domination, 91, 101, 103–07, 110
     Appropriate responses to, 98–112
     Global crisis of, 93, 111–12
     Hierarchical dualism, 95–98, 100, 105–08, 184n.102
     Historical account as catalyst for transformation, 98
     Relative to family structure, 94, 111
     Sexism as model for other forms of, 95
     Transcendence as support for, 95–98, 106–08
   Ecological sciences, 94–101
   Emerging consciousness, 91–93, 102–03
   Ethic, summary of, 90–93, 99–100, 113–14, 181n.1
     Coevolutionary interdependency, 101
     Interrelation and cooperative independence, 101, 110
     Laws of consciousness and kindness, 101–03
     Laws of Gaia, 98–101
   Evil, 107
   Evolution and God, 5, 90, 100, 102–03, 108–10
   Evolution and human norms, 5, 90
   Experience as primary source for theological reflection, 92
   God/ess, 109–110
   Human boundedness, 5–6, 90, 100, 147–49, 182n.58
   Human consciousness, 101–03, 109–10, 183n.70
   Human freedom, 5, 14, 90–91, 95–98, 100, 102–06, 109–10, 147–49, 183n.70

Humans
- As mind of the universe, 100, 109–10
- As universe conscious of itself, 102, 109–10
- Jesus, 107–108
- Life drives, 91
- Mary, 108
- Moral realism, 90, 149
- Natural evolutionary development, 92–93, 98, 103, 149
- Naturalist moral realism, 4–6, 8, 16, 26, 90, 105
- New humanity, 99
- Political realism, 8, 90
- Realism, 16–17, 149
- Religious language, 92–93
- Scientist as new prophet, 99
- Scripture, 104–05
  - Prophetic liberating strand, 105
- Self, 30–31
- Sin, 93–98, 107, 111
- Social change, 110–12
- Theology, 104–13
  - Norms of, 104–05
  - Sources of, 104–05
- Transcendence, origins of, 95–96
- Women, full humanity as norm, 104, 106
- *See also* Feminist Christian realism

Saiving, Valerie, 34
Self-transcendence. *See* Human freedom
Sin, 14, 18, 24, 34–36. *See also* Niebuhr, Reinhold; Ruether, Rosemary
Smith, Ruth, 30, 33

Theological realism, 4, 7–8, 119, 149
Teilhard De Chardin, Pierre, 23, 90, 92, 102–03
Thistlethwaite, Susan, 162n.39
Tillich, Paul, 60–61, 132

Vaughan, Judith, 30–31, 33, 43–46, 48–49

Welch, Sharon, 3–6, 10, 13, 16–17, 26–27, 120–46, 149–50
- *A Feminist Ethic of Risk,* 121, 142
- Beloved community, 136, 138, 188n.113, 189n.135
- Of Martin Luther King Jr., 138, 189n.135
- Christianity, crisis of, 123
- Communicative ethic, 137
- Communitarian ethics, criticism of, 137, 150
- Community as locus of moral reflection, 137
- Criterion for truth, 124–25, 127
- Criticisms of, 139–144, 189n.131
- Divine immanence, 121–123, 132, 135–136, 153
- Divine transcendence, 121, 123–124, 132–135, 150, 153
- Dominant ethic, criticism of, 124
- Ethic of control, criticism of, 124, 130–131
- Ethic of risk, 121–23, 133–34
  - Definition of power, 134
  - Goal of responsible action, 134
  - Locus of responsible action, 134
  - Role of African American literature in, 133
  - Strategy for responsible action, 134
- Foucault, Michel, as resource, 124–25, 126, 128, 130, 186n.29, 189n.127, 189n.135
- God, 121–24, 132–36. *See also* Divine transcendence; Divine immanence
- Habermas, Jürgen, criticism of, 138
- Hauerwas, Stanley, criticism of, 137
- Horizontal transcendence, 121–22, 132–33, 135–36
- Human boundedness, 121, 131, 134–35, 146–47, 149–50
- Human communities and God, 5, 8, 16, 23, 27, 122
- Human communities and moral norms, 5, 16, 27
- Human freedom, 5, 27, 33, 120–21, 131, 136, 146–47, 149–50
  - In community, 120, 131, 133
- Individualism, criticism of, 131, 137
- Judgments across cultures, 128–31, 137
- Liberation theology
  - Contrast with, 130
  - As new episteme, 124
- Lindbeck, George, criticism of, 138
- MacIntyre, Alasdair, criticism of, 137–38, 188 n.119

Welch, Sharon, (*continued*)
   Marshall, Paule, criticism of, 129
   Models of divine power, criticism of, 132–33
   Moral judgments, 128
   Nihilism, 16
   Ontology, 122
   Philosophical and methodological assumptions, 121, 128–29
   Political realism, 4–6, 8, 16–17, 27, 120, 141, 150
   Power
      definitions of, 134
      as domination and control, 131
      of the erotic, 136
   Realism, 149–50
   Relativism, 120–28, 130, 142, 149–50
      Epistemology, 121, 130, 146
   Religious language, 122
   Rejection of moral realism, 8, 120, 149–50
   Suspicion of theory, 127, 129, 141
   Theology of domination, 131
   Theology of immanence, 135–36
   Universal claims in ethics, criticism of, 131
   Vertical transcendence, 135
   See also Feminist Christian realism
West, Cornel, 141
Williams, Delores, 162n.46
Womanist theology, 11–12, 87

HIEBERT LIBRARY

3 6877 00173 8243

BT
83.55
.M49
2001